LEARNING TO READ
IN AMERICAN SCHOOLS:
Basal Readers and Content Texts

PSYCHOLOGY OF READING AND READING INSTRUCTION

A series of volumes edited by **Rand Spiro**

LEARNING TO READ
IN AMERICAN SCHOOLS:
Basal Readers and Content Texts

Edited by

RICHARD C. ANDERSON
JEAN OSBORN
ROBERT J. TIERNEY
The Center for the Study of Reading
University of Illinois at Urbana-Champaign

LEA LAWRENCE ERLBAUM ASSOCIATES, PUBLISHERS
1984   Hillsdale, New Jersey   London

Lawrence Erlbaum Associates, Inc., Publishers
365 Broadway
Hillsdale, New Jersey 07642

Library of Congress Cataloging in Publication Data
Main entry under title:

Learning to read in American schools.

(Psychology of reading and reading instruction)
Bibliography: p.
Includes indexes.
1. Reading—United States—Addresses, essays,
lectures. 2. Basal reading instruction—Addresses,
essays, lectures. 3. Reading comprehension—Addresses,
essays, lectures. I. Anderson, Richard C. II. Osborn,
Jean. III. Tierney, Robert J. IV. Series.
LB1050.L383 1984   428.4'07   83-20701
ISBN 0-89859-219-4

Printed in the United States of America
10 9 8 7 6 5 4 3 2

Contents

Preface

The past ten years have seen unparalleled growth in research-based knowledge about the nature of reading comprehension, the characteristics of readable texts, and the instructional practices that will maximize comprehension. This new scholarship already occupies the course of study of graduate seminars in reading at major universities, but has had as yet only a modest impact on the teaching of reading in school classrooms. The goal of *Learning to Read in American Schools* is to communicate this research to the diverse group of people engaged in reading education.

A great deal of the recent research about the reading process and reading instruction has emanated from the University of Illinois in Urbana-Champaign. The Center for the Study of Reading was established at the University of Illinois in 1976 under a contract with the National Institute of Education. This contract called for basic research on the processes underlying the development of reading comprehension. Center researchers represent a variety of disciplines—education, linguistics, cognitive psychology, and computer science.

The Center has not only been given the task of conducting research about reading, but is also responsible for disseminating the results of its research to schools, teachers, colleges and universities, as well as to publishers of instructional materials. Common experience, as well as systematic classroom observation, indicates that published basal reading programs and content area texts have an enormous, even overriding, influence on how reading, social studies, and science are taught in the nation's schools. It stands to reason, therefore, that researchers who wish to have scholarship influence practice ought to give a high priority to interacting with publishers. And since teachers in school districts use basal reading programs and content area texts, it also stands to reason that researchers give equal priority to interacting with teachers, the trainers of teachers, and school administrators. *Learning to Read in American Schools* has been written to foster this kind of interaction.

Some of the most important and most school-relevant research done at the Center, and at other universities and institutions as well, is summarized in *Learning to Read in American Schools*. The book is organized around five major topics: reading comprehension instruction, stories in basal readers and trade books, appraising text difficulty, content area textbooks, teachers' guides, and workbooks. Each topic is the subject of one or more chapters; each chapter summarizes what is known about the topic, discusses the most recent research, and offers conclusions that are relevant to classroom instruction. Most of the chapters are followed by critiques written by people well known to the field of reading education. The hope of the editors is that reading educators using the book will interact with the ideas presented, evaluate them, and apply them to those aspects of reading education that are their major concerns.

Currently, there would appear to be a lag as long as 15–20 years in getting research findings into practice. The lag is this long in one area in which there is a clear connection between research and practice, namely, the application of readability formulas to monitor the difficulty of stories and texts. The formulas now in use are based on research done in the 1940s, 1950s, and 1960s. Old ideas are not necessarily bad ideas, but readability is an area in which the new research has outstripped current practice, practice that is grounded in old research. Recent studies, based on the linguistic analyses of student texts, reveal that the "readability" of a text is not an adequate gauge of its comprehensibility. Readability formulas direct authors and editors to use short, simple sentences and easy words. One frequent result of this kind of writing is that the explicit connectives between phrases and sentences are omitted. The linguists contend that such a text can be more difficult to understand than one that contains explicit connectives to bind its ideas together.

In the spirit of communicating this kind of information to those people on whom it would have immediate impact, the research on readability (as well as the rest of the research represented in *Learning to Read in American Schools*) was first presented as a paper at a conference for educational publishers. The conference was sponsored by the Center for the Study of Reading, in cooperation with the National Institute of Education and the Carnegie Corporation. According to one estimate, the participants included executives or authors representing educational publishing companies controlling 93% of the United States market for educational programs and 75% of the Canadian market. The conference provided researchers and publishers a forum for an exchange of ideas and information. Often the give and take was lively; the researchers appreciated the opportunity to discuss with publishers the changes to educational materials that the research findings suggested, and to hear the publishers discuss the applicability and practicability of the research findings. For example, several publishing house executives emphasized that, far from promoting simpleminded controls on readability, most editors abhor them. But they follow them because most of their customers demand absolute adherence to readability formulas.

Some valuable communication took place between the researchers and publishers who attended the conference. We hope that the same quality of communication will occur with other members of the reading education profession who read *Learning to Read in American Schools*. We have attempted to communicate the most recent research based information about reading comprehension and reading instruction. What is described in the book should be considered and reflected upon by anyone involved in any way with the teaching of reading, social studies and science to elementary and middle school students.

Richard C. Anderson
Jean Osborn
Robert J. Tierney

LEARNING TO READ IN AMERICAN SCHOOLS:
Basal Readers and Content Texts

1 Developing Comprehension: The Impact of the Directed Reading Lesson

Isabel L. Beck
University of Pittsburgh

Over the last five years I have spent an enormous amount of time poring over commercial reading materials. My initial work was an analysis of strategies used to teach decoding in eight beginning reading programs (Beck & McCaslin, 1978). A second endeavor was an examination of all aspects of instruction (except code breaking) that might affect comprehension. For this study, we selected two widely used basals as our information base (Beck, McKeown, McCaslin, & Burkes, 1979). Most recently I have examined the decoding and comprehension dimension of three additional programs. The course of my research on reading programs has encompassed a moderate to in-depth look at 13 basal programs. (See also Beck, 1981; Beck & Block, 1979; Beck, McCaslin, & McKeown, 1981; Beck & McKeown, 1981; Beck, McKeown, & McCaslin, 1981; Beck, McKeown, & McCaslin, in press.)

The following assumptions motivated my analysis of commercial programs: first, that basals represent the state of the art of reading instruction; second, that to offer suggestions for the improvement of instruction, researchers must understand existing practice at a detailed level; third, that information about instruction contained in the literature at large or in publishers' descriptions of their programs was too global to promote understanding of practice beyond its surface features.

With that brief overview of my work with reading programs and my reasons for pursuing that research, I now turn to the specific issues that are the focus of this chapter. The issues to be discussed were identified in a 1979 monograph. I should point out, however, that since publication of that monograph I have worked with several other programs and have

3

found the issues identified in the monograph relevant to the additional programs. Hence, the information base can be considered larger than two programs.

The reading education field in general and the programs we worked with in particular view comprehension instruction as occurring through the directed reading lesson (a series of events surrounding a textual selection from the children's reader), and the skills sequences (exercises aimed at promoting what are considered specific "skills," such as finding the main idea or following directions). Our work has focused on the directed reading lesson because it is the most traditional format for reading instruction and because it consumes a major portion of the instructional time devoted to reading. This assumption is made by looking at the amount of material present in the teacher's guides and by teachers' own reports about how they spend instructional time during reading periods.

The implicit objective of a directed reading lesson is to provide students with meaningful encounters with text so that they can build habits of comprehending. The typical lesson plan followed by teachers involves preparing students for an upcoming selection, having students read the selection, and finally, a discussion of the selection. From examination of these components in randomly selected lessons, we have identified seven issues that may play a role in student comprehension of the selections they read.

As a background to a discussion of these issues, the view of reading comprehension that underlies our work should be presented. Reading comprehension is not a unitary process. Rather, it is a complex process comprised of a number of interacting subprocesses. Nor is reading comprehension a single ability. Rather, it is highly dependent upon the reader's decoding accuracy, decoding fluency, vocabulary knowledge, previous background with the content in a given selection, and more. It would seem to follow, then, that attempts to improve comprehension are more likely to be productive if consideration is given to the components of the comprehension process *and* the abilities and knowledge required to perform these processes *and* the instructional procedures used to promote the abilities and teach the knowledge.

Also underlying our work are some notions about conditions that should facilitate the comprehension of a specific text. Here we acknowledge that new knowledge is more readily acquired by oral/aural language experiences until children are able to comprehend as efficiently by reading as they are by listening. Sticht, Beck, Hauke, Kleiman, and James (1974) suggest this occurs around the seventh or eighth grade. Hence, an oral language to written language sequence is inherent in our notions about comprehension instruction.

Now the discussion can proceed to the issues we identified. The first issue concerns the very earliest texts that children encounter.

PROBLEMATIC ASPECTS OF THE EARLIEST
TEXTUAL MATERIALS

In virtually all reading programs, children are required to interact independently with pieces of connected text early in the process of learning to read. That is, they are assigned to read a story selection silently. To be sure, at the beginning, the texts read are just several sentences—but they are meant to convey meaning. It is during the time that each child interacts with the text independently that comprehension is constructed and the meaning of the text becomes represented in memory.

Since it is important that children be taught to develop a meaning-detection rather than a word-recognition orientation to the process of reading, it is necessary that they have all the elements needed for constructing meaning. Young readers can recognize so few words in print, however, that developers of beginning reading materials must of necessity work within a severely restricted vocabulary pool to create textual materials. Such vocabulary limitations imposed upon the earliest texts often preclude the most direct way of conveying meaning.

We found that these restrictions can lead to two types of problematic texts in beginning reading materials: (a) those for which the best words to describe a story concept are unavailable, and are replaced by roundabout language or by referring expressions, such as *here* and *this;* and (b) those that partially or totally omit information needed for story development. I will present an example of a text that has both roundabout language and omitted information.[1] This text attempts to communicate that a character is running so fast that he cannot stop in time to avoid falling into a pond. The children read:

> I can run fast.
> I see a pond.
> I must stop.
> I can't stop.
> The pond is bad luck.

Certainly these words do not represent the most direct way of communicating the intended message.

To compensate for the incomplete nature of the early texts, program developers often rely on accompanying pictures and information that is to be provided by the teacher or elicited from the children to carry the story content.

We selected a number of problematic texts and analyzed and evaluated the mechanisms (pictures and orally provided information) the programs used to compensate for incomplete texts. In some cases, the program

---

[1] The example was altered to make program attribution difficult.

mechanisms seemed successful for maintaining textual coherence. In other cases, the mechanisms did not seem adequate to make texts from which young readers would be likely to construct meaning.

Recommendations. Since the limited vocabulary of all early reading materials is inadequate to carry well-formed story lines or even well-formed messages, we make the recommendation that developers view these early texts as stories that are partly told to children. Some of the story would be read but the remaining elements necessary for textual coherence should be provided by the teacher through judicious use of questions and discussion during the reading lesson. The major concern here is that children be given *all* the elements necessary for constructing meaning. This is particularly important because reading at this early level is a new enterprise; children need to be made aware that the reading process is directed toward constructing meaning.

Picture Characteristics

There is some research that indicates that pictures whose content agrees with that of a printed text improve children's comprehension, but that pictures whose content is out of keeping with a printed text reduce comprehension (Peeck, 1974). In addition, some evidence suggests that stylistic factors of pictures (the way in which pictures are drawn) affect children's comprehension of a story (Poulsen, Kintsch, Kintsch, & Premack, 1979). Our work focused upon isolating specific aspects of pictures, under the two broad categories of *style* and *content* that may help or hinder comprehension.

First, let us consider style. In our review of the pictures included in the first two grades of several programs, we identified artistic stylization as a potentially problematic factor. In an effort to expose children to a variety of artistic styles, recent programs have included story illustrations that range from the very realistic to very abstract, and from very simple to highly elaborate.

It is our view that in some cases, abstract or elaborate stylization may increase the task demands for identifying an important picture element. For example, in one story, stylization takes the form of elaborate costumes worn by the story's animal characters. In the story, the words for some of the animals (e.g., boar, ox, dragon, rooster) are just being introduced into the children's reading vocabulary. It seems that children might gain clearer conceptions of any animals that may have been previously unknown if the pictures were less ornate. Indeed, Poulsen et al. (1979) have suggested that excessive elaborate detail distracts children. In another story, a grasshopper is a major character. Here, the grasshopper is drawn in colorful Picasso-like style. When several adults were questioned about the picture, they could not identify the creature.

Another stylistic factor that may cause comprehension difficulties is change of perspective. Poulsen et al. found that children experience difficulty in understanding a story in which the pictures undergo "gross changes in perspective" (p. 398). We found a number of selections exhibiting what we considered to be radical shifts in perspective. For instance, a squirrel family is pictured smaller than a human family; on a subsequent page it is larger than the human family.

We suspect that difficulties in comprehension can also arise because of the *content* of the art, that is the elements of a story that are included in pictures or the overall view of a story that is depicted. One problem of picture content is that of a conflict between the picture and the text; we did indeed find some pictures that were truly in defiance of the basic tenets of the stories they accompanied.

Recommendations. It would seem that problematic picture situations could be reduced by giving more deliberate consideration to the role of pictures in early reading materials. Since pictures are often an integral part of the texts in early grades, efforts should be made to design pictures and the discussion around them so that they highlight, clarify, or complement text concepts. Certainly they should not confuse text concepts. Accordingly, attempts by developers of programs to include a range of artistic styles in their student materials should not take precedence over the goal of devising pictures that children understand easily.

Divisions Within a Story

In the primary grades children are usually assigned a portion of a text to read and then are stopped for a questioning/discussion period. In our review of teacher's manuals, we found instances where little attention had been given to the suitability of stopping points. We think that interrupting reading at an inappropriate point in a story episode might impede comprehension in much the same way that inappropriate paragraphing or punctuation can disrupt a more mature reader's comprehension. For the mature reader, when the discourse unexpectedly continues in the same vein as before the interruption, comprehension may suffer. The questioning/discussion period between the ending of one silent reading unit and the beginning of the next can be as long as several minutes. When this period interrupts in the middle of a story episode and lasts a long time, comprehension may suffer.

Recommendations. When narratives are to be divided into smaller portions for the purposes of questioning/discussion, it would seem wise to divide them in accordance with a plan that takes into account the sequences of events in the stories. We suggest the episodic structures that story grammars describe may provide some helpful constructs for identifying appropriate division points. Applying these constructs of episodic structure may emphasize the unified nature of the episodes and may thus help to promote story comprehension and recall.

Previous Knowledge Assumed by the Texts

I now discuss the relationship between previously acquired knowledge and the content of what is being read in the directed reading lesson. The importance of prior knowledge in comprehension is not a new discovery, but it recently has received a good deal of research attention. Prior knowledge is seen as providing the framework that helps the reader to assimilate new information. Anderson, Reynolds, Schallert, and Goetz (1976) note that "it may turn out that many problems in reading comprehension are traceable to deficits in knowledge rather than deficits in linguistic skills narrowly conceived" (p. 19).

In our examinations of selections from later primary-grade and intermediate-grade books, we became concerned with what could be mismatches between the previous knowledge important for understanding certain selections and the actual knowledge of the children who would be reading the selection. Consider, for example, a fifth-grade story that assumes knowledge of the antebellum South and an understanding of various facets of a slave's life. Comprehension of the story would be likely to suffer unless students have an appropriate background in which to fit such concepts as: Quaker, Underground Railroad, free states, overseer, trader, bloodhounds, runaway, patrol, and hummocks. Or consider a sixth-grade story that is heavily dependent upon nautical and sea-related knowledge; or a fourth-grade story that relies upon knowledge of the interdependence of animals in nature. Sophisticated knowledge structures are needed to comprehend these stories.

Setting the stage for comprehension through the prereading discussion appears rather perfunctory in some recent programs. We did not see within the teacher's guides any systematic preparation for those selections that are obviously more difficult than others in terms of the prerequisite knowledge required for understanding.

Recommendations. For texts that require considerable prior knowledge, the prereading discussion should certainly be given more serious consideration. Of course, wide individual differences among students using the program make it impossible for program developers to accommodate the multitude of variations in the backgrounds of those students. But it would appear that designing more suitable prereading activities, eliminating unnecessary terminology, and discarding certain selections would make selections more appropriate for general use. Program developers also have the obligation to continually remind teachers that children come to texts with varying degrees of relevant previous knowledge, and that their teaching must be adjusted accordingly. Reading programs can preclude some comprehension problems by providing activities that will help children acquire knowledge appropriate to a specific reading selection, for example, pre-reading-time oral discussions structured to develop knowledge frameworks relevant to the upcoming reading selection.

There has been about for a long time the notion of teaching reading through the content subjects. I support that notion, but I think we should become aware that we need to be teaching content in the reading class, as well.

Vocabulary

Very closely related to the background knowledge required for reading a text is vocabulary knowledge. In this section my emphasis is on single words rather than networks of ideas as was the case in the section on background knowledge.

By about the third grade, and certainly by the fourth grade, most of the selections in the newer reading programs are drawn from independently published materials, as compared to selections created by a publisher for inclusion in their series. The newer basals are virtual anthologies. Authors of the selections are professional writers using the best words available from the general vocabulary to communicate their ideas. Thus the kind of vocabulary control found in the older basals is not in evidence in current programs. The sophisticated vocabulary in the selections from the newer basals has both positive and negative potential for students reading the books. The negative potential is obvious—too many unfamiliar words will cause comprehension problems. The positive potential is also obvious—children can add words to their store of vocabulary.

Vocabulary development strategies created for each story lesson begin with the identification of a subset of words that developers believe may cause decoding or meaning difficulty. These words are listed in the teacher's manuals. By the third or fourth grade the programs assume competent decoding; most of the words noted in the teacher's manuals are of the meaning difficulty variety. These words become "target words" for vocabulary development activities. Traditionally, the development of word meaning is attended to by instructional events that occur *prior to reading, during reading,* and *after reading.* I will summarize briefly the vocabulary instruction found at each of these points.

Prior to Reading

In the teacher's manuals of most intermediate reading programs, the developers provide specific instructional strategies for dealing with the meaning of target words. One of the programs we studied is very atypical in this regard, as no such strategies are detailed. There is simply a general suggestion that the teacher may want to preintroduce target words by writing them on the board and using them in strong oral context. The other programs we studied do reflect the traditional tendency to preteach at least a subset of the target words. In most cases of prereading instruction, target words are presented in sentences constructed to provide enough context to allow the students to infer the meaning of the target word. Besides this "context" method there are other traditional defining tasks and sentence generation tasks.

During Reading

In all the programs we examined, the main vehicle for vocabulary instruction is the reading selection itself. Children are expected to learn new words by inferring their meanings from the text. But the texts children are using have not been specifically constructed to provide the context necessary for conveying the meaning of target words. Rather, as I noted previously, the selections were written by professional writers whose concern is the communication of ideas rather than the specific demonstration of the meanings of particular words. Since the texts are not constructed specifically to establish the meanings of target words, it seems that the extent to which a context is likely to lead a reader to the meaning of a target word depends on chance rather than on design.

We conducted a small study to see how helpful these contexts were. Two stories were selected from the basal readers, and the target words were blacked out. Adults were then asked to read the stories and determine the target words, or close synonyms. The adult readers were able to identify an average of only 51% of the target words (or synonyms) from context. These target words were already in the vocabulary repertoires of our adult subjects; it would seem that children unfamiliar with the words would be much less likely to get meaning from the contexts. We have developed a categorization scheme that predicts which words will be identified, but a discussion of that is not germane to this paper (see Beck, McKeown, & McCaslin, in press). The point here is that natural contexts are not a reliable way of conveying meaning of potentially unfamiliar words.

Most programs include a glossary in the student reader. Children are expected to refer to the glossary for meanings of unfamiliar words encountered in their reading selections. Unquestionably, knowing how to use a glossary is a highly valuable skill. But there is evidence that expecting children to look up unfamiliar words as they are encountered during reading is questionable as a major strategy for teaching word meaning. Beyond third grade, children read selections independently; they are on their own to identify and look up unfamiliar words. Studies have shown that children have difficulty isolating words whose meanings they do not know (Anderson & Kulhavy, 1972; Harris & Sipay, 1975); many children may be unlikely to recognize the need to use a reference. Even when they identify an unknown word, it seems that only highly motivated students choose to interrupt their reading to check on its meaning. The teachers we have informally questioned report that they rarely see their students refer to the glossaries in their books.

The programs' reliance on story context and independent use of the glossary as methods of vocabulary development are at best appropriate only for the most motivated and competent readers. Children most in need of vocabulary development, the less skilled readers who are unlikely to add to their vocabulary from outside sources, receive little benefit from such indirect opportunities.

After Reading

In most programs, after-reading activities include a variety of "skills" development exercises. For vocabulary they consist mostly of independently completed exercises. In one of the programs we worked with, after-reading activities in the vocabulary strand are oriented toward reinforcing target words. For each story lesson, after-reading exercises are provided for the same set of target words found in the story. These activities provide *one* more encounter with the words. The words do not reappear on any regular basis in later reading selections. In another program (the same program that detailed no vocabulary preteaching strategies), after-reading vocabulary activities introduce an entirely new set of words. No effort is made to provide experience with the target words introduced in the stories.

The Best and Worst in Juxtaposition

Let us now for a moment consider the best case of vocabulary instruction that we found in the programs we studied. A new vocabulary word is presented in a sentence that elucidates the meaning of the new word; the word is encountered in the text selection, and the student looks it up in the glossary if she/he does not remember its meaning; the word appears a third time in an independently completed, after-reading activity. The word does not appear again in subsequent selections or in vocabulary work. Remember, this is the *best* instance of new word experience that we encountered. It does not necessarily occur with any regularity.

At worst, a new word appears solely in a selection and the student skips over it because she/he either does not recognize it as an unknown word or does not want to be bothered with the disruptive glossary step.

Recommendations. Clearly, there is a big difference between these instances in the chances that a new word will be learned. However, we believe that even in the best case presented, it is likely that a new word has not had enough exposure for its meaning to be readily accessed even a short time after the instruction. Indeed, it is our assertion that it takes an extended series of fairly intense exposures before one "owns" a word, that is, before it can be quickly accessed and applied in appropriate contexts.

We believe this is particularly so since words introduced at this level are not of the type heard in everyday conversation, and thus not reliably reinforced. Therefore, we believe that neither the frequency conditions nor the instructional strategies in intermediate grades reading programs are effective for enhancing word knowledge.

Toward the end of this chapter, I discuss an instructional experiment that we have conducted that investigates the relationship between vocabulary and reading comprehension. There are implications for program developers inherent in this work.

SETTING THE DIRECTION FOR STORY LESSON READING

We next examined the traditional practice of setting a purpose for reading each selection. In closely examining the direction-setting activity through the intermediate grades in several programs, we found examples that might have a positive effect on the reader's comprehension of the text, and examples that might have a generally negative effect on reading behavior and, in turn, on comprehension. We agree with a statement made by Frase (1977) that "purpose in reading may lead a reader to stray from, as well as move toward, desirable learning outcomes" (p. 43). In the present discussion, the "desirable learning outcome" is, of course, good comprehension of the text.

First, I consider some examples of interfering direction-setting activities and discuss the reasons they may affect comprehension negatively. Interfering direction-setting activities err in three different ways. There are instances of direction-setting activities that could set the reader off in the wrong direction; these misdirective activities seem likely to evoke inappropriate expectations, expectations that are not confirmed when the story is read.

Secondly, activities in which the direction setting seemed right but the scope too narrow. That is, the focus of the direction-setting activity was on only a small portion of the selection, usually found at either the beginning or ending of the story. The activity, therefore, excludes most of the story's content from its focus.

Thirdly, instances of direction-setting activities that in themselves give away information that should be determined by *reading*. While such "give away" activities can set the reader off in the right direction, they often take him or her through the whole journey, and make the reading of the story either unnecessary or anticlimactic.

Ideally, a positive direction-setting activity, by evoking a network of relevant associations, should prepare children to construct the meaning of text. It should not just elicit one or two bits of information. A direction-setting activity should provide a framework for the organization of events and concepts in a selection so that many aspects of the text become interrelated. To identify the key ingredients of direction-setting activities that would further these objectives, the notions of Anderson (1977) and others about *schemata* are helpful.

Schemata, which have variously been called *scripts, frames,* or *plans,* are already existing structures into which new concepts can be incorporated. Anderson describes a schema as a framework for ideas that can be thought of as containing "slots" to be filled.

Recommendations.   Direction-setting activities should be formulated to conform to a schematic design. A schema promoting a network of ideas relevant to the content of a text might transform a direction-setting activity from an information-gathering directive into a plan that would help children identify, interrelate, and remember important story elements. The schematically oriented direction-setting activity differs from the information-gathering type in that it is more concerned *with setting children thinking in ways that will help them to understand the story* than specifying particular story elements to be located and remembered.

AFTER-READING QUESTIONS

I turn now to a consideration of questions asked in conjunction with story reading. Questioning students on what they have read is the most extensively used form of comprehension guidance. Conventional wisdom would indicate that questions are asked for two purposes. First, because comprehension occurs inside the head and cannot be observed, teachers ask questions to determine whether students have understood a text. Answers can function as a measure of comprehension. Second, questions are seen as an aid to the development of comprehension that does not take place spontaneously during reading; that is, questions can function as post hoc probes for organizing and integrating story content. It is this latter function of questions with which we were concerned.

Since after-reading questioning is such a prevalent instructional practice, it has received much attention in the literature. The study of questions generally revolves around taxonomic notions of comprehension; there are several levels of comprehension from low to high, or simple to complex. Numerous studies have analyzed after-reading questions from basal readers or teacher-generated questions. The most often cited recommendation from such studies is that more attention be given to higher levels of comprehension, for example, questions that elicit inferences, evaluation, and appreciation.

It should be noted, however, that questions from higher levels of taxonomies, those considered to be "better" in the taxonomic view, do not necessarily require greater interaction with text information. For example, a question that asks children to identify with a story character— "How would you feel if you had been Goldilocks?"—would be labeled an appreciation question, the highest category on one taxonomy. Yet, a response to such a question would probably require less reliance on text information than a question that required a synthesis of story events. Such a question would be found on a lower level of the taxonomy.

Questions for promoting comprehension cannot be evaluated as "good" or "poor" unless we know, within the story framework, the role of the information tapped by the question. The importance of the information tapped by questions was emphasized by Kintsch and Vipond (1978) in discussing the usefulness of questions in measuring comprehension. We think this notion applies to promoting comprehension as well.

Through an extension of Kintsch and Vipond's notion, we are able to describe how we believe questions should function to promote comprehension of a story. Our view is quite simple. Questions should tap information that is central to story development. But it is not enough for questions solely to elicit discrete bits of important story content. Questions for a story should be generated to promote the development of a unified conception of the story, or a *map* of the story. Any coherent story map must interweave explicit and implicit story concepts. Here we register our concern with the tendency to structure questions according to taxonomic notions to the extent that question sequences begin by eliciting a "literal" recitation of a story without acknowledging that a basic understanding of what is read requires that inferences be drawn. Questioning that attempts to develop a story map does recognize the importance of making certain inferences as well as recalling explicit story events.

Recommendations. To promote the development of a story map, information elicited by each question should build on what has preceded. There are two notions here. First, questions should proceed in a sequence that matches the progression of ideas or of events in the story. Second, questions should be framed to highlight the interrelationship of story ideas.

After a story map has been established, additional questions can then appropriately extend discussion to broader perspectives. Text extension questions could develop a story interpretation, explore a general theme or lesson embodied in the story, probe the use of literary conventions within the story, or act to extend the text by making story ideas a springboard for more general discussion. In our view, the extension of story ideas can enhance comprehension of a story *if* a map of the story has already been developed; story extension questioning, however, cannot substitute for the development of a story map.

FOLLOWING THROUGH ON THE ISSUES

We have identified some of the issues that might affect comprehension of a given text. Throughout the published versions of our work we cited existing theory and/or research and/or logical argument and/or our own teaching experiences as backdrops for our discussion of practices that appeared problematic. We view our work as issues generating, or as the plowwork needed before empirical studying of some of the issues.

We have now completed the first phase of two experimental studies about the issues we identified. The first study was an attempt to redesign a story lesson from a basal program and to assess comprehension of the redesigned version and the original version. The second study was a very large vocabulary development program that investigated the relationship between vocabulary knowledge and reading comprehension.

I am not able to report either study in any detail. For the vocabulary study I discuss the findings in several sentences. For the story study I present slightly more information, as it covers a number of the issues I have discussed in the present chapter.

The Vocabulary Study

To investigate the relationship between vocabulary knowledge and reading comprehension, we designed and implemented an extensive vocabulary program that taught approximately 100 words to fourth-graders over

a five-month period (Beck, McCaslin, & McKeown, 1980). Fourth graders from the same school who were matched on vocabulary and reading
achievement served as controls. The two groups were compared on tasks
using instructed and control words. Gains in specific word knowledge, in
comprehension at the word, sentence, and discourse levels, and in general word knowledge and reading comprehension were made by the experimental group children. In contrast to some previous vocabulary
training studies, our work indicated that a vocabulary training program
can lead to gains in comprehension (Beck, Perfetti, & McKeown, 1982).

The Story Lesson Study

For the story work (Beck, Omanson, & McKeown, 1982), we selected a
late-second-grade narrative about a raccoon who inadvertently frightens
some bandits. When they flee, they drop a money bag which the raccoon
picks up and eventually drops on a woman's doorstep while looking for
food. The woman finds the money and attributes her good fortune to
having made a wish on a star. A concept critical to understanding the
story is that it revolves around a series of coincidences. The program
developers have designed lesson elements for the story that do not promote the concept of coincidence. Rather, these elements promote a variety of concepts that are often distracting to this and other key aspects of
the story.

The program lesson focuses on a discussion of raccoons as clever,
playful animals. Our redesign of the lesson attempts to introduce the
concept of coincidence and set up conditions that might help young
readers understand story events as coincidental. These conditions include
that bandits and raccoons share the physical characteristics of a masked
face, that animals behave in a routine manner, that they focus on seeking
food and avoiding danger, and that raccoons habitually pick up objects
that are in their paths.

The pictures that accompany the original story are drawn in a fanciful
style. They promote the idea that a fairy tale is happening rather than a
plausible story. Although the pictures are quite engaging, the conflict of
their style with the story is potentially problematic to comprehension. In
the redesign of the lesson, the pictures were redrawn in a realistic style.

The questions provided by the reading program that are to be asked
after each silent reading unit are uneven in quality. While some aim to
elicit important story content, others tap information that is irrelevant to
the story line. For example, one question asks where one might find out
why raccoons swish their food in water before eating it. Since these
questions appear between silent reading units of the story when children
are in the process of constructing meaning from the story, they seem

potentially distracting. The redesigned questions systematically require the reader to establish connections between important story states and events in such a way that the plot is constructed.

We presented the story in its original form and in a form that included all redesigned components. We also attempted to explore the effects of the separate revisions. For these partial revision conditions, only one revision element was presented in the lesson while the other elements remained as in the original version. We used a narrative analysis developed by Omanson (in press) to derive a method for scoring children's recalls of the story. This analysis identifies the events and states of a story, and the relations that connect them, and on the basis of these relations classifies the content of narratives as Central or Noncentral. Central content describes the gist or plot of a narrative.

The basic data for the story task is the proportion of content units recalled. The two clearest results are: The total revision group recalled more central content at final recall than the original story group, and none of the partial revisions was sufficient to enhance recall. We then conducted a second study that used the raccoon story and the original and revised forms of an additional story. The study had a larger sample and an additional dependent measure, which was a set of forced-choice questions based on explicit and implied story information. The result was that children reading the revised stories recalled more from the stories and correctly answered more questions than children in the original story group. Thus we have reliable evidence that comprehension of a text can be enhanced through the careful crafting of the lesson elements surrounding the text.

I would like to say something more about the generalizability of enhanced comprehension of a specific text. The approach of redesigning a single reading lesson stems from a notion that daily encounters with reading lessons that consistently facilitate text comprehension may lead to the development of general comprehension fluency. Any attempt to test the validity of such a global notion must begin with a demonstration that comprehension of a single story can be enhanced by a careful structuring of the lesson elements surrounding that story. If this can be demonstrated with several individual stories, then the idea that the lesson elements surrounding a text can be "engineered" to enhance comprehension of specific materials will have some empirical basis. However, evidence of the enhancement of comprehension of specific texts is necessary, but not sufficient, to permit the claim that general comprehension will thus be affected. Yet it is intuitively compelling to think that reading experiences designed to maximize conditions for the construction of comprehension will better prepare children to comprehend subsequent texts. An attempt to measure the validity of the notion concerning general comprehension would require large-scale instructional manipulation and longitudinal assessment. Such an undertaking is beyond the scope of the present program of research, but needs to be considered eventually. At present, we believe we have taken a useful step and believe that the issues we have raised can be used by developers now.

COMMENTS

If I have one major criticism of current basals, it could be summed up by remarking that the basals are attempting to be everything to everybody and thereby have conflicting goals. I would like to consider some of these.

It appears that the basals want to expose children to "good" art and variety in styles of illustration; yet, as I mentioned, some of that good art (and it is often very good) seems in conflict with a given text. Well, what is the primary goal, exposure to the art or enhancement of the text? Basals want to expose the children to variety in discourse types and topics, so some of them include many content selections in their readers. What is the goal, learning something about the temperature in the arctic and the desert in both farenheit and centigrade (an actual selection from a second-grade reader) or having a suitable selection on which to practice lower-order processes? Basals want to teach reference skills, so in the middle of a complicated narrative, the children are questioned about where they think the author got the information he needed to write the selection. What is the primary goal, understanding the narrative or learning that there are sources available for finding information? I could go on and on, but I do not want to belabor the point.

My conclusion is that in an attempt to be everything to everybody, the basals sometimes set for themselves too many goals for individual lessons. All the things I previously mentioned are good things in themselves and can be incorporated over time. The problem is that they cannot be done at once, or all the time, and that there are better places for some of them to be incorporated. For instance, certainly there are better places to discuss reference sources than in the middle of a complex narrative; certainly some texts are not harmed by abstract drawings; indeed, they might be enhanced; certainly a text about centrigrade and farenheit temperatures is better placed beyond second grade. But again the recommendation is for a more careful crafting of each story lesson.

Before concluding I should like to point out a conflict that can be derived from some of the things I have discussed and a resolution to that conflict. Throughout this chapter, I have implied an equating of the ease of comprehensibility with good reading instructional practice. However, I also discuss the need to challenge students in ways that add to their store of knowledge and vocabulary, and extend their thinking about text ideas. The notions of easy material and the need for challenge would seem to leave us with conflicting recommendations. Perhaps what is needed is a two-track system of reading instruction: A daily reading assignment of an interesting but conceptually easy selection and also a regular presentation of conceptually more difficult selections grouped around the same knowledge domain. Since the conceptual load of the easier selections would not require a great deal of processing, they would allow children to build reading fluency. The stories with a greater conceptual load would help to build students' knowledge structures. Grouping texts around the same knowledge domain (e.g., nautical selections), would efficiently use the time spent preparing children to read about specific content. Each successive story in the strand could serve to reinforce the children's previous knowledge of the topic and then proceed to build on that knowledge base.

For the most part, I have dealt with conditions that we viewed as potentially problematic—and not those we found facilitative. My purpose in this is not to disparage commercial programs. Indeed, we found many conditions in each of the programs that we viewed as helpful in promoting comprehension. And I remind you that we did not quantify any of the problematic conditions. Rather, I have stressed problematic aspects in order to point out that they exist. The issue is not whether they exist 5% or 25% of the time. The issue is that they be remedied when they exist.

While certain instructional practices have been negatively assessed in this chapter, it must be noted that many children do learn to read under those very conditions. It must be recognized equally, however, that there are also children who have difficulty learning to read. For those children, reading instruction should be carried out in the most effective way possible. This does not mean the application of some instant instructional panacea, for none exists. Fluent reading ability develops slowly, over time. Improvements in instructional practice must be matched to this gradual evolution. A refinement of strategies, aimed at more careful development of each daily lesson, seems an appropriate course to follow.

REFERENCES

Anderson, R. C. *Schema-directed processes in language comprehension* (Tech. Rep. No. 50). Urbana: University of Illinois, Center for the Study of Reading, July 1977. (ERIC Document Reproduction Service No. ED 142 977)

Anderson, R. C., & Kulhavy, R. W. Learning concepts from definitions. *American Educational Research Journal*, 1972, 9, 385–390.

Anderson, R. C., Reynolds R. E., Schallert, D. L., & Goetz, E. T. *Frameworks for comprehending discourse* (Tech. Rep. No. 12). Urbana: University of Illinois, Center for the Study of Reading, July 1976. (ERIC Document Reproduction Service No. ED 134 935)

Beck, I. L. Reading problems and instructional practices. In T. S. Waller & G. E. MacKinnon (Eds.), *Reading research: Advances in theory and practice* (Vol. 2). New York: Academic Press, 1981.

Beck, I. L. & Block, K. K. An analysis of two beginning reading programs: Some facts and some opinions. In L. B. Resnick & P. Weaver (Eds.), *Theory and practice in early reading.* Hillsdale, N.J.: Lawrence Erlbaum Associates, 1979.

Beck, I. L., & McCaslin, E. S. *An analysis of dimensions that affect the development of code-breaking ability in eight beginning reading programs.* Pittsburgh: University of Pittsburgh, Learning Research and Development Center, 1978.

Beck, I. L., McCaslin, E. S., & McKeown, M. G. *The rationale and design of a program to teach vocabulary to fourth-grade students.* Pittsburgh: University of Pittsburgh, Learning Research and Development Center, 1980.

Beck, I. L., McCaslin, E. S., & McKeown, M. G. Basal readers' purpose for story reading: Smoothly paving the road or setting up a detour? *The Elementary School Journal,* 1981, *81,* 45–51.

Beck, I. L. & McKeown, M. G. Developing questions that promote comprehension: The story map. *Language Arts,* 1981, *58,* 913–918.

Beck, I. L., McKeown, M. G., & McCaslin, E. S. Does reading make sense? Problems of early reading texts. *The Reading Teacher,* 1981, *34,* 780–785.

Beck, I. L., McKeown, M. G., & McCaslin, E. S. Vocabulary development: All contexts are not created equal. *The Elementary School Journal,* in press.

Beck, I. L., McKeown, M. G., McCaslin, E. S., & Burkes, A. M. *Instructional dimensions that may affect reading comprehension: Examples from two commercial reading programs.* Pittsburgh: University of Pittsburgh, Learning Research and Development Center, 1979.

Beck, I. L., Omanson, R. C. & McKeown, M. G. A study of instructional dimensions that affect reading comprehension. *Reading Research Quarterly,* 1982, *17,* 462–481.

Beck, I. L., Perfetti, C. A. & McKeown, M. G. The effects of long-term vocabulary instruction on lexical access and reading comprehension. *Journal of Educational Psychology,* 1982, *74,* 506–521.

Frase, L. T. Purpose in reading. In J. T. Guthrie (Ed.), *Cognition, curriculum, and comprehension.* Newark, Del.: International Reading Association, 1977.

Harris, A. J. & Sipay, E. R. *How to increase reading ability* (6th ed.). New York: McKay, 1975.

Kintsch, W., & Vipond, D. Reading comprehension and readability in educational practice and psychological theory. In L. G. Nilsson (Ed.), *Memory: Processes and problems.* Hillsdale, N.J.: Lawrence Erlbaum Associates, 1978.

Omanson, R. C. An analysis of narratives: Identifying Central, Supportive, and Distracting content. *Discourse Processes,* in press.

Peeck, J. Retention of pictorial and verbal content of a text with illustrations. *Journal of Educational Psychology,* 1974, *66,* 880–888.

Poulsen, D., Kintsch, E., Kintsch, W., & Premack, D. Children's comprehension and memory for stories. *Journal of Experimental Child Psychology,* 1979, *28,* 379–403.

Sticht, T., Beck, L., Hauke, R., Kleiman, G., & James, J. *Auding and reading: A developmental model.* Alexandria, Va.: Human Resources Research Organization, 1974.

Guided Reading: A Response to Isabel Beck

P. David Pearson
Center for the Study of Reading
University of Illinois at Urbana-Champaign

In responding to Isabel Beck's close descriptive analysis of basal reader practices that may inadvertently block students' comprehension of reading selections, I find myself in the ignoble position of a critic with little to criticize. Having recently completed two close analyses of basal reader content with my colleagues at the Center for the Study of Reading, and having participated in the construction of a basal reading series, I recognize all too readily the reality of the practices she has identified.

Instead of taking issue with her, I try to amplify each of the points she makes by providing other evidence to support them and alternative or modified recommendations to basal reader publishers about changes they could make to turn each potential weakness into a strength. After dealing with specific issues, I close by discussing the more pervasive issue of how professionals who serve different but complementary roles (such as teachers, publishers, teacher educators, and researchers) can facilitate program changes that are both professionally advisable and economically acceptable.

A RESPONSE TO BECK'S ANALYSES OF PROBLEMS

Problematic Aspects of the Earliest Textual Materials

Beck's first point is that basal authors use indirect or roundabout language in the earliest texts because of their need to control vocabulary for frequency and/or symbol-sound predictability. What this practice does is to place a tremendous *inference* burden on the young child. Granted, pictures and teacher questions help to clarify situations in the stories; however, the use of anaphoric terms (pronouns and general terms like *thing*) and indirect phrases like "The pond is bad luck," remains a source of ambiguity for the children, especially if they are asked to read a story silently before they read and discuss it orally with a teacher.

There are no easy solutions to this problem. While I would like to see vocabulary control eased up to allow for the use of more explicit (but maybe hard-to-decode) words, I recognize that consumers are demanding even heavier vocabulary control. Two possibilities occur to me. Why couldn't peripheral characters (ice cream vendors or van drivers) be given real names, like Mr. Gonzalez or Ms. Van Neuman, just for that story? Why couldn't the words *garbage can* or *trailer* be used rather than *it* or *this?* Both research and experience with young children reading primers suggest that such long and novel words will be easier for the children to recognize in these early stories than will shorter and more visually confusable words like *cat, car, rat*, etc. In addition, text references to characters or objects in the pictures would be less ambiguous. Further, teachers need not be worried about complete mastery of such words when they first occur.

Short of changes in wording in the text, publishers could encourage teachers to preview stories to clarify potentially ambiguous terms or phrases. Manuals could direct teachers to tell students that *thing* or *it* means "garbage can" or that *he* refers to the ice cream vendor. In addition, since pictures often carry the story in these early stories, manuals could direct teachers to establish the story framework via a discussion of pictures prior to reading. Then, when children read the text, they would, to use Beck's words, "possess all the elements necessary for constructing meaning."

Picture Characteristics

The debate among reading researchers about the effect of pictures on word identification (Arlin, 1980; Singer, Samuels, & Spiroff, 1974) and comprehension (Levin & Lesgold, 1978; Pressley, 1977; and Schallert, 1980) parallels a similar debate within the basal reading community. Both groups have claimed either that pictures are aids to word identification and comprehension or that they are irrelevant cues that only postpose the ultimate task of learning what sounds the letters represent or what the text really says.

One interesting research finding (e.g., Poulsen, Kintsch, Kintsch, & Premack, 1979) is that excessive picture detail does not facilitate comprehension of related text. In fact, simple stick-figure drawings that support story details have been shown to be as effective or more effective than elaborate or stylized pictures.

The question that has always fascinated me is why it is that publishers use complex or sylized art in early materials at all. I suspect that they do so for two reasons. First, appreciation of good art is an end in itself, needing no justification in terms of facilitating comprehension. Second, clever art may add a motivational element to the selection, thus increasing the probability that children will attend to the selection. If the assumption about this second rationale is accurate, than it parallels an implicit motive for certain kinds of intrusions that we have found in expository selections in basal readers (Pearson, Gallagher, Goudvis, & Johnson, in preparation). Authors of expository selections seem to implant motivational tidbits about a topic in order to increase interest. For example, in a description about the travels of the sea turtle, there is an intrusion about the possibility that the fish that got away from you when you went fishing at the mouth of the river may, in fact, have been a sea turtle snapping at your bait. Such an intrusion may prove interesting and motivational, but what effect does it have on a student's understanding of the sequence of a sea turtle's travels. Like unnecessarily elaborate pictures, high interest tidbits may deflect a student from focusing on what is truly important in a text.

Regarding Beck's recommendations, I can do little save support them. Art is important in its own right. But the goal of reading programs is to facilitate children's comprehension. That goal should remain foremost in the minds of authors, editors, and designers as they try to create complementary text/art gestalts in basal selections.

Divisions With Stories

Silent reading units (SRUs) are particularly crucial in materials for the early grades, when teachers are more likely to guide the reading of a selection page by page. In the intermediate grades, the SRU is much more likely to be the entire selection. Beck's point is that breaks between episodes are more appropriate than breaks within episodes (as defined by a story grammar). I find little to argue with here. All I can add is that publishers should attempt to match pages or divisions with natural episodes so as not to fractionate the development of critical story elements.

Previous Knowledge Assumed by the Texts

Perhaps the single most significant contribution of recent research and theory within the cognitive tradition has been to validate the central role of prior knowledge in explaining variation in the comprehension of specific texts. In fact, two recent studies (Johnston & Pearson, 1982; and Johnston, 1981) suggest that prior knowledge can account for more variation in performance than either IQ or measured reading achievement scores. And the critical role of prior knowledge in text interpretation (e.g., Anderson, Reynolds, Schallert, & Goetz, 1977) or perspective (e.g., Pichert, & Anderson, 1977) seems beyond question. But the critical question from both a publisher's and a teacher's point of view is what to do when students lack appropriate background knowledge.

As a researcher who has worried extensively about this issue, I admit that we have little guidance to offer either publishers or teachers. We do know that the conventional wisdom on this issue (bringing up key concepts in a discussion prior to reading) does little more than activate appropriate knowledge structures if they already exist in students' long-term memory. When student knowledge about a topic is weak we have little hard evidence to suggest that some techniques work better than others.

From a publisher's point of view, the problem is exacerbated by the recognition of wide individual and group differences in background knowledge. Even if we know which techniques worked best to develop background knowledge, how would we ever determine the critical group for whom manual suggestions ought to be written? Should publishers write manuals geared toward the mean or toward those students who are likely to be wholly deficient in background knowledge? The issue is not trivial; manual directions to teachers would vary widely depending upon the stance that a particular publisher chose to take.

Frankly, I am not convinced that publishers of basal readers can ever address the lack-of-background-knowledge issue in all its dimensions. Here, I think, we must rely on the good faith and judgment of teachers to intervene when they perceive an abnormal mismatch between text requirements and student knowledge. The problem lies more in the domain of teacher education than text development. The best publishers can reasonably expect to do is to raise the issue for precisely those texts in which there is a high probability of mismatch.

Vocabulary

As Beck suggests, background knowledge and vocabulary issues are highly correlated; vocabulary terms are, after all, nothing more than the surface linguistic references for knowledge structures. In fact, when we talk about building knowledge structures, we tend to do so in terms of vocabulary. Ironically, though, we can talk about teaching and do teach vocabulary in a way that does not necessarily help to build integrated knowledge structures. This occurs, I think, because publishers strive for variety of topics within units. A word like *federal* is presented because it occurs in Story X rather than because it occurs within a thematic unit in which it will be compared with terms like state, local, executive, judicial, legislative, rights, and so on. Consequently, children learn definitions; they do not develop what Beck calls ownership of a word, an event that can occur only when a student learns where that word fits within his or her store of related terms.

One can view the problem of learning a new concept as a process of learning how that concept is like and how it is different from other concepts related to it. In this light, I think we have usually asked the wrong question in generating activities to help students learn new concepts. Insteading of asking, "How can I get this word into the student's head?" we should be asking, "What is it that the student already knows about that I can use as an anchor point, as a way of accessing this new concept?" If we ask the latter question then we will always be directing our vocabulary instruction to the ownership issue—Where does this word fit?—rather than to the definition issue—What does this word mean?

Setting the Direction for Story Lesson Reading

Few traditions in reading instruction have the support of common sense, research validation, and the wisdom of practice to the degree that setting purposes prior to reading does. Yet a purpose-setting question, as Beck notes, can be a double-edged sword: A child reading to find out X may not learn about Y (see Frase, 1977).

Beck notes that purposes (*directions,* she calls them) can mislead children in several ways. They can lead students in the wrong direction, be too narrow, or be too informative. I concur. Nonetheless, I remain convinced that purpose setting is useful. In our experience at the Center, we have found three kinds of purpose-setting activities useful. One is geared toward stories and involves little more than directing the children to read to find out what X's problem is and how X solves the problem. Since most good stories have a problem-solution theme, that general question directs children toward the central flow of events in a story, a goal that Beck advocates for post-reading questions. A second activity stems from our research on this issue (Gordon, 1980; Hansen & Pearson, 1980; Hansen & Pearson, 1982). Purposes are generated prior to reading by having students make predictions about what a character's problem will be, how the problem might be solved, and whether an attempt will succeed. The students' purpose for reading is to evaluate the accuracy of their predictions. If during the prediction session teachers have focused attention on important story elements, then students end up reading at an appropriate level of detail. Children receiving such a prereading activity perform better on both literal and inferential questions asked after stories are read than do students receiving a business-as-usual treatment. Further, after 10 weeks of instruction, the technique transfers to stories the students are asked to read without any such teacher support; apparently they internalize the strategy. We think the technique works because children read for story elements that are important and because the personal involvement of evaluating predictions sustains attention and motivation while reading.

For expository selections, we have had a lot of teachers trying out a pre- and post-reading semantic mapping strategy. Prior to reading, the teacher asks students a "What do you know about X" question (where X is the topic of the expository selection). Through a series of associations and probe questions, the teacher elicits the group's collective knowledge, which he or she displays on a chalkboard, overhead, or chart. Then the students read the selection. After reading they meet again to modify their group semantic map in accordance with information presented in the text. No explicit purpose need be set; the students' implicit purpose is to "update their knowledge about X" (see Spiro, 1979), which is precisely what it should be for expository selections. The map serves as a visible demonstration of prior knowledge, new knowledge, and the sum of the two. Such an approach, we think, meets Beck's goal (see p. 19) of providing children with the appropriate framework (schema, script, frame, or plan) into which new knowledge can be incorporated.

After-Reading Questions

All I can do here is to concur with Beck. In examining the questions that follow a story (and those presented to guide the page-by-page reading in earlier stories), I sometimes think that the questions were generated by a committee, each member of which had responsibility for a single page of the text and was not allowed to discuss his or questions with any other members. As a result, the questions made sense in a local, but not a global context. There is no logical flow from one question to the next. Beck wants that logical flow; she wants to impose the criterion that each question makes the most sense in precisely the serial position in which it is asked.

Further, she wants to avoid the questions that are either irrelevant (off the main point of the story) or too picky. Questions should elicit the *causal* flow of the narrative; children should see how one event leads to a second, and so on. Narratives are rarely *merely sequential;* things happen in a particular order because that is the way they *had to happen.*

I do not think it would be very difficult for publishers to apply Beck's story map heuristic to the selections they include and impose the criterion that in the initial part of a follow-up discussion, no author or editor can ask a question that does not elicit some element of that story map. Questions about background knowledge, comparisons with other stories and questions about author craft should be reserved for a second pass. First, however, walk the students through the causal flow of the narrative.

MORE GENERAL ISSUES

Beck concludes her paper by speculating about why and how the bright, well-trained, and professionally responsible people who work in publishing houses generate programs that exhibit all the problems she has noted. She argues that publishing houses are pulled in too many directions, trying to be "all things to all people." Therefore, they are beset by internally conflicting goal orientations. For example, they want good art and good comprehension, and sometimes the one gets in the way of the other.

I agree, but I think the problem cuts deeper. In my view the publishing industry has some difficulty deciding whether its primary responsibilities are professional or economic. It is this underlying tension between doing what one thinks is best (e.g., facilitates comprehension) and what a market survey says most teachers want or what a state committee mandates that leads to conflicting goals and activities within a program.

To illustrate, suppose a publisher took seriously my recommendation about pre- and post-reading semantic mapping activities for expository selections. These activities might prove to be very unpopular, especially since they demand so much of what we know is a precious teacher commodity—time. The series might fail to sell and these professionally sound books would collect dust in an inventory warehouse somewhere.

In this volume, reading researchers make a lot of suggestions about changes in basal programs that involve taking risks. Risks are risky! Ideally what a marketing executive wants is a product that is just enough like its competing products and predecessors so that the sales staff and consultants can point out that the new product is really "an old friend" and just different enough so that they can argue that it has unique features no other product possesses. Publishers are willing to take risks that are small. They are also willing to deviate from the conventional wisdom if and when they believe that a new or deviant idea has enough currency among some substantial subset of the population of potential consumers.

And now we come to the professional responsibility of researchers and teacher educators. It is irresponsible for us to tell publishers to take risks that we feel will improve reading skills among students unless we are also willing to undertake the complex and difficult task of disseminating new ideas to that population of consumers. In short, if we are professionally committed to an idea for change then we must—through courses, in-service activities, writing, and other mechanisms of change—be willing to share in the task of "creating a market" for what we know or believe will affect the literacy standards of our schools. That is not to say that researchers and publishers should not work together to change the materials. They should.

Here, I think, is a classic instance where we must "play both ends toward the middle."

REFERENCES

Anderson, R. C., Reynolds, R. E., Schallert, D. L., & Goetz, E. T. Frameworks for comprehending discourse. *American Educational Research Journal*, 1977, *14*, 376–382.

Arlin, M. Teacher transitions can disrupt time flow in classrooms. *American Educational Research Journal*, 1979, *16*, 42–57.

Frase, L. T. Purpose in reading. In J. T. Guthrie (Ed.), *Cognition, curriculum, and comprehension*. Newark, Del.: International Reading Association, 1977.

Gordon, C. J. *The effects of instruction in metacomprehension and inferencing on children's comprehension abilities*. Unpublished doctoral dissertation, University of Minnesota, 1980.

Hansen, J., & Pearson, P. D. *The effects of inference training and practice on young children's comprehension* (Tech. Rep. No. 166). Urbana: University of Illinois, Center for the Study of Reading, April 1980. (ERIC Document Reproduction Service No. ED 186 839)

Hansen, J., & Pearson, P. D. *An instructional study: Improving the inferential comprehension of good and poor fourth-grade readers* Technical report #235. Urbana: University of Illinois, Center for the Study of Reading, March, 1982.

Johnston, P. *Prior knowledge and reading comprehension text bias*. Unpublished dissertation, University of Illinois, 1981.

Johnston, P., & Pearson, P. D. *Prior knowledge, connectivity, and the assessment of reading comprehension*. Technical report No. 245. Urbana: University of Illinois, Center for the Study of Reading, June, 1982.

Levin, J. R., & Lesgold, A. M. On pictures in prose. *Educational Communication and Technology*, 1978, *26*, 14–35.

Pearson, P. D., Gallagher, M., Goudvis, A., & Johnston, P. *An analysis of the flow of text structures in informational writing for children*. Manuscript in preparation.

Pichert, J. W., & Anderson, R. C. Taking different perspectives on a story. *Journal of Educational Psychology*, 1977, *69*, 309–315.

Poulsen, D., Kintsch, E., Kintsch, W., & Premack, D. Children's comprehension and memory for stories. *Journal of Experimental Child Psychology*, 1979, *28*, 379–403.

Pressley, M. Imagery and children's learning: Putting the picture in developmental perspective. *Review of Educational Research*, 1977, *47*, 582–622.

Schallert, D. L. The role of illustrations in reading comprehension. In R. J. Spiro, B. C. Bruce, & W. F. Brewer (Eds.), *Theoretical issues in reading comprehension: Perspectives from cognitive psychology*. Hillsdale, N.J.: Lawrence Erlbaum Associates, 1980.

Singer, H., Samuels, S. J., & Spiroff, J. The effect of pictures and contextual conditions on learning responses to printed words. *Reading Research Quarterly*, 1974, *9*, 561–574.

Spiro, R. J. *Etiology of reading comprehension style* (Tech. Rep. No. 124). Urbana: University of Illinois, Center for the Study of Reading, May 1979. (ERIC Document Reproduction Service No. ED 170 734)

2 Do Basal Manuals Teach Reading Comprehension?

Dolores Durkin
Center for the Study of Reading
University of Illinois at Urbana-Champaign

The Center for the Study of Reading has been charged with a tremendously important responsibility: To improve reading comprehension instruction in elementary schools. Since "improvement" is meaningless unless what is done now is known, a classroom-observation study was conducted in order to uncover the kind and amount of reading comprehension instruction that exists in Grades 3–6 (Durkin, 1978–79). (The definition of "instruction" used in that study is provided in Table 1.) Those grade levels were selected on the assumption that more comprehension instruction is offered in the middle and upper grades than at the primary level.

During the study, teachers in 39 classrooms in 14 school systems were each observed for three successive days while reading and social studies were taught. Everything that was done during the 17,997 minutes of observing was timed and described. Because data from this study prompted the research described in this chapter, it is necessary to summarize a little of what was found during the observations.

FINDINGS FROM CLASSROOM OBSERVATIONS

To begin, comprehension instruction was never seen when social studies was taught. Of the 11,587 minutes spent observing the reading period, only 45 minutes went to comprehension instruction. It is important to note that the 45 minutes was divided among 12 separate episodes, which means that the average length of an instance of comprehension instruction was only 3.7 minutes.

Although the amount of time spent on teaching comprehension was unexpectedly small, the time spent on assessing it was ten times greater. Large amounts of the teachers' time also went to giving and checking written assignments. The constant presence of assignments in workbooks and ditto sheets reinforced a conclusion reached by Taylor in her book *Transforming Schools* (1976). She observed that, "Teachers keep their classes so perpetually occupied with busy work that neither chaos nor learning takes place" (p. 169). The generous number of assignments given in all the classrooms was associated with "mentioning": saying just enough about a skill, requirement, or topic to allow for an assignment related to it.

To sum up, then, very little reading comprehension instruction was seen. Instead of being instructors, the 39 observed teachers were mentioners, assignments givers, assignment checkers, and interrogators.

BASAL READER MANUAL RESEARCH

After the classroom observation study had been concluded, it was only natural to wonder why the observed teachers were so similar in the way they spent their time, which was supposedly devoted to teaching students how to read. Because basal reader series are thought to exert considerable influence on teachers, it was evident that an examination of basal reader manuals was called for.

Such an examination was carried out in a subsequent study. It took the form of a word-for-word reading of manuals from kindergarten through Grade 6. The purpose was to learn what these manuals offer for comprehension instruction and, in the process, to see whether a connection existed between what had been observed in classrooms and what was contained in manuals. The five basal series examined were chosen because each had a current copyright date and, in addition, each met at least one of the following criteria: (a) was a leading seller, and (b) was widely promoted.

Categories for Manual Suggestions

It was assumed for the basal reader research, as it had been for the classroom observation study, that manuals offer not only comprehension instruction but also suggestions for application and practice. It was further assumed that comprehension instruction would be reviewed periodically in the manuals. How all these categories were defined and how frequently instances of each were found in the examined manuals is shown in Table 1.

TABLE 1
Number of Procedures Related to Comprehension
in Five Basal Reader Series, Kindergarten through Grade 6

Series	Instruction	Review	Application	Practice
A	128	346	436	693
B	122	158	253	746
C	98	418	538	832
D	92	121	303	662
E	60	85	111	495

Instruction. A manual suggests that a teacher do, say, or ask something that ought to help students understand or work out the meaning of connected text.

Review. A manual suggests that a teacher do, say, or ask something for the purpose of going over instruction offered previously.

Application. A manual suggests a procedure that allows for the use of what was featured in instruction. This is carried out under a teacher's supervision.

Practice. A manual suggests a procedure that allows for the use of what was featured in instruction. This is carried out by students working independently.

The table indicates, to cite an example, that in one series, procedures for what was classified as comprehension instruction appeared 128 times from kindergarten through Grade 6. In the same series, suggestions to review comprehension instruction occurred 346 times. Activities called "application" were found 436 times, and suggestions for practice appeared 693 times.

Comprehension Instruction

What was counted as an instance of comprehension instruction varied considerably both across the five series and within each one. More specifically, a recommendation that was a sentence in length and one that was, in contrast, well developed were counted as one example. Since all the series contained both kinds of recommendations, it is unlikely that any was penalized by this procedure.

In examining the frequency data for instruction, it should also be remembered that certain recommendations were called comprehension instruction even though the procedures that teachers were to follow were unclear. For example, what is the meaning of manual directives like: "Lead the children to generalize that . . . Guide the pupils to conclude that . . . Help the students to understand that. . . ?" Or, to cite another example, what are the teachers supposed to do or say when, in preparation for work with main ideas, a manual directs them to "Introduce the word *idea*"?

All this points to what was common in all the series: They offer precise help (e.g., obvious answers to assessment questions) when it is least needed, but they are obscure or silent when specific help is likely to be required. Even some of the specific help is of questionable value. To illustrate, teachers who say to children exactly what manuals tell them to say would use with first-graders such advanced language as *literal meaning, logical, infer, main idea, pause momentarily, evident, situation, refer to,* and *prepositional phrase.*

Lest anyone think that the judgments made for the basal reader study were based on excessively demanding criteria, it should be pointed out that many manual recommendations categorized as "comprehension instruction" were one sentence in length. To be more specific, if a manual recommended that a period be described to children as something that shows where a sentence ends, that was called comprehension instruction. Although lean, the directive was judged to be both relevant and instructive since readers do need to know where sentences end if they are to understand them. However, *prior to* being told about this function of periods, they need to know what a sentence is; but manual authors overlooked this. That students need to understand what a question is before they are ready to learn about the question mark was not recognized either.

All this is to say that what was counted as comprehension instruction was not always dealt with in a way, or in a sequence, that made sense. Is it sensible, for example, to offer information about an ellipsis (in this case, three dots) as early as Grade 1 (as did two of the five series), or as early as Grade 2 (as did two others), and then restate that information on 24 subsequent occasions? Or, for example, does it make sense to explain the function of italics *after* students read a selection in which italicized words appear? (Providing instruction after it would have been useful with a selection is characteristic of all the series. If what was taught was applied to the next selection, the sequence would not be questioned. That was not the practice, however. Instead, it is typical for something entirely different to be highlighted in the next selection.)

When considering the frequency with which comprehension instruction is offered in manuals, it is also important to remember that a manual procedure may meet the criteria established in the study for comprehension instruction, yet not be instructive for the target audience. To illustrate, one of the five series deals with the linking function of *and* in a first-grade manual by recommending that children be told that *and* is used to connect two words. Following that, a list is to be put on the chalkboard to allow the children to name the words connected with *and* (e.g., *Mary and John, up and down*).[1] Although this recommendation was judged to fulfill

---

[1]Throughout the paper, the wording of examples is altered to avoid identifying a series. The essence of the recommended procedure, however, remains intact.

the requirements of the definition of comprehension instruction, it is highly unlikely that first-graders would be able to grasp the intended meaning of "connect." It is possible, therefore, that all they would derive from the recommended procedure is word-identification practice. Nonetheless, it was classified for the research as "comprehension instruction."

An unexpected characteristic of a sizeable number of manual recommendations for comprehension is that they are more pertinent for writers than for readers. One manual, for example, directs teachers to show students how simple, brief sentences can be made more interesting by adding adjectives and adverbs, but makes no suggestion for relating this to how the meaning of long, seemingly complicated sentences can be worked out by readers. Or, to cite another example, instead of emphasizing that a rhetorical question may be followed by the answer (which is pertinent for readers to know), another manual describes rhetorical questions as something authors use to hold readers' attention.

Teachers who adhere to another manual's recommendation would tell students that whatever is at the beginning or end of a sentence attracts attention. Elsewhere, the same series teaches that variety in sentence structure serves to keep a reader's attention. With still another series, instructors would teach that short sentences can function to convey excitement. Meriting attention in all these cases is the fact that the possible significance for reading of what was being discussed was never treated. (Whether what *was* discussed is correct is a different but also important matter.)

Another questionable pattern found in all the series relates to what could be interpreted as an eagerness to get to written exercises. Such a pattern can be illustrated with what is done with pronouns. In this case, manuals suggest that teachers use one or two sentences to point out that pronouns refer to other, previously mentioned words, and that they then switch to application. That is, teachers are directed to use additional sentences with pronouns in order to see whether the students can name their referents. And that is all that is done. Predictably, workbook or ditto sheet assignments come next.

What needs to be emphasized about this illustration is that no suggestions are made for what to do if students are unable to name referents, nor are teachers ever encouraged to link what is being done *with reading*. For example, they are never directed to explain that understanding a sentence may require knowing who or what a referent is; and that if a mental substitution cannot be made for pronouns or for certain adverbs, rereading may be necessary. Instead, what is suggested is a brief, isolated event that is never linked to how to read. To put it differently, a means is treated as an end in itself. It is as if doing little exercises and getting right answers are all that count.

Earlier, when a reference was made to the classroom-observation study, "mentioning" was said to characterize the teachers' behavior. You may have noticed that what manuals do with pronouns exemplifies mentioning: saying just enough about a topic to allow for an assignment. Mentioning can be further illustrated by what is done in manuals concerning the reader's use of contexts to learn the meaning of unfamiliar words. Essentially, manual "instruction" for that topic is as vague and circular as: The meaning of a word is sometimes suggested by the context. The context sometimes suggests what a word means. Next comes application and practice. That is, teachers are told to list sentences and have the students explain the meaning of specified words. All the while the concern is for right and wrong answers; consequently, encouragement is not given to probe with questions like: How do you know it means that? What words in the sentence tell you what it means? Why couldn't it mean _____ in this sentence? Whether this brief, nonspecific kind of "instruction" with little or no probing inhibits transfer to those times when students are reading on their own is a possibility that both authors and users of manuals need to consider.

What may also inhibit transfer is the failure of manual authors to keep in mind that reading is the concern. Examples of a concern for writing without relating it to reading were described earlier. Another example of forgetting the goal is in a series in which grammar seemed to be the issue. At the start, the series offered grammar instruction in a way that made its relevance for reading clear; but as the instruction became more advanced, explicit attention to the link between sentence grammar and sentence meaning disappeared. Instead of continuing to relate what was being taught about grammar to how to comprehend sentences, the recommended instruction turned into a technical treatment of grammar as an end in itself. In this case, the common practice of turning a means into an end not only deprived students of information relevant for working out the meaning of complicated sentences, but also required them to learn new terms concerned with grammar. This might be unwise, especially for students who have to struggle to become readers even when a reading program stays on target.

One more noteworthy pattern in all the examined series is a tendency to equate definitions with comprehension instruction and, by so doing, to stop just short of being helpful for reading. The tendency of manuals *not* to go beyond definitions can be illustrated with the way first-person and third-person narration is handled. Characteristically, much attention goes to defining each; receiving far less coverage (or no coverage) are (a) the limitations of first-person narration in contrast with the omniscience allowed by a third-person perspective, and (b) the implication of this for reading.

What is done with fact and opinion reinforces the same conclusion. All the examined manuals encourage teachers to spend considerable time on defining *fact* and *opinion,* and on having students do exercises in which they make a distinction between sentences that state facts and sentences that express opinions. Neglected, on the other hand, is the way knowing the difference between a fact and an opinion should enter into the reading process—for instance, the reading of an editorial or an ad in a children's magazine. It is as if definitions are all that count when, in fact, defining terms is just a start insofar as improving comprehension is concerned.

Review

When considering the data in Table 1 that describe the frequency of review, it is important to keep in mind that suggestions for review in all the series are often one sentence long; consequently, they are also nonspecific (e.g., "Remind pupils that authors sometimes give clues to when things happen"). When *how* to review is specified, the suggested procedure merely repeats what was recommended earlier for instruction. This is the case even with the series that explicitly promises "alternative lessons."

Important to keep in mind, too, is that the frequency with which information or a skill is reviewed appears to have no connection with difficulty or importance for reading. Instead, the amount of review in all the series seemed more like the product of random behavior than of a pre-established plan.

How review is spaced throughout a manual also appeared to be the result of random decisions. This is suggested by the fact that sometimes a topic is covered, then reviewed frequently. At other times a topic is introduced, then forgotten for a long while or forever. Like its amount, then, the timing of review did not point to a carefully constructed, predetermined plan for developing the manuals.

Had there been one, it is likely that efforts to review as a whole what had been said intermittently about a given topic would have been common, not unusual. An obvious need to synthesize can be illustrated with the series that first taught that shifting the placement of phrases changes the meaning of sentences; but then, in a subsequent manual, showed that rearrangements do not alter meaning. Nowhere were the two opposite conclusions ever brought together and compared so that students could see when a change affects meaning and when it does not. Better coordination among the individual manuals of a series could remedy what may have been a problem of the left hand not knowing what the right hand was doing.

Application

Before the manuals were analyzed, it was assumed that a suggestion for comprehension instruction would be followed by another for application. (The definition in Table 1 reflects the assumption.) While this did not rule out the possibility of there being more than one instance of application for each instance of instruction, the large discrepancy actually found between the frequency of instruction and the frequency of application was unexpected (see Table 1).

The large discrepancy stems from the tendency of all the examined manuals to teach by implication rather than with direct, explicit instruction. This means that if an objective has to do with the ability to draw conclusions that are not stated, it is highly *un*likely that manuals will describe an instructional procedure for teaching students *how* to reach unstated conclusions. Instead, they are apt to provide teacher-supervised exercises (application) in which the concern is to see *whether* the students can arrive at them.[2] If they are unable to do the exercises, all that is offered is more exercises.

Since application is a type of assessment, the frequency data shown in Table 1 for application suggest one possible reason why the teachers who were observed for the research referred to earlier spent so much time assessing and so little teaching. The data about application might also help to explain the frequency of "mentioning" in the earlier study. (As was indicated before, another possible explanation for the mentioning is the brevity of many of the manual suggestions categorized as comprehension instruction.)

Providing for application even when what is to be applied was not taught is one reason why labels assigned to manual segments by their authors were ignored during the analyses. Why they were not useful can be illustrated with a manual page that urges teachers to read a paragraph aloud, after which students will be questioned about the sequence of events that it describes. Even though the paragraph contained signal words like *first* and *after that,* they were never referred to in the suggestions. Only assessment questions were offered. Nonetheless, the activity is explicitly described in the manual as "instruction for following a sequence." For the study, it was classified as "Application."

Practice

Even a cursory look through basal manuals makes it abundantly clear that the one thing that is *never* forgotten at any grade level is practice in the

---

[2]Because application procedures sometimes replaced (rather than followed) instruction, strict adherence to the definition in Table 1 was not always possible.

form of workbook and ditto-sheet exercises. For that reason, the large numbers shown for practice in Table 1 should come as no surprise to anyone who knows even a little about basal reader materials.

What effect large numbers of exercises have on students' conceptions of, and attitudes toward, reading is a question worth considering. Whether too much of this practice has too little relevance for reading also merits discussion. Too obvious to miss, for example, is the tendency of practice exercises to focus on brief pieces of text even when what is to be practiced seems to call for larger units of discourse. This characteristic means that if the concern is for something like making predictions while reading fiction, practice is likely to be with sentences, not stories. The job for students, for instance, might be to connect sentences listed in one column *(Suzie was cold)* with other sentences listed in a second column *(Suzie went inside)*. Although such practice ought to help clarify the meaning of "making a prediction," its value for helping a person make predictions while reading a story must be questioned, especially since the manuals never urge teachers to point up the relationship—if one exists—between the practice exercises and reading a story.

In addition to the reliance of practice on brief pieces of text, manual descriptions of practice are themselves brief. Typically, too, one brief reference to practice is followed by another for still more practice that deals with something entirely different. The result is a large number of manual pages that flit from one topic to another as they make suggestions for practice. One page in a manual, for example, deals in quick succession with: word meanings based on context, finding titles in the Table of Contents that include a person's name, classifying given words under the categories *fruit* and *meats*, telling whether specified words have the same vowel sound, and writing a story using certain listed words.

In another series, one manual page refers to practice for: identifying words using contexts and sounds, distinguishing between main idea and supporting details, recognizing time order, interpreting figurative language, recognizing descriptive words, using dictionary skills, and getting information from diagrams. Ditto-sheet practice exercises accompany all the topics just named with the exception of the descriptive words. Why none was included for that is not explained.

All this can be summed up by asking, is it any wonder that the 39 teachers in the classroom-observation research ended up classified *not* as instructors, but as mentioners, assignment givers, and assignment checkers? Why they were also called interrogators is clearly explained even with a quick check through manuals. The more careful analysis done for the research points to the conclusion that if teachers ever used all the questions found in manuals, they would end up questioning students to death, sometimes about trivia.

CONCLUDING COMMENTS

Presumably, those responsible for preparing basal reader series have a rationale for what they do and do not do with comprehension. While it is recognized that data from marketing departments must be considered when decisions about the content of manuals are made, everyone who purchases, uses, or analyzes a series has the right to expect publishers and authors to assign equal importance to pedagogy. With that in mind, it seems appropriate to pose questions for which the research that has been partially reported here did *not* uncover answers.

1. How do those who are responsible for manuals make decisions about what will be taught for comprehension and when it will be presented? A similar question has to do with the content, timing, and frequency of review.
2. What is the reason for relying on practice to teach instead of on direct, explicit instruction, which is then followed by practice?
3. Why is there *so much* practice, typically carried out with brief exercises that may not even help when students read longer discourse?
4. When manuals attend to what writers do, why don't they also attend to the significance of that for readers? More generally, why are means so often treated as ends in themselves? Stated still differently, why do so many procedures in manuals stop short of being instructive for comprehension?

Although nobody can claim that all that needs to be known about helping students become proficient comprehenders *is* known, I believe that those who prepare and publish basal reader series should be fully prepared to respond to questions like those just posed.

REFERENCES

Durkin, D. What classroom observations reveal about reading comprehension instruction. *Reading Research Quarterly,* 1978–79, *14,* 481–533.
Taylor, P. *Transforming schools.* New York: St. Martin's Press, 1976.

Reaction to "Do Basal Manuals Teach Reading Comprehension?"

Roger Farr
Indiana University

If one were tempted to dismiss the Durkin review of basal reader manuals, that dismissal would most likely rest on a charge that Durkin's definition of the teaching of reading comprehension is too narrow. After all, don't students learn to comprehend better by being given the opportunity to read stories and then to answer questions that probe literal, inferential, and evaluative reactions? And isn't it possible that students learn reading comprehension skills by being asked to complete assignments in which tasks such as arranging events in chronological sequence, determining cause/effect relationships, and identifying supporting details are assigned? Even more important, don't students learn comprehension skills by reading different types of selections for a variety of purposes? If students do learn comprehension skills through these activities, then has Durkin misrepresented the amount of reading comprehension instruction included in the manuals of basal readers?

A reaction article to Durkin's study of the amount of reading comprehension instruction observed in classrooms (Durkin, 1978–79) criticized Durkin's definition of reading comprehension instruction, arguing "that an alternative and more plausible definition of comprehension instruction leads to a much higher estimate of the time teachers devote to comprehension instruction" (Hodges, 1980, p. 299–300). Since what is relevant to teaching is relevant to texts, and especially to their manuals, it may be expected that Durkin's study of basal manuals will be subject to the same attacks. So it is imperative to point out the contributions these two studies have made: They have helped a whole field to rethink the distinction between teaching and assessment, instruction and practice.

It is also important to note that Durkin does not argue that assigning exercises, checking on students' comprehension of a selection they have read, or giving students directions for completing an activity are *unrelated* to reading comprehension instruction. Nor does she argue that such activities cannot improve a student's reading comprehension. What she does argue is that while there are many teacher activities *related* to teaching reading comprehension, these activities are not necessarily the teaching of reading comprehension. Durkin would have us focus precisely on those teaching activities that make up the direct teaching of reading comprehension. She does not want us to confuse assignment giving, assignment checking, and assessing reading comprehension with comprehension instruction. She wants to examine those things a teacher does to teach.

An analogy may help to clarify the distinction between directly teaching a behavior and engaging the learner in activities that may or may not develop that behavior: A child learning to propel himself on a playground swing is likely to first be placed on the swing and pushed by a parent or friend. Even though the child is "engaged in" swinging, he has not learned to swing. Although he may be able to tell about swinging or describe feelings of swinging, he has not learned to swing. By observing how others pump themselves by pulling on the ropes and swinging their legs, he may learn to swing. But because *some* children may learn from observation and experience does not mean that all will. Others seem to need more direct teaching in the form of explanations, demonstrations, and *guided* practice. Independent practice and testing may follow teaching, but they are not equivalent to teaching. So to argue that some children learn to comprehend by imitation and practice is to ignore the fact that many do not, or that they may learn to read faster or better with direct instruction.

There are three other kinds of critical reactions to Durkin's research that I have identified. The first argues that students learn to comprehend better by the kind of automatic learning that may come through experience. Certainly there is evidence that better readers learn to read almost automatically, yet often have these children failed to learn the higher-level reading/thinking skills necessary to enable them to be critical readers. Even if the question of whether students learn better by inferring skills from activities or with direct instruction is open to debate, we do know that students can learn from both approaches. Therefore, it seems obvious that both should be included in basal reader manuals.

It is important and useful that Durkin has focused directly on teaching reading comprehension. Numerous studies in the reading area have concluded that the teacher makes the difference in how well children learn to read. What is still unknown is that which the teacher does to teach reading comprehension effectively.

By equating assignment/giving and assessing reading comprehension with teaching reading comprehension, there is danger of producing a very limited student response and then accepting it or failing to accept it as comprehension. Mosenthal (in press) has hypothesized that student responses in high-risk situations are quite different from responses in low-risk situations. High-risk situations are those in which a student is completing a task to show what he knows. Students often relate such tasks to receiving a grade. In these situations—which include answering questions after an assignment is read, completing a written exercise, or taking a comprehension test—the student will offer the response which he believes is the one the teacher desires. On the other hand, low-risk situations—such as discussions of stories—provoke student responses that are more divergent, that cause students to seek a variety of plausible explanations, and that focus on the act of comprehension rather than on merely determining the most acceptable response. Durkin's definition of teaching reading comprehension is more akin to low-risk activities, while assignment completion and test taking are high-risk activities. Certainly, we want to develop reading comprehension as thinking rather than as merely attempting to come up with the correct answer.

There are two additional reactions that seem to question the validity and usefulness of Durkin's findings. These include the arguments that a basal reading program is not supposed to constitute a total teacher training program, and that it is not necessary or possible to give a teacher specific directions about how to teach reading comprehension.

The first of these reactions may come from publishers and authors of basal readers, who might argue that a basal reader is not supposed to be a total reading program. The instructional materials, they might insist, are merely provided for teachers as a means to teach reading comprehension. They may argue further that the instructional activities and teaching suggestions in their materials should relate only to the content of the stories in their particular series—that it is the teacher's responsibility to come up with ways to teach the skills and then help to generalize those skills in other materials.

There are several problems with this argument. First, it is not uncommon for publishers of basal readers to promote their programs as complete reading programs. Furthermore, publishers do provide teacher directions to teach word recognition skills. Why shouldn't they do this for broader comprehension skills? Basal readers are the predominant influence on reading instruction in the country today. Publishers and authors, therefore, have an obligation to see that adequate reading comprehension instruction is included in their manuals. Durkin's earlier study, which observed classroom instruction, reveals that teachers do not teach reading comprehension. She is searching for the reasons for this state of affairs. She has now examined basal reader manuals, and I suspect she may next turn to a review of reading methods texts and teacher education programs. My knowledge of those indicates that Durkin will find even less guidance on how to teach reading comprehension in those sources.

The third reaction to Durkin's study may come from those who object to Durkin's search for specific teacher directions for teaching reading comprehension. After all, one may argue that a teacher doesn't need to be told step by step how to teach, and that basal manuals are not teacher training texts. Basal reader manuals, however, do seem to include an extensive amount of step-by-step directions for many other activities. Moreover, if specific teaching directions are provided, teachers may choose not to use them or to make modifications or substitutions.

Before examining the specific implications of Durkin's research findings for publishers, it might be interesting for us to briefly review other studies on reading comprehension. It is not surprising that the most promising emphasis of research on learning to read has come to focus on comprehension. Comprehension is, after all, the *sine qua non* of reading; for without an understanding of what is read, there is no reading. It is only the most naive of lay persons who would equate reading with the act of pronouncing words. Researchers of the reading process from Edward Thorndike in 1917 to Frank Smith in 1978, have demonstrated that the central focus of all aspects of reading is comprehension.

Moreover, the emphasis on comprehension has included more than a narrow emphasis on the literal meaning of text. In 1949, Gates stated that reading was neither simply a mechanical skill nor merely a "thought getting" process. Gates said that reading "can and should embrace all types of thinking, evaluating, judging, imagining, reasoning, and problem solving." He further emphasized that the reading act is completed or nears completion when the reader applies his understanding in some practical way.

Yet, while many researchers have focused on comprehension, their efforts have often been to identify the components of reading comprehension. They have attempted to study reading comprehension as the associating of word meanings with symbols, selecting correct meanings of phrases, organizing separate ideas that are read, retaining concepts, and evaluating and critiquing ideas. Some researchers have attempted to study reading comprehension by examining a reader's ability to handle increasingly larger segments of texts—moving from separate facts and details to the meaning of a larger, unitary idea. Seldom, however, have researchers investigated what it means to teach reading comprehension.

Early studies attempted to view reading as a set of separate and distinct skills; they tried to determine the components of reading comprehension; and they sought to understand how a reader comprehends a single meaning from printed material. Building on those studies, researchers and theorists today have begun to truly understand reading comprehension as a much broader concept. Studies that are being conducted today focus on the logical process when one reads: building on the background of concepts, experiences, and language that the reader brings to the printed page. In a sense, the author's ideas are seeded in the reader's background. As the reader attempts to explore his or her own ideas, to modify them, to fit new ideas into the organization of his or her thinking, and to construct still new ideas, the reader is involved in a constant process of concept development.

Future research will certainly bring increased understanding of the comprehension process, with a myriad of implications and challenges for teaching reading. That challenge for educators was framed very cogently by Robert Thorndike in a 1974 review of research on reading comprehension:

> If reading is reasoning, we face at one and the same time a barrier and a challenge. The barrier is that set by the child's limited comprehension of what he reads, which we see now as not primarily a deficit in one or more specific and readily teachable reading skills but as a reflection of generally meager intellectual processes. And this barrier promises to stand in the way of a wide range of future learnings. The challenge is to overcome this barrier *by better and more inventive teaching—not solely to read, but also to think.* Because as we improve the understanding with which a child reads, we may concurrently improve the effectiveness with which he processes a wide range of information important in his development. The challenge is also to learn to exploit for educational advantage the individual's resources for reasoning through other media than words, so that the barrier of verbal limitation may be bypassed whenever it is not relevant. (p. 147 italics mine)

What we now need to determine is how to get that *"more inventive teaching"* which Thorndike mentioned embedded in our instructional programs.

To that end, Durkin's research is, I believe, a very valuable contribution. As a lesser contribution, I would like to propose the following set of questions that may serve as a guide to publishers who would like to review their basal reader manuals in order to determine if the direct teaching of reading comprehension has been included. I would note that although these questions have been derived from a review of Durkin's study, she has neither reviewed nor endorsed this list. The questions are merely suggestive.

1. Is each reading comprehension skill explicitly taught?
2. For each reading comprehension skill practiced and assessed, is specific instruction provided?
3. Are reading comprehension skills taught as explicitly as are word recognition skills?

4. Is guidance provided to help children understand the thinking pattern needed to arrive at an answer to a comprehension question?
5. Has attention been given to the interrelation of reading comprehension skills?
6. Has immediate application been provided for reading comprehension skills after they have been taught?
7. Are explanations for teachers about reading comprehension substituted for specific suggestions for teaching reading comprehension?
8. Do teaching suggestions provide guidance for teachers to follow when students do not know the answer to a question?
9. Do reading comprehension skills that are developed at one basal reader level relate to and build on those taught at other levels?
10. Do *defining* and *identifying* substitute for teaching?
11. Do teacher suggestions merely aim for correct responses from children, or do they go far enough to help children understand?
12. Are alternative teaching suggestions provided for teaching reading comprehension skills?
13. Is there a specific plan for the inclusion of review of reading comprehension skills?
14. Does instruction and practice of reading comprehension skills utilize only short written segments when the skill in normal use involves much longer printed segments?
15. Is there some logical plan for the introduction of comprehension skills?
16. Is the focus of questions on teaching comprehension or merely on checking whether a student has comprehended?

REFERENCES

Durkin, D. What classroom observations reveal about reading comprehension instruction. *Reading Research Quarterly*, 1978–79, *14*, 481–533.

Gates, A. General considerations and principles. In N. B. Henry (Ed.), *Reading in the elementary school: Forty-eighth yearbook of the National Society for the Study of Education*. Chicago: University of Chicago Press, 1949.

Hodges, C. A. Toward a broader definition of comprehension instruction. *Reading Research Quarterly*, 1980, *15*, 299–306.

Mosenthal, P. Reading comprehension research from a classroom perspective. In J. Flood (Ed.), *Understanding reading comprehension*. Newark, Del.: International Reading Association, in press.

Smith, F. *Understanding reading: A psycholinguistic analysis of reading and learning to read* (2nd ed.). New York: Holt, Rinehart & Winston, 1978.

Thorndike, E. L. Reading as reasoning: A study of mistakes in paragraph reading. *Journal of Educational Psychology*, 1917, *8*, 323–332.

Thorndike, R. L. Reading as reasoning. *Reading Research Quarterly*, 1973–74, *9*, 135–174.

3 The Purposes, Uses, and Contents of Workbooks and Some Guidelines for Publishers

Jean Osborn
Center for the Study of Reading
University of Illinois at Urbana-Champaign

This chapter concerns the reading workbooks that are used in elementary school classrooms. Workbooks that are designed to be a component of reading instruction are a part of essentially every basal reading program. In this chapter the term *workbook* is used generically, and indicates a consumable material that is associated with a basal program and is to be used by individual students. Included in this discussion are workbooks, practice books, skill sheets, mastery lessons, and any other pieces of paper provided by a publisher for students to write on. Also included are ditto masters that are available for teachers to use with their own pieces of paper.

THE PURPOSES OF WORKBOOKS

What purposes do workbooks serve? Do teachers and students use workbooks? Are workbooks important to reading instruction? And, to carry this line of questioning to its extreme, "Are workbooks necessary?" The first two questions, "What purposes do workbooks serve?" And "Do teachers and students use workbooks?" are discussed in the next sections of this chapter. But to the questions "Are workbooks important to reading instruction?" and "Are workbooks necessary?" in the absence of data, I give a personal response: for some students, maybe, for others, a very definite yes. I know of no hard data from any carefully undertaken studies that contrast a reading program that uses workbooks with a reading program that does not. But, given that the *practice* of what is being learned is

45

a time-honored concommitant to learning, and that workbook activities are supposed to give students practice in what they are learning, it does not sound too risky to say that workbooks are important to the kind of reading instruction that takes place in American classrooms.

What They Say about Workbooks

What do we really know about workbooks, their design, their effectiveness, and their use? Part of the difficulty of discussing workbooks arises from the lack of previous study on workbooks. An investigation of the literature of reading education reveals that very little has been written, for example, about the relationship of the content of workbooks to that of teachers' guides and student readers, about the sequence of tasks that occurs in workbooks, about the instructional design or quality of the activities that appear in the workbooks, or about the relevance of those activities to the acquisition of reading.[1] The few papers about workbooks that have been published in the past 10 years are based primarily on the observations and concerns that their authors have about the uses of workbooks. These papers are not intended to be an extensive analysis of the design, relevance, and efficacy of workbook tasks.

Better-than-typical examples of such papers are two 1974 articles by Dolores Durkin who, as a result of visiting elementary school classrooms for a period of six years, made some observations about the use of instructional materials. In one of these papers she presents findings about classroom instruction that were "readily apparent and surprisingly persistent." She found that: (a) teachers were spending time on unnecessary and even erroneous instruction, and (b) such instruction often was the result of an unquestioning use of basal reader manuals, basal readers, and workbooks. She described several workbook-based teaching events that: (a) were unnecessary, or (b) represented "turning means into ends-in-

---

[1] Until very recently there has been very little scholarly analysis of *any* of the components of basal programs, with the exception of the following topics: racism, sexism, and readability. Whether it is the academic interest in these topics or other reasons closer to the consumer, the developers of basal programs *have* attended to these aspects of their programs. It is my belief that work on these topics represents the easiest part of the task of analyzing what is in basal programs. The major component of these analyses has been *counting;* researchers have counted the number of minority group members represented in stories, the number of women who appear in stories, and the number of syllables and words that appear in sentences. Granted that such analyses should also examine the context in which minority group members and women are presented, the quality of how the sentences are put together, and what the sentences are about, this kind of research is manageable and possible. More difficult are the analyses of the psychological, linguistic, and instructional content of basal programs and the relating of that content to what is known about the teaching and learning of reading.

themselves," or (c) constituted irrelevant and non-essential practice, or (d) were incorrect instruction. Each of these events was based on what was in the workbooks the teachers were using and was carried out because "the children have to know that in order to fill out the next two pages in their workbook" or "the manual said to do it" (Durkin, 1974).

What do teachers in training learn about workbooks? The authors of some much used reading methods textbooks give workbooks either short discussion or no discussion. A survey of recent editions of 12 such books reveals that what was said about workbooks ranged from one line to four pages (and these are all *very* long books). One book lists some strengths and weaknesses of basal reader workbooks. The weaknesses included "are boringly factual," "emphasize mechanics, word recognition more often than comprehension," "often too hard for lower third of class, yet lacking in challenge for superior pupils," "often lacking in clarity of directions and inadequate explanation of purpose of." The strengths include "stress sequential learning, help develop skills," "aid in diagnosing difficulties," "save teacher time for preparation," "are prepared by skilled persons," "provide for extensive, effective drill" (Spache & Spache, 1978).

The authors of another book advise teachers to consider several factors in examining workbooks: the adequacy of practice on more critical comprehension skills such as summarizing, drawing inferences, and sequencing; the sufficiency of workbook exercises—Are there enough to allow students to develop mastery?; the control of vocabulary in the exercises; and the likelihood that the exercises can be worked independently (Carnine & Silbert, 1980).

Another author points out that workbooks can have educational value and that they can serve as diagnostic instruments. This author says that a study of errors made by children "will suggest to the alert teacher where further instruction is needed." Like many other authors, he cautions that the way teachers use workbooks determines how effective workbooks are (Heilman, 1971).

Still another textbook author lists criteria for the selection of workbooks. These include the need for workbook exercises to: (a) be related to the reading lesson of the day, (b) be matched to the reading levels of the children using them, (c) be used discriminatingly, (d) be used for a small portion of the working day, (e) be used for appropriate reading skills, (f) be matched to the children's ability (Zintz, 1977).

THE FUNCTION OF WORKBOOKS

Let's move from what authors say about workbooks to a discussion of how workbooks are used in classrooms. Workbooks function in a variety of ways for teachers and students. How workbooks serve teachers will be discussed first.

How Workbooks Serve Teachers

Some ways that workbooks serve teachers are obvious and others are not so obvious. Among the obvious is that workbooks permit teachers to keep some students occupied so that other students in the class can be taught in small groups.

An equally obvious but much less frequently mentioned function of workbooks is that they provide the teacher with what is often the only clear and uncompromised feedback about what each student can do. No such unequivocal feedback about student performance is available to a teacher during other parts of a reading period. Typically, a teacher working with a group of students will ask one student to read a passage or to answer some questions. If that student's response is acceptable, the teacher will move to another student. The teacher must assume that the students who are not responding are able to read that passage and answer those questions.

In contrast, workbook activities require students to work independently. How students perform in their workbook activities gives a teacher information about the performance of each student on all parts of a task. This knowledge permits the teacher to make decisions about whether or not additional instruction is needed for students, or whether they can move ahead. From this point it follows that workbook tasks can be diagnostic and prescriptive tools that teachers can use to evaluate the performance of their students.

Workbooks not only provide the teacher with information about each student, but they also allow the teacher to provide individualized instruction. They can be and usually are an essential component of individualized instruction plans. Sets of workbook tasks permit students to learn a body of information at their own rate and do so independently of the teacher.

In addition to these obvious functions, workbooks also include a function that is not so obvious. I hesitate to bring up this final point for fear that it will be interpreted as "Workbooks are good because they serve supervisors in their roles as classroom snoops." However, I would like to say that workbooks *can* serve supervisors of classroom reading programs in their roles of helping teachers become instructionally effective. When supervisors check student workbooks, they can not only gain information about how students are learning, but they can also make some very strong inferences about how teachers are teaching. I agree that supervisors must also observe teachers teaching and students learning for a more complete picture of what is happening, but I argue that a supervisor can acquire a lot of information about what has been going on in a classroom by checking student workbooks.

I spend a certain portion of my life working with teachers in classrooms; one of my routine procedures is to walk around the desks and pick up and flip through students' workbooks. I check to see (a) if the work pages have been done, (b) if they have been graded, (c) what the error rate is on each page, and (d) what type of errors the students have made. Two minutes spent in this activity is worth hours of classroom observation; it is a first pass at gathering information that will help me help a teacher.

In concluding this section on how workbooks serve teachers, it seems appropriate to say that well-designed workbooks containing useful activities can be partners with teachers in the initial teaching of what is new and in the maintenance of what has already been taught.

How Workbooks Serve Students

How do workbooks serve students? Well developed workbooks containing well constructed tasks can serve students in many ways:

1. Workbooks can provide students with a means of practicing details of what has been taught in the reading lesson.
2. Workbooks can provide *extra* practice on aspects of learning to read that are difficult.
3. Workbooks can provide intermittent review of what has been taught in a reading program.
4. Workbooks can provide activities in which students must synthesize what they have learned or make applications to new examples or situations.
5. Workbooks can provide students with a sense of accomplishment, when the work is "do-able," worthy, challenging, and has some "payoff." (This is not to imply that *all* tasks simultaneously have all of those qualities, but only that they should be incorporated into tasks as often as possible.)
6. Workbooks can provide practice in following directions (an aspect of learning whose importance extends far beyond following directions in order to do workbook tasks).
7. Workbooks can provide students with practice in a variety of formats that they will use when they take tests. The ability to cope with complex instructions is a characteristic of the successful test taker.
8. Workbooks can provide students with practice in working independently (another aspect of learning whose importance stretches far beyond doing workbook tasks). Most workbook tasks are to be

done by students who are working without the help of a teacher; such training, beginning in the primary grades, probably does prepare students for the teaching and learning modes of the upper elementary grades and secondary school.

9. Workbooks can provide students with practice in writing, an often neglected area in the elementary curriculum. In some workbook tasks, students write words, sentences, and paragraphs. These workbook activities are in a sense a bridge between the requirements of "pure reading" and those of "pure writing."

This list represents some, but not all, of the ways workbooks serve students. Workbooks are not without their critics, however. A frequently heard criticism of workbook activities is that they serve no students, only the teacher. The contention is that if a student has already mastered the goal of a workbook task, the practicing of it in a workbook is trivial and usually boring. Conversely, if a student does not know how to do a workbook task, the attempts at the task are nonproductive, sometimes counterproductive, and almost always frustrating. When workbook tasks have no relation to what is done in the rest of the lesson, when workbooks consist primarily of tasks that are assessments of what only some students already know (from sources other than the reading program, as well as from the reading program), when workbooks consist of tasks that are out of sequence or peripheral to the main line instruction of the reading program, then such a criticism has some validity. But, is such a pessimistic view of workbooks warranted in view of how workbooks are actually used?

The Use of Workbooks

Do teachers and students use workbooks? A classroom observation study we did last year gives some idea of how extensively workbooks are used in classrooms. For this study, observers watched a total of 90 reading periods of 45 teachers working in first- through sixth-grade classrooms in three different school districts. The observers recorded the use of basal program readers, teachers' guides, workbooks, and other supplemental materials during reading periods. (They also recorded the use of materials not associated with the adopted basal.) The classrooms in which the observations took place were in school districts that had adopted one or more basal programs. The adopted programs had been in use in their school districts for more than three years.

Central to this discussion are some well-documented observations from this study. The first has to do with how extensively the materials provided by the adopted programs were used, and the second has to do with how much student time was spent with workbooks associated with the programs.

How extensively (and exclusively) are procedures and materials from an adopted program used in classrooms? We found that during the periods allocated for reading instruction, the adopted basal materials—readers, teachers' guides, charts, workbooks, and other supplements such as practice cards and audio-visual materials—were used almost exclusively. If one is willing to generalize from our sample, it can be said that teachers and students do use the components of a basal program as "a package." It can also be said that during reading periods what the teachers do and say in order to teach reading (the procedures they follow), and what the students use as the medium for the practice of reading (the books, workbooks, and other supplements) derive primarily from the procedures described and the materials provided by the adopted basal program.[2]

How much time do students spend doing workbook tasks? Workbooks were a regular feature of instruction in every classroom we observed. In most classrooms students spent as much or more time with their workbooks as they did with their teachers. Put another way, our observations indicate that these students spend as much time reading and writing in their workbooks as they do interacting with their teachers. This is not to say that students spend all of the reading period with either their teachers or their workbooks; they also spend time reading in their readers and occasionally working in or reading other materials. Sometimes they are fooling around and aren't doing much of anything.

When and for what purpose the workbooks were used depended upon how reading instruction was organized in the classrooms. Our observations in self-contained classrooms revealed that the teachers typically taught one group of students while other groups of students worked at their desks. Cross-class grouping was used in a number of the classrooms, especially the upper grades. In these rooms one teacher worked with a group of students drawn from one or two more classrooms while in a different room another teacher worked with other children from the same classrooms. (Cross-class grouping permits teachers to work with larger groups of children of similar ability and usually reduces the number of groups a teacher works with each day while at the same time increasing the amount of time a teacher can spend with each group.)

We observed that in each type of classroom organization, workbooks were used for about the same amount of time. It is useful to reflect about

---

[2]In some schools two adopted basal programs were used, one for the "regular" students and the other for the slower students. In these schools procedures and materials from two programs were in evidence, but students in one program seldom, if ever, were given materials from the other program.

why this is so. In self-contained classrooms, workbooks have an obvious management function; that is, the teacher can teach one small group of students with undivided attention and with an untroubled conscience only when the other students are doing something that engages them and when the teacher considers what they are doing a worthwhile activity. In cross-class groupings, the observed functions of workbooks were more varied. In most of these classrooms, a teacher taught only one group at a time. Even in the one-group classrooms, work in workbooks was a part of the reading lesson. While the students did their workbook activities, the teachers did a variety of things—graded papers, helped individual students, and walked around the room. These teachers organized their reading periods to include time for students to work in workbooks and did so even though there was no need to provide something for students to do independently.

Implications for Developers of Basal Programs

Three conclusions from our study are of particular relevance to a discussion of workbooks. (a) Teachers follow the procedures that are described in basal program teachers' guides, and they use the workbooks and other supplementary materials that make up the basal program almost exclusively. (It must be added, however, that this does not imply that teachers follow *all* of the suggested procedures and use all of the available materials, nor that they always do what is suggested as the "right way" or with unfailing competence.) We concluded, however, that the basal programs accounted for most of what the teachers and students were doing during reading periods. (b) During reading periods, students often spend as much or more time working in workbooks as being taught by their teachers. (c) Teachers use workbooks because they think they are an important component of the reading program.

The conclusion that the teachers so fully and almost exclusively used the adopted basal programs is relevant to a point frequently raised by the trainers of teachers who oppose or question the use of basal programs. They contend that good teachers are professional people who do not feel constrained by any one program, but who will develop their own programs instead. They advise teachers to pick and choose from a variety of commercial programs and, in addition, to create their own "teacher-made" materials. They argue that only in that way can a program be developed that will match the needs of a particular group of students as well as the teaching styles of individual teachers.

This notion of what teachers should do is in direct contrast to what we saw teachers doing. The 45 teachers whose classrooms we observed had an average of 12 years of teaching experience; they were all trained and certified and probably had taken many courses from professors who advised a more eclectic mode for the teaching of reading. We do not care to formulate an explanation for why their teaching behavior has been more affected by basal reading programs than by their professors.[3] It should be noted, however, that we saw many good teachers and some excellent teachers, we also saw some inadequate teachers. We saw students who were doing well, but we also saw students who, to use an old-fashioned term, were not "being reached." What was consistent across these classrooms was the presence of those procedures and materials from the adopted basal programs. Although other books were in the classrooms, typically they were on the shelves and not in use, at least during the reading period. And of particular interest to the discussion of workbooks—although we saw some workbook materials from other sources, we saw few teacher-made workbook-type materials.

That these teachers did not seem to be making major adjustments and alterations in the programs they were using is certainly a reason for developers of programs to be exceedingly thoughtful and careful about the instructional content of their programs. But, even if it could be assumed that teachers always made radical changes in the programs they used, it would still seem essential to the integrity of a basal program that it be as instructionally viable as possible.

A final point: Workbooks are consumable items; schools buy new workbooks every year. We have been brought up to believe that the best products will be the best sellers. The economic interests of program developers might be well served by the creation of good products.

We think our classroom observations have implications for developers of basal programs, and especially for the developers of the workbook components of those programs. If teachers' guides direct what is taught, student readers provide what is read, and workbooks provide what is practiced, then what is in these materials must have within them a sufficient amount of instructional clout to assure that students can be taught and will learn the content of the program being used.

The Sufficiency, Efficiency, and Effectiveness of Workbook Tasks

Before proceeding to the next section I would like to make one point very clear. In our classroom study, we documented how time was spent; in this chapter I am discussing workbooks. Neither in the study nor in this pre-

---

[3]One third-grade teacher made a comment that may be illuminating. She said that when the children are tested on tests that come from the basal program, and the teachers are evaluated by how well the students do on the tests, everyone is, of course, going to spend all the available time teaching what will help the students do better on the tests.

sentation do I comment on or question the basic philosophy or instructional basis of a program—there *are* differences among the basal programs. But the amount of time I saw students engaged in workbook activities has led me to ask some questions about how what is taught in a program appears in its workbook component. The primary questions are about sufficiency, efficiency, and effectiveness. Are there a sufficient number of workbook activities to provide support for the instruction in the content of the program? Are the activities efficient in that they provide for practice that is integral to the content of the program? Are the activities effective in that their use is likely to make a difference to student performance in reading? Workbooks are a part of a delivery system. How well do they support the rest of the system?

Not many reading educators would oppose the notion that workbook tasks be designed so that they are relevant to students and to the program with which the tasks are associated. Relevant and challenging workbook tasks are desirable for many students, but (and this is another statement based on intuition) they are critically important to those students for whom learning to read is hard.[4] It is for these children especially that teachers turn to the tools for teaching reading that are in their classrooms. For most teachers, the tools consist of materials that are associated with the basal program they are using.

Keeping in mind the children for whom learning to read is hard, I surveyed a number of basal program workbooks. As I did this, I also followed along in the teachers' guides to see what was going on in the rest of a unit or lesson. Some of what I saw seemed inefficient, some insufficient, some seemed needlessly labored, some seemed impossibly difficult, some seemed irrelevant to the instructional plan of the program, a few seemed simple-minded—and some seemed clever, fine, and well done. What I saw prompted me to put together a set of "workbook guidelines." In this final section these guidelines are presented along with examples from workbooks. These examples are actually "counter-examples"; that is, they show aspects of workbook design that are *not* exemplary. The counter-examples were chosen to illustrate some of the factors workbook designers may want to consider if their goal is to provide materials that will help students learn to read, especially students for whom learning to read is hard.

Before beginning this final section, I would like to describe how I picked the workbook tasks that I use as counter-examples. I was intent on

---

[4]The controversies about how to teach reading are well known and are not discussed here. What even the most opinionated of those engaged in these controversies just might agree on is that arguments about how to teach reading are not nearly as important to students for whom learning to read is easy as to students for whom learning to read is hard.

combining what I had learned from watching students use workbooks in the confusing reality of classrooms, with what I could learn from reading workbook tasks under the cold light of the lamp on my desk. I looked through somewhat randomly selected workbooks from five different basal programs. I selected five representative programs, each of which is used extensively in schools. I used the most recent editions available to me. I avoided beginning-level books (more teacher direction is implied at this level) and most upper-level books (for a number of reasons, but primarily because I did not want to deal with advanced-level curricula). I did not do a complete analysis of all workbooks found at every level of every series; rather, I tracked the tasks in one series for a while, then moved to another, and then picked and chose from still others. I looked at hundreds of tasks in about 20 books.

My overall impression is that workbooks are the forgotten children of basal programs. Like forgotten children they have both good points and bad points. A remedy for the bad points of forgotten children is to attend to the details of their existence. To those of you reading this text who have something to do with the development of workbooks, I urge that you consider the guidelines that are discussed in this final section to see if any of the "forgotten children" aspects of the examples I give apply to what you are doing.

One final point, I do not wish to give the impression that I am a crabby, uncharitable woman—a nitpicker, who sits in an office with a real magnifying glass in her hand and a metaphorical one in her head, looking for trivial errors and only occasional unsatisfactory workbook tasks; rather, the impression I want to convey is that I am a reasonable and rather charitable woman who sat in her office looking through a pile of workbooks. It is this woman who has to admit that she had absolutely no trouble finding the examples for this paper, and who could come up with lots more by simply flipping through some more pages of some more books.

SOME GUIDELINES FOR WORKBOOK TASKS

1. *A sufficient proportion of workbook tasks should be relevant to the instruction that is going on in the rest of the unit or lesson.*

To get some sense of how much of what is taught during a lesson is reflected in what students do in their workbooks, I analyzed the contents of a lesson in one level of a basal series and related to it the portions of the two workbooks that accompany that level. How the events of the lesson listed in the teachers' manual are represented in the two workbooks is outlined in Example 1.

EXAMPLE 1
Lesson X

Teacher's Guide	WB 1	WB 2
1. Word recognition 46 words	1) Word meaning task with 9 words from Lesson X	5) Word meaning task with 8 words from Lesson X
2. Word and phrase meaning 22 words		
3. Sequencing of story events (6 events)	2) Sequence task with 2 sets of 5 events (independent story)	6) Sequence task with 6 events (based on Story in X)
4. Phonetic skills introduce /sp/ *sp* review /ft/ *ft*	3) Sentence completion task with 13 *sp* words (1 word from Lesson X story.)	7) Sentence completion tasks with 6 *sp* words (3 story words) 8) and 6 *ft* words (no story words)
5. Locating information on a contents page	4) 1 page task with table of contents	9) 1 page task with table of contents
6. Optional a) Noting action and conversation as a means of characterization b) Dramatizing good safety habits		

There are five major events in the lesson (in addition to those events having to do with the reading of the story and some other optional activities.) Aspects of each of those five events appear as workbook tasks. There are nine pages of workbook tasks to be done in conjunction with the lesson.

Forty-six words that at least some of the students using the program are not likely to have seen in print before appear in the story of this lesson. The teacher is directed to write on the board (or have students look up in the glossary) and discuss 22 of these words. The letter combination *sp* is introduced as a phonetic skill. A discussion of sequencing is also a part of the teacher directed lesson, as is locating information on a contents page.

Available for the students to work on in the workbooks are two vocabulary tasks, two sequencing tasks, three phonetic skills tasks, and two information locating tasks. Of the 46 new words that appear in the story, only 21 of these appear as words to be "worked with" in these tasks. Each word appears only once. The question of sufficiency has to be asked; is the amount of exposure to these vocabulary words sufficient for the hard-to-teach students? Does the practice with 19 *sp* words provide enough practice so that students will know how to handle the letter combination in future reading?

The sequencing task in Workbook 1 requires that students number two sets of events from 1 to 5, and then from 6 to 10, whereas in Workbook 2 the students sequence 6 events. Two tasks are devoted to working with tables of contents.

All of the tasks in the nine pages I examined were relevant to the rest of the lesson. This was not the case in all of the series I examined.

2. *Another portion of workbook tasks should provide for a systematic and cumulative review of what has already been taught.*

Workbook tasks are an obvious place for the systematic reivew of the vocabulary and phonics skills that are taught in the rest of a program. The vocabulary introduced in the lesson just described is *not* used in various contexts in workbook tasks throughout the rest of that level of the program. Only one of the letter combinations taught in that lesson occurs in

EXAMPLE 2
Lesson Y

Teacher's Guide	WB 1	WB 2
1. Word recognition 36 words 2. Word and phrase meaning 17 words	1) Word meaning task with 14 words from Lessons X and Y	4) 10 sentence completion exercises based on story in Y 5) 10 sentence completion exercises with words from Lessons X and Y
3. Inferring story details	2) Inferring details from pictures task (unrelated vocabulary)	6) 10 inferring detail sentences, based on story in Y
4. Phonetic skills introduce /str/ *str* review /un/ *ew* /yuw/ *ew*	3) Word meaning task with 12 *sp* and *str* words	7) Word meaning exercise, 7 *str* words (3 words from Lesson Y)
5. Locating words in a glossary, using guide words		8) Page task with guide words 9) Page task with table of contents
6. Optional a) Pantomiming story characters b) Noting action and conversation as a means of characterization		

EXAMPLE 3
Lesson Z

Teacher's Guide	WB 1	WB 2
1. Word recognition 34 words 2. Word and phrase meaning 18 words	1) puzzle with 8 words from Lesson Z	5) 10 sentence completion exercises with words from Lesson Z
3. Spanish words 6 words		6) Writing 10 Spanish words
4. Predicting outcomes		7) Predicting outcomes of three paragraphs
5. Phonetic skills review /ft/ *ft* /sp/ *sp*		8) Review of 12 *ft* words in sentences 9) 5 *sp* words in a sentence completion exercise
6. Reading a map		10) Map reading exercise
7. Optional a) Playing the role of a new student in a foreign land b) Plot and character development c) Elaborating story elements	Review 2) inferring the main idea (unrelated vocabulary) 3) Responding to provocative questions (unrelated vocabulary) 4) Recognizing supporting details unrelated vocabulary)	

the next lesson. Letter combinations introduced in previous lessons appear only once or twice or not at all in subsequent lessons.

A crude analysis of the vocabulary and phonics skills taught in a sequence of three lessons reveals that some things are reviewed and some are not (see Examples 1, 2, and 3). In the lesson (Lesson Y) following the lesson just described (Lesson X), 14 words from Lesson X are used in Lesson Y workbook tasks, indicating an attempt to use some of the words once again. However, there were 46 new words presented in Lesson X and 36 new words in Lesson Y. In workbook tasks in the next lesson (Lesson Z) none of the Lesson X words appears and only a few words from Lesson Y can be found. These are used incidentally, not as target words. The letter combinations taught in Lessons X and Y also have a spotty appearance in the subsequent workbook tasks. In Lesson Y workbook tasks, students practice a new combination (/str/ *str*) and review one of the combinations (/sp/*sp*) from Lesson X. Another combination reviewed in the teacher presentation part of that lesson does not appear in a workbook task. Three combinations are reviewed in the teacher presentation part of Lesson Y (/str/*str*/uw/*uw*/yuw/*ew*). Of these only one (/str/ *str*) appear in workbook tasks. The *ft* and *sp* combinations get two more tasks in Lesson Z.

There are three specific comprehension activities taught in these three lessons: sequencing of story events, inferring story details, and predicting outcomes. The teacher is directed to teach each of these lesson segments as the students follow along in workbook tasks from Workbook 2. What is troublesome is that additional workbook tasks on these topics are cast in a very different form from the initial teaching task. The vocabulary in these additional tasks is usually unrelated to the vocabulary of the lesson. I suspect that for the hard-to-teach student, working with a difficult comprehension concept in such a different context and with such different (and perhaps unmastered) vocabulary is hazardous and often not beneficial.

Why certain vocabulary and letter combinations are selected for more practice than others is not clear. It is clear that there is not an ongoing, systematic, and cumulative review of vocabulary and phonic skills. The assumption seems to be that students will master the content of each page and that that content will be assimilated into general reading skill. I think such an assumption is optimistic. My classroom experience indicates that for hard-to-teach students, lots of monitored practice is required for content to be mastered and assimilated into general reading skill. I also know that, on the other hand, some students need much less practice. A simple in-workbook testing procedure for determining which students need extra practice on any given task would be really helpful.

3. *Workbooks should reflect the most important (and workbook appropriate) aspects of what is being taught in the reading program. Less important aspects should remain in the teacher's guide as voluntary activities.*

In each of the lessons just described, the teacher is directed to present several different kinds of skill activities as well as to conduct the story reading activities. (There are also additional optional activities.) In Lesson X the activities include word recognition, word meaning, sequencing of story events, phonetic skills, locating information on a contents page, and noting action and conversation as a means of characterization. In Lesson Y there are word recognition, word meaning, and phonetic skills activities that are similar in form to the previous lesson but contain different words and skills. The different activities in this lesson include inferring story details, locating words in a glossary with guide words, and pantomiming story characters (as well as noting action and conversation as a means of characterization). In Lesson Z the different activities include predicting outcomes, Spanish words, and reading a map.

Which of these activities is reinforced with workbook tasks, and how sufficient are the tasks in number and in quality? As discussed in the previous guidelines, only some of the phonics skills and new words that are taught in the lessons appear in the workbooks. But what about the other activities? Sequencing story events appears in two workbook tasks, locating information on a contents page in two tasks, practice with guide words in one task. Three of the tasks are about inferring details, one about reading a map and two are extra—one on main idea and one on "provocative questions." Inferring details was in previous lessons; the other topics from a previous level of this series.

At least some elements of the most important activities of Lessons X, Y, and Z appear as workbook tasks and there are (in Lesson Z) a couple of review tasks. Careful observations of hard-to-teach students could determine if what is in the workbooks is sufficient. My hunch is that the sequencing of story event tasks are much too difficult and that hard-to-teach students make a lot of mistakes in them. I also suspect that one of the tasks on inferring details requires so much prior knowledge on the part of the reader that students who lack that knowledge have no way of approaching the task. But, in comparison to some of the other programs that I examined, the workbook tasks in this program do reflect the major teaching activities of the lessons.

4. *Workbooks should contain, in a form that is readily accessible to students and teachers, extra tasks for students who need extra practice.*

There are alternate and supplementary workbooks available with basal series that have been written for students who need extra practice. Frequently, what is on each page is well labeled, and there are several examples of each type of task. My concern is that the tasks that have been created should be especially effective tasks, and not just more of the same, or worse yet, some kind of busy-work activities that might keep the students busy and perhaps even amused, but that have minimal "instruction power."

Example 4 is a supplementary task for students who are having trouble with syllabication. I submit that students who have trouble with syllabication need to spend their time with words, and not cutting and pasting. In addition, these students are not likely to follow the complex set of directions this task requires, nor are they likely to appreciate "another way in which the words of each square are alike." If the realization that a red square of one-syllable words contains only animals and a blue square for three syllable words contains words that begin with the syllable *be* does anything for syllabication, I have not figured out what it is, except per-

Say the word in each shape. If you hear one syllable, color the shape red. If you hear two syllables, color the shape green. If you hear three syllables, color the shape blue. Then cut out each shape.

Put the red shapes together to make a red square. Put the green shapes together to make a green square, and put the blue shapes together to make a blue square. Make sure the words are not upside down.

The words in each square will have the same number of syllables. See if you can discover another way in which the words of each square are alike.

■■■ = red   (words that name animals)
■■■ = green   (words that name people)
_ _ _ = blue   (words that begin with the common syllable be)

becoming

dog

father

belonging

goat

mother

beginning

children

cat

horse

SL 21; TU 14; D 113g

EXAMPLE 4   61

Story Vibrations

Follow the directions given belov

Underline words that would give a feeling of mystery to a story.

dark, shadowy figures in the night
eyes peeking from behind a curtain
a bright yellow sports car
a dark underground passageway
boats rocking lazily in the harbor
strange creaking sounds at night
sun shining through the window
an unusual steady tapping
a robin perched on a branch
strange footprints in a flower bed

Underline words that would show hostile feeling in a story.

a playful, young brown bear
eyes blazing with anger
a faithful friendship
stamping their feet and shouting
children wrestling on a mat for fu
a scowling frown
children laughing at a funny joke
cheerfully chasing the cat
slamming the door in his face
yelling angrily

Underline words that would give a peaceful feeling to a story.

a noisy birthday party
soft music playing
fluffy white clouds floating along
bands marching in a parade
soft snow falling silently
a crowded subway in New York
sun slipping behind the mountains
people cheering at a baseball game
a whispering brook
moonlight on a quiet lake

Underline words that would show feeling of confusion in a story.

lost in a busy downtown store
a smile of delight
hustle and bustle of a busy statio
whistling a merry tune
a cat sleeping in a basket
alarms blasting and people hurryin
watching a sunrise
a bag tearing and apples rolling
a peaceful ride in the country
six telephones ringing at once

EXAMPLE 5

haps to convey the false notion that *all* words that begin with *be* have three syllables. This is a task that seems neither efficient nor effective.

How much practice should be provided is a problem. In the absence of hard data, I offer several suggestions:

a. better too much than too little, particularly if there are procedures available (for example, check-out tests) to determine how many of the available tasks students need to do;

b. better more on what is *known* (from classroom observation) to be difficult, and less on easier aspects of reading;

c. better for workbook designers to go into classrooms and watch hard-to-teach children to get a sense of what aspects of reading need the most practice.

5. *The vocabulary and concept level of workbook tasks should relate to that of the rest of the program and to the students using the program.*

The task in Example 5 is from a primary-level book. First of all, this task is difficult for a hard-to-teach child. It assumes prior knowledge of the distinction between words and phrases—the directions say *words* but may mean *phrases;* it is not clear. It also assumes this child can pick from a rather confusing, unpunctuated array of phrases those words or phrases which reflect the concepts *mystery, hostile, peaceful, confusion.*

For a hard-to-teach child the content of this task is neither sufficient nor effective. In order to complete this task, this child would have to be taught how to do it. (The teaching would surely include showing him how to separate the lines by some sort of punctuation.) The task form would have to be available many times and on successive days (it appears only once in the entire workbook), and the vocabulary used in each example should not only be used in those examples but in other parts of the reading lesson as well. For students who can figure out how to do the task and who know the meaning of these descriptive words, this task would provide independent work that will help them reflect on the meaning of language.

6. *The language used in workbook tasks must be consistent with that used in the rest of the lesson, and in the rest of the workbook.*

The directions in the teacher's guide for Example 6 have the teacher teach the students about word *syllables;* in the workbook tasks the students are told to identify the word *parts.* The directions in the teacher's guide for another lesson (Example 7) have the teacher teach the students the differences between fiction (which they also describe as "make-believe") and nonfiction. In the workbooks the students must decide if paragraphs are *real* or *not real.*

How Many Word Parts?

Follow the directions given below.

Say each word to yourself. Write the number of parts you hear beside it.

bicycle	_____	whistle	_____	apple	_____
table	_____	expert	_____	jingle	_____
exchange	_____	invisible	_____	exercise	_____
flexible	_____	extra	_____	needle	_____
uncle	_____	handle	_____	bustle	_____
bottle	_____	excited	_____	people	_____
candle	_____	jiggle	_____	excuse	_____
exactly	_____	kettle	_____	gurgle	_____
bundle	_____	bubble	_____	nibbled	_____
circle	_____	little	_____	cattle	_____
giggle	_____	exclaimed	_____	handed	_____
explore	_____	middle	_____	explain	_____
hustle	_____	mumbled	_____	turtle	_____

EXAMPLE 6

The Real Thing?

Read each story. Then decide if the story is real or make-believe. If the story is real, write real on the line. If the story is make-believe, write not real.

1. Della made a paper airplane. She put it outside on her front porch. Suddenly there was a big gust of wind. It lifted the airplane high into the air. Della ran after the plane and tried to catch it. It flew over a tree and around the house. It landed on her front porch.

real

3. Oscar's socks wanted to play a joke on him. They ran around the drawer and mixed themselves all up. When Oscar reached inside the drawer, he got two different socks. But the joke was on the socks. They had forgotten one little thing. They were all the same color!

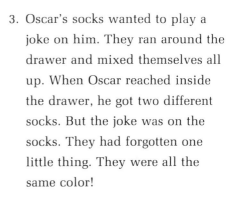
not real

2. Don wanted to grow some flowers. He found a big, empty box. He filled it with dirt. Then he put some seeds in the dirt. When the dirt was dry, he watered it. Soon the seeds grew into tiny plants. Then the plants got bigger and bigger. At last they were flowers!

real

4. Lisa found an old coin in the garden. She took it inside to clean it. Suddenly there was a puff of smoke. A voice said, "I am the magic genie. I will give you your wish."

Lisa wanted to make a special wish. Finally she wished for a new bike.

not real

EXAMPLE 7

Circle the word above each sentence
that completes the sentence.

pump   cramp   damp

1. Bob got a _____ in his leg while swimming.

bumper   hamper   whimper

2. The puppy began to _____ when it was left alon

bump   ramp   jump

3. The car went slowly down the _____

bumper   plumper   hamper

4. Ann put the dirty shirts in a_____

Circle the word that completes each sentence.

silkier   sillier

1. The kitten has _____ fur than the cat.

dirtier   drier

2. After planting the seeds, my hands were _____
than Tom's hands.

crunchier   chillier

3. The weather seems _____ today than it was
on Monday.

scratchier   scrawnier

4. This wool jacket is _____ than that one.

fluffier   fuzzier

5. The TV picture is _____ now than it was
last Thursday.

EXAMPLE 8

Whether such changes are due to lack of coordination between teacher's guide writers and workbook writers, or are done to adapt to the constraints of readability, or for some other reasons, such workbook tasks represent some inconsistent—and therefore ineffective and inefficient—instruction for hard-to-teach students.

Consistency of language from the rest of the lesson to the workbook is critical, as is consistency from task to task within a workbook.

Parts of two tasks from adjacent pages are pasted together in Example 8. The direction in the first says that students are to circle the word "above" each sentence, whereas in the very next text, they are to circle each word. A small difference, but one that causes some confusion to the easily confusable student.

Consistency is also important within tasks. The initial instruction in Example 9, which seems clear, tells the student to read and find the main idea of each paragraph. The second instruction says to number the sentence that gives the main idea for each part. There are eight sentences and four paragraphs (or parts). Suppose I am a hard-to-teach student who has some arithmetic skill. Does this mean every paragraph has two parts? Am I supposed to use up all those sentences? Does it mean that I'm supposed to find two main ideas for each paragraph? Maybe those sentences with lines in front of them are parts. For the easy-to-teach student, such ambiguity is simply a problem to solve; for other students, such ambiguity may result in confusion about some barely set understandings. The inefficiency of such a task seems evident.

7. *Instructions to students should be clear, unambiguous and easy to follow; brevity is a virtue.*

The language used in instructions is a topic that needs serious investigation. Perhaps this kind of research will tell us more about characteristics of effective instructions. Meanwhile, the comments on examples presented here are based on the performance of students I have observed in classrooms, and on my intuition. I would like to begin by saying something based on classroom observation. Students often do not read instructions, but simply go ahead and do the tasks. When easy-to-teach students decide to read instructions, they are usually able to follow them, even if the instructions are confusing, ambiguous, or unclear. My hypothesis is that these students regard such instructions as a problem-solving activity. They solve the problem and then proceed with the task. In contrast, when hard-to-teach students are confronted by confusing, ambiguous, or unclear instructions, their inability to follow them only confounds their tenuous ability to perform the tasks. Clear instructions *are* likely to make a difference for such students.

Instructions accompany most workbook tasks. Intuitively, it seems that brevity is a virtue and verbosity is less than virtuous. Thus, "Read

Moving West

Read the paragraphs. Then skim the sentences to find the main idea of each paragraph.

1

Some of the first people to move west had to walk. The trails over mountains and through forests were often very narrow. These people took pack animals loaded with the things they needed most.

2

Later, as trails became wider, covered wagons pulled by oxen carried families and the things they would need in their new homes. People were able to take along household goods, supplies, and tools.

3

Many families made at least part of their trip to the West on the Ohio River or on other rivers in that part of the country. They put all their goods on flatboats and floated downstream.

4

It was often difficult for wagon trains to cross rivers, though some wagons could be floated. There were strong currents, and even getting to the water might be hard because of steep banks or quicksand.

Number the sentence that gives the main idea for each part.

_____ Covered wagons carried people and their goods.

_____ Pack animals carried household goods and farming tools.

_____ Some early travelers walked and used pack animals.

_____ One way of traveling west was to float down a river.

_____ Covered wagons could travel on wider trails.

_____ Quicksand made crossing of rivers difficult.

_____ Crossing rivers was difficult and dangerous.

_____ The Ohio River was on the way to the West.

EXAMPLE 9

the sentences below. Fill in each blank." seems easier to follow than "Read the first sentence in box 1. Use the words letters stand for and the sense of the other words to find out what the new word in heavy black print is. Find the word that makes sense in the second sentence and print it where it belongs. Then do what the last sentence tells you to do. Do the other boxes the same way" (Example 10).

The goals of this instruction include a praiseworthy effort to coordinate what the teacher is directed by the program's teacher's manual to say about reading with what the students do when they are working independently. Thus, "Use the words letters stand for and the sense of the other words to find out what the new work in heavy black print is. Find the word that makes sense. . . ." are words that represent how reading is being taught in this program. But, the question that has to be asked is, does language in such "long form" function in a direction-giving mode? The "middle-sized" form of this instruction would be "Read the words and use the context of the sentence," the short form would be "Read the sentence." I suspect most students, even our hard-to-teach students, eventually use the short form and skip such an instruction.

In addition to being a counter-example to the guideline of brevity rather than verbosity and an example of an instruction that is not efficient, this instruction illustrates several additional points that relate to the use of instructional language.

a. *Instructional language must be unambiguous.* The easy-to-teach child who reads this instruction will figure out that the horizontal rules indicate the space that the instructions are referring to as "boxes" and then understand that in each box the *first sentence* is followed by the *second sentence,* and that by the *last one.* But consider the student who does not make the translation from horizontal rules to boxes and who is used to the numeral 1 being associated with *first* and the numeral 2 being associated with *second.* The instructions may be very confusing for that child. (This would be especially so if the child does not bother to read the instructions all the way through and does not see the last line "Do all the other boxes the same way." That line does give some help with how to do the task.) In this task, the use of the words *box, first, second,* and *last* is not clear and, for some students, is likely to be ambiguous and therefore inefficient.

b. *Critical elements of the instructions should be emphasized.* Even for children who can perform this task without reading the instructions, there is one response criterion that cannot be reliably figured out by looking at the print and at the pictures. Whether the correct work is to be *circled* or *printed* in the blank has to be determined by reading the instructions (If the students do not look for the words that tell *how* to respond, and *circle*

Read the first sentence in box 1. Use the sounds
letters stand for and the sense of the other words
to find out what the new word in heavy black print
is. Find the word that makes sense
in the second sentence and print it where it belongs.
Then do what the last sentence tells you to do.
Do the other boxes the same way.

1. The girl **dashed** along the beach.

   To **dash** means to _____.

       wet   brighten   race

   Put an **S** on the one who is **dashing**.

2. **Mash** up the carrots for the baby.

   Mashed carrots are _____.

       uncut   soft   loud

   Put an **A** on the **mashed** carrots.

3. We put the **cash** in here.

   Cash is   _____ ___.

       cakes   noise   money

   Put an **S** on the one with **cash**.

4. Where did this **trash** come from?

   I'll need a _____ for the **trash**.

       basket   doctor   dress

   Put an **H** on the **trash**.

EXAMPLE 10

70

right answers, they stand in danger of being told by their teacher they just do not know how to follow instructions and that every answer is wrong even if all of the correct words have been circled.) Easy-to-teach children learn how to search out what they need to know so that their teachers will write "Good work," "Fantastic!" on their work sheets; hard-to-teach children do not learn such strategies so readily. (Please note that I am not saying such strategies are undesirable—in fact, I believe students who do not figure them out should be taught them, but not when the goal of the task is the teaching of something else.)

c. *Instructions should become less complex as students do repeated examples of the same type of task.* Many of the tasks in this series (from the beginning of this workbook to the end) include this "long form" of the instruction "read"; there does not seem to be an acknowledgment of the notion that as students become experienced, the length and elaborateness of instructions can (and should) be diminished. I noticed this in many workbooks of many series, and I suggest that the continuing use of "long forms" encourages students *not* to read instructions. For hard-to-teach students, not reading instructions is an especially hazardous workbook strategy. One series started every instruction (in two levels of the series) with the words "you should understand." I suggest this teaches all students *not* to read the first words of the first sentence of *any* instructions.

d. *Components of instructions that appear frequently should be taught so that students will understand a "short form" of those components.* This program uses boldface type in many of its tasks to identify words students will do something with. Wouldn't it be more efficient to teach the meaning of *boldface type* than to continuously require the students to process "the word (or words) in heavy black print."

e. *Tasks should be designed so that "punch lines" are obvious.* In this task, students who have correctly followed the third line of each box have made a word by writing letters on the pictures. The task would be improved by providing a line on which they write those letters and indicate a picture of the word they have written.

Lest you think I am picking on this one task because I could find no other instances of problems with instructions in workbook tasks, let's move on to some other examples of ambiguity in instructions. In Example II, *first* refers to two sentences that are next to a picture, and *last* implies a sentence with a blank that is under the picture, but, is the first *last* on top of the second picture? Does the second picture have a first sentence? The pictures and sentences are layed out in a confusing order. Surely the students are confused.

Another task with ambiguous instructions is shown in Example 12. There are two sets of instructions, Part A and Part B. The students are first asked to identify consonant letters by circling them and to underline

Vowel Sounds

Read each sentence. Look at the words in dark print.
Write the word that does not have a long vowel sound
on the line.

1. The **boy** is in the **boat**.

boy

2. If you press too hard with the
   pencil, the **point** will **break.**

point

3. I hope you **enjoy** your **day** at the
   zoo.

enjoy

4. If I had my **choice,** I'd pick the
   green one.

choice

5. **Please** remind me to buy **foil** at
   the store.

foil

6. Debbie planted the **seeds** in the
   soil.

soil

EXAMPLE 14

the vowel letters before them. The instructions in Part A seem reasonably clear, if the students are comfortable with the notion that a word can "name a picture," if they can cope with the concept of *before* and if the widely-spaced letters under each picture don't bother them. The real trouble comes with Part B; first of all, it's hidden at the bottom on the page. Will it be seen and done? Next, the students have already underlined the vowel letter that comes *before* the consonants; now they are supposed to underline the first vowel letter in each word, and to determine if the vowel stands for a short or long vowel sound. To an unsure child, this second instruction might imply that there is supposed to be a line in some other part of the word. The instructional assumptions of the final line will be mentioned here; they are considerable and have to do with the sufficiency of examples, singular and plural confusions, and the basic nature of the response demands of the rest of the task (knowledge of vowels and consonants) as compared to the response demanded by this part (oral discrimination).[5]

Successful performance on the task in Example 13 assumes that students understand the instructional concepts *first*, *above*, and *below*. (There is very little teaching of the language used to express instructional concepts in the workbooks. The few attempts I saw were at best inadequate, at worst ludicrous.) But even granted an understanding of how these words are used in printed instructions, I would like to point out a problem for hard-to-teach students. The instruction in Part C of this task *implies* that words from Part A are supposed to be used to fill in blanks in Part C. However, the instruction *says* to use the words "*above*" (from Part B). If students use only the Part B words to fill in the Part C blanks, they will have some very strange answers. The easy-to-teach child will see through the small fallacy in the Part C directions and go to the list of words in Part A. More careful instructions would make it more likely that hard-to-teach children would go to the right list.

I will now list several more points about instructional language.

f. *When possible, avoid the use of negation in instructions* (see Example 14). Instructions that require students to process words indicating negation are more difficult than those written without such words. Thus, "Write the word with the oi or oy sound." would be better than "Write the word that does not have a long vowel sound."

By the same token, "Circle the word in each row that has a short vowel sound" is much easier than "Circle the word in each row that does not have a long vowel sound." The content of tasks of this sort require the students to make difficult discriminations. Hard-to-teach students do not need a difficult language processing task along with a difficult content task.

---

[5] Permission to reprint examples 11, 12, and 13 was refused by Holt, Rinehart and Winston.

• You should understand that when you meet an unfamiliar word, you can sometimes figure out what it is if you divide it into syllables and then pronounce each syllable as if it were a word.

In each sentence below, the underlined word is one you have probably heard but may not have seen in print. Use the sense of the other words and what you have learned about letter sounds and syllables to decide what the word is. Then write that word on the line at the right, dividing it into syllables as you do so. A starred example has been done for you.

★ Industrial waste is an environmental crisis.   cri   sis

1. The archer hit the target with her first arrow.   arch   er

2. The speed limit on most highways is fifty-five miles per   lim   it
   hour.

3. She has good credit at all stores.   cred   it

4. Automobile fumes can pollute the air.   pol   lute

5. What is Steve's favorite flavor of ice cream?   fla   vor

6. A carelessly tossed match can be a real fire hazard.   haz   ard

7. Suzanne burned her hand, and a blister developed.   blis   ter

8. My tennis racket needs to be restrung.   rack   et

9. Since the meeting will begin on time, do not be tardy.   tar   dy

10. People should figure their income tax by April 15.   fig   ure

11. Most newspapers contain comic strips.   com   ic

12. Each year people are asked to donate to the United Fund.   do   nate

13. Mr. Grouch is known to have a nasty temper.   nas   ty

14. She wore a black velvet cloak over her gown.   vel   vet

15. Eddie has a habit of cracking his chewing gum.   hab   it

16. Please get away from my desk, and do not meddle with   med   dle
    my papers any more.

17. A country's major city is usually its capital city.   ma   jor

18. A group of cows grazed peacefully in a large field of   clo   ver
    clover.

EXAMPLE 15

g. *Avoid instructions that are too ambitious*. Many instructions are too ambitious in that they attempt to combine goal setting, explanation, and instruction. Such a reasonable sounding practice often makes instructions long and cumbersome. The instruction in Example 15 includes: (a) goal setting, "You should understand; (b) explanation, "Use the sense of the other words and what you have learned about letter sounds and syllables to decide what the word is"; and (c) instruction, "Write that word on the line at the right, dividing it into syllables." The content of this task is very difficult for many students because it requires the knowledge of several syllabication rules. Does the incorporation of goals, explanation, and instruction in the instructions affect student ability to divide the underlined words into syllables? The best way to get answers to this question is by working with students, and especially with hard-to-teach students. My hunch is that the goal setting is confusing, the explanation is not sufficient, and the instructions are too embedded in everything else.

h. *Instructions should contain sufficient information*. Although I found a lot of examples of too many words in instructions, here is an example of insufficient information (Example 16). The instruction asks that the word with the *same sound* as the word that names the picture be underlined. It seems that the student must identify the *vowel* sound of the picture word. But, does it seem that way to the hard-to-teach student, or even to the unwary adult?

I conclude this section on instructional language by stating the obvious: The problems associated with writing adequate instructions are numerous. In the absence of firm rules about instruction writing, it would seem important for developers of workbooks to spend more time in classrooms observing children as they read instructions, and questioning them about their interpretations of instructions. These research efforts should contribute to the creation of instructions that will permit more students to understand the demands of their workbook tasks.

I would like to make one additional point: Some of the instructions are fine. All of the programs I looked at have instances of clear instructions. I do not want to give the impression that every instruction in every workbook needs a major overhaul.

The first 7 guidelines have been discussed in a rather lengthy manner. The next 13 will not be discussed as fully, not because they are less important or because they are unworthy of a more thorough examination, but simply because there is not space. The 20 guidelines are not listed in order of importance, although I would select several as *most* important. Of the first 7 guidelines, the most important include those about the relevance of workbook tasks to the rest of the program, coordination of vocabulary and concept level to the rest of the program, and importance

Me or My?

Underline the word that has the same sound as the word that names the picture.

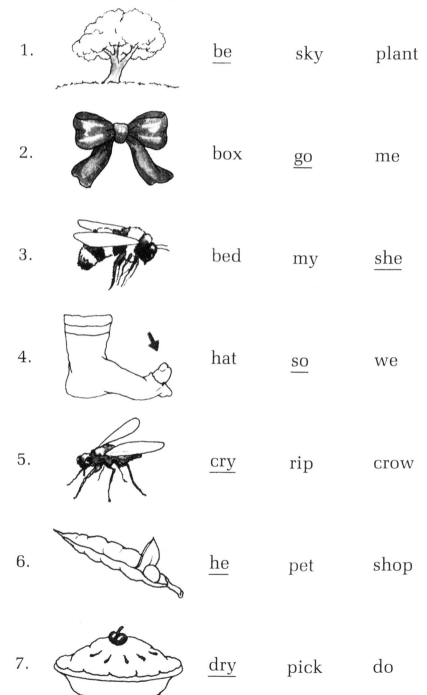

1.   <u>be</u>   sky   plant

2.   box   <u>go</u>   me

3.   bed   my   <u>she</u>

4.   hat   <u>so</u>   we

5.   <u>cry</u>   rip   crow

6.   <u>he</u>   pet   shop

7.   <u>dry</u>   pick   do

of instructional language. From the next 13, I would select the topics of instructional design and appropriateness of art as most important.

8. *The layout of pages should combine attractiveness with utility.* I suspect that reading long lines of type that stretch all the way across a page is more difficult than reading shorter lines; certainly shorter lines *look* less onerous.

Rules dividing sections of tasks are usually disapproved of by layout designers, but instructionally they often make sense. In addition, many workbook pages would become a lot easier to work if the sections of tasks were labeled. Example 17a is a page from a workbook. The addition of rules and labels in 17b does seem to clarify the content and make the instructions easier to follow.

9. *Workbooks should contain enough content so that there is a chance a student will learn something and not simply be exposed to something.*
Teaching, rather than exposing, has to do with both the nature of the task and the amount of times similar tasks appear in a given workbook. In example 18, the difficulties of following the first instruction are not discussed here, other than to say that for some students what represents a group is probably no more bewildering than what is meant by "the same way." I believe the first part of the task is conceived as a sort of warmup for the second part. The instruction is clear enough, but the task itself assumes the students are able, without previous instruction in this lesson or any other lesson, to operate with seven different analogy rules. If they cannot do this page, they will never get another chance—at least not in this level of the series this workbook is in.

Another task that only exposes is shown in Example 19. For children who have trouble identifying words that indicate *when, where,* and *how,* this task is difficult and probably important. Such a task appears only once in this workbook. The hard-to-teach child is only being exposed to something that is worthy of being taught.

Example 20 is primarily a language task. For students who understand part-whole relationships and have a vocabulary that includes a lot of knowledge of the world, this task is nice enough. For students who are unsteady about what is a whole and what is a part, and whose vocabulary does not include such words as *cells, lining,* and *henhouse,* this task presents lots of problems. But because this type of task appears only once in the entire workbook, I suspect that a hard-to-teach child will not be much affected by it. If this child gets a lot of teacher help and does the task well, then more examples of the task are in order. If our child does not get help and does poorly on the task, then it is just one more bewildering workbook page.

None of these tasks, which expose rather than teach, is in any way sufficient.

Word Parts

Draw a line between the parts of each word. Then write the number
numbers of the rule you used.

1. between double consonant letters
2. between unlike consonant letters
3. between a vowel letter and a consonant letter
4. between two vowel letters

rat|tle	1	circle	_____	holly	_____
ro|de|o	3, 4	hammer	_____	museum	_____
winter	_____	usual	_____	orbit	_____
widow	_____	duty	_____	cider	_____
castle	_____	poem	_____	after	_____
sister	_____	wander	_____	summer	_____
radio	_____	cabin	_____	quiet	_____
water	_____	dizzy	_____	accuse	_____
jelly	_____	idea	_____	lumber	_____
jumbo	_____	paper	_____	bonnet	_____
penny	_____	cruel	_____	lady	_____
fuel	_____	coffee	_____	giant	_____

EXAMPLE 17a

78

Word Parts

Follow the directions given below.

Draw a line between the parts of each word. Then write the number or numbers of the rule you used.

Rules
1. between double consonant letters
2. between unlike consonant letters
3. between a vowel letter and a consonant letter
4. between two vowel letters

Words	Numbers	Words	Numbers	Words	Numbers
rat|tle	1	circle		holly	
ro|de|o	3, 4	hammer		museum	
winter		usual		orbit	
widow		duty		cider	
castle		poem		after	
sister		wander		summer	
radio		cabin		quiet	
water		dizzy		accuse	
jelly		idea		lumber	
jumbo		paper		bonnet	
penny		cruel		lady	
fuel		coffee		giant	

EXAMPLE 17b

79

In each group of pictures below, circle the pair of things that are related to each other in the same way as the first pair.

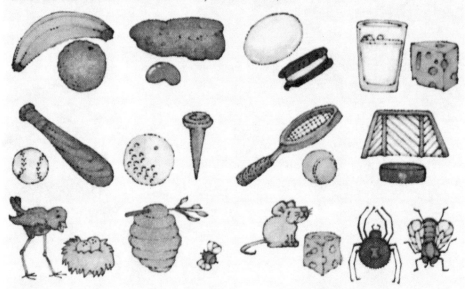

Complete each of the following sentences by underlining the word that best fits in the blank.

1. *Hay* is to *horse* as *gas* is to _____   telephone   tractor   light

2. *Girl* is to *woman* as *boy* is to _____   father   girl   man

3. _____ is to *sight* as *nose* is to *smell*.   Eye   Ear   Foot

4. *True* is to *false* as *in* is to _____.   down   out   side

5. *Children* are to *parents* as _____ are to *bears*.   ponies   cubs   kittens

6. *Drops* are to _____ as *flakes* are to *snow*.   rain   dust   hail

7. *Wheel* is to *car* as *runner* is to _____   sled   train   wagon

EXAMPLE 18

80

In each sentence the part that is underlined tells
when or **where** or **how.**

Read each sentence. After the sentence you will
see three words. Make a line under the one word
that shows what the underlined words of the sentence
tell. The first one is done for you.

	When	Where	How
1. We saw a funny clown at the circus.	When	<u>Where</u>	How
2. Our cat likes to stay out at night.	When	Where	How
3. The rain came softly.	When	Where	How
4. The kitten is behind the door.	When	Where	How
5. He ran as fast as he could.	When	Where	How
6. Some bushes are growing near the house.	When	Where	How
7. I'll be there in a minute.	When	Where	How
8. He eats a few cookies every day.	When	Where	How
9. He seemed to feel better after lunch.	When	Where	How
10. Put the cards near the telephone.	When	Where	How
11. After school, he watched TV.	When	Where	How
12. He is waiting at the corner.	When	Where	How
13. She answered us with a smile.	When	Where	How
14. Next week she will visit us.	When	Where	How
15. He carried the eggs carefully.	When	Where	How
16. She has never come to visit.	When	Where	How
17. She asked nicely if I was feeling better.	When	Where	How

EXAMPLE 19

Four things are named in each row. Three of the things named are parts of the other thing. Put a ring around the thing that the others are part of in each row. The first one has been done for you.

1. tail   (airplane)   cabin   wings

2. floor   walls   corners   room

3. barn   henhouse   hayloft   farm

4. motor   wheels   bus   seats

5. coat   buttons   lining   cloth

6. sandwich   lunch   milk   grapes

7. swings   slide   playground   sandbox

8. cells   bones   body   blood

9. cover   words   book   pages

10. plant   leaf   root   stem

EXAMPLE 20

10. *Tasks that require students to make discriminations must be preceded by a sufficient number of tasks that provide practice on the components of the discrimination.* For example, tasks in which students must decide in which words *y* must be changed to *i* to make plurals, or must determine which expressions are metaphors and which are similes, require them to make discriminations. Only after hard-to-teach students have practiced and mastered component tasks do they have a good chance of successfully coping with tasks that require them to apply this kind of knowledge to complex situations. More careful observation of students working with complex tasks would give workbook developers a better sense of how much component task practice should precede those kinds of tasks.

11. *The content of workbook tasks must be accurate and precise; workbook tasks must not present wrong information nor perpetuate misrules.* Phonics, word analysis, and comprehension tasks should be looked at with a cold and critical eye to make sure students are not taught, for example, that the sound of *o* in *hope* is short, or that "the main idea is in the first sentence of a paragraph."

12. *At least some workbook tasks should be fun and have an obvious payoff to them.* This guideline does not ask that *all* tasks be fun and games, but occasional puzzles, word games, cartoons, and other gamelike tasks would relieve the page-after-page seriousness of many of the workbooks I looked at. Caution: I am suggesting instructionally *effective* tasks that are fun, not pointless tasks that are fun.

13. *Most student response modes should be consistent from task to task.*

For example, if *x* is used to indicate something is wrong, don't have students use *x* to indicate that something is right in the next task. These are instructions from two tasks in the same workbook:

1. Circle the word that completes each sentence. Put an X on the word you do not need.
2. Mark an X before the sentence that gives details of the story. You will mark *six* sentences.

The dual role of *x* probably makes these tasks more confusing for a hard-to-teach student.

14. *Student response modes should be the closest possible to reading and writing.* Except for first-level workbooks, used by students who have not developed writing skill, it would seem desirable to provide for student response modes that call for *more* writing rather than less writing (see Example 21). The writing of the letter or number that *stands* for a word is

Write the letter for the word that belongs in each blank.

a. buttons   d. Scat   h. hopscotch

b. wrong   e. scraps   i. soap

c. caught   f. scrawny   j. angry

              g. pouring

1. What is __b__ with your old bicycle?

2. She was __j__ at him for teasing her.

3. Judy washed her hands with __i__.

4. My dog likes to eat __e__ from his dish.

5. The girl found a tan, _____ cat.

6. Judy's brother was _____ milk for her pet.

7. She _____ the beach ball with both hands.

8. Grandma put three new _____ on her coat.

9. The children were playing _____ on the playground.

10. To chase the cat away, the man shouted "_____!"

EXAMPLE 21

84

Some Things Change

Write the root word of the words in dark print on the
lines below.

1. Bella is not the **biggest** frog in the pond.
2. Many frogs are much **larger** than she is.
3. Bella is not the **prettiest** frog either.
4. But **Bella's** stories are wonderful.
5. All the frogs come **hopping** from miles around just to hear stories.
6. Bella makes you feel **happier** just listening to her.
7. Raymond has **loved** Bella for years.
8. He will never stop **loving** Bella.
9. It is not because she is the best **swimmer** in the pond. It is because Bella makes Raymond ˙ feel proud to be a frog.

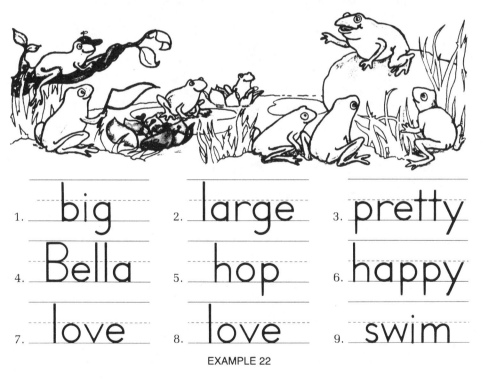

1. big
2. large
3. pretty
4. Bella
5. hop
6. happy
7. love
8. love
9. swim

EXAMPLE 22

85

- You should understand that if you can make up a statement of the main idea of a paragraph, you will know the most important idea about the topic of the paragraph.

As you read each paragraph below, decide what its main idea is. Following each paragraph are three sentences. Choose the sentence you think tells the main idea of that paragraph, and write an **X** in the blank before it.

1. Glacier National Park in northwestern Montana has numerous attractions for many summer visitors. Those who enjoy scrambling over steep cliffs can climb high mountains and explore deep canyons. Hundreds of well-stocked lakes and streams delight and reward those who like to fish. The park abounds in interesting wildlife, but no hunting is allowed. There are miles of wilderness trails for hiking and horseback riding. From an automobile, breathtaking landscapes may be seen, including the glaciers for which the park is named.

___ A lot of fishing is done in Glacier National Park.

___ There are many attractions in Glacier National Park.

___ In Glacier National Park, there is plenty of wildlife.

2. Some of the lakes in Glacier National Park lie in low, wooded valleys. Others are in the mountains where the air is nearly always cold. Lake McDonald, the largest, is completely surrounded by mountains. One of the smallest, Swiftcurrent Lake, is famous for the clearness of its reflections of neighboring mountain peaks. Although only a half mile long, Iceberg Lake is on such a high mountain that icebergs can be seen floatin in this lake, even on very warm summe days. There are about two hundred fift lakes in this park.

___ Swiftcurrent Lake is the smallest lak in the park.

___ All the lakes have icebergs.

___ The lakes of Glacier National Par differ in size and location.

3. The glaciers in Glacier National Par were once part of a vast sheet of ice tha covered much of North America thousand of years ago. Today there are betwee fifty and sixty glaciers in the park; onl one of which has a surface area of abou one-half square mile. This is Grinne Glacier, and it has an area of almost 30 acres. Sperry Glacier is the second larges with an area of about 287 acres. Only seve glaciers in the park have areas greater tha one-fourth square mile. Most of th glaciers are much smaller with areas c only a few hundred square yards.

___ There are glaciers of varying sizes i Glacier National Park.

___ Fishing is permitted in the lakes.

___ A vast sheet of ice covered Nort America years ago.

EXAMPLE 23

much less likely to produce a meaningful sentence, phrase, or word pair than the writing of the word itself.

Often, more writing would make tasks more instructional (see Example 22). This task would be more useful if the students had to write the ending to a given base word and then use the base word in another sentence right under the first sentence.

If there is a purpose for finding the main idea in real-life reading, it is to pick what is important in what has just been read. Underlining a main idea sentence *in* a paragraph is more like real life than finding it in a multiple choice item below a paragraph. Requiring students to write out the implied main idea of a paragraph would be more useful than having them select one best sentence from three different sentences (see Example 23).

15. *The instructional design of individual tasks and of task sequences should be carefully planned.* A well-designed task is one that makes the performance requirements of the task clear, causes the student to attend to those elements of the task that are central to what the task is attempting to teach, and permits the student to move without hazard through the task from beginning to end. Well designed tasks are often part of a sequence of tasks that are instructionally connected. The performance requirements of task design were discussed in the section on instructional language. In this section a few examples of less than adequate instructional design are given.

In the task presented in Example 24, students are supposed to determine the appropriate use of homographs by matching one of two sentences with a picture. In the first pair of sentences the student only has to read as far as *flowers* to get the correct answer. The student does not even have to read the word *earth* as it is used in two different ways in two different sentences. The third pair of sentences forces the student to read both sentences all the way through to determine which of them is represented by the picture. This pair of sentences is the only set on the page that makes the students attend to the target words. In all of the other sentences that students can identify the correct sentence by attending to other words in the sentence.

Tasks should be designed so that students can move without hazard through the task from beginning to end. Some of the tasks I looked at were two-part tasks. And in some of these the success of working Part 2 depends upon getting all of the items correct in Part 1. If there is no way for students to check their responses in Part 1 before moving on to Part 2, they stand a good chance of doing some very counterproductive work in Part 2.

Student responses should indicate to the teacher whether the students understood the task. In the task in Example 25, the lines drawn between the pictures do not let the teacher know if the students understand *before*

Use the sounds the letters stand for and the sense
of the other words to read each new word in heavy black
print below. The two sentences in each box use two
different meanings of the same word. Put a circle
around the sentence that goes with the picture
at the right.

1. Flowers grow well in soft **earth**.

2. The **earth** moves around the sun.

1. This **clip** will hold the papers together.

2. May I **clip** this picture from the paper?

1. My dog sleeps in that **shed**.

2. I wish my dog didn't **shed**.

1. Wash your hands in the **sink**.

2. We watched the toy boat **sink**.

1. Our car **stalls** on a cold morning.

2. The horses live in **stalls**.

EXAMPLE 24

88

Draw lines from the pictures that show
before to those that show after.

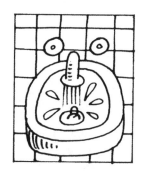

Draw lines from one sentence to the
other to show what the pictures tell.

The boy fell on the doorstep.   Mail fell on the doorstep.

The mailbox was stuffed.   The boy hurt his knee.

The stopper was in the drain.   Water filled the sink.

EXAMPLE 25

89

and *after*. The sentences about the pictures are at the bottom of the page; the students need not relate them to the pictures. (On the other hand, the pictures are pretty unclear and ambiguous. Maybe the boy is running for the mail. Maybe the wash basin is a clown face.) This is an example of a task that is not well designed for the students, nor for the teacher.

Workbook developers should be *reasonable* about what they expect students to process. In Example 26, students are supposed to be able to underline the letters for nine consonant blends as they appear in words that make up 15 sentences. It took me a long time to do this task, and I soon adopted the rather tedious strategy of going through each sentence with one blend in mind, then with another and another until I had finished the nine blends. In order to finish this rather punishing task, I often did not read the words in which I found the blends. I made lots of mistakes. I suspect that hard-to-teach students will not have the patience even to begin this task. I also know that a better-designed task can be created to get them to attend to consonant blends.[6]

In Example 27 the students are to decide which consonant letter is used the most in each sentence. What the task has to do with reading is a little unclear; what is clear is that the task takes a lot of time and that to do it correctly a student has to use lots of counting and matching skills and does not have to read (in the sense of looking at words and sentences) at all.

The task in Example 28 only requires children to copy words that are underlined. Although the task takes up an entire page and lots of time, there is no requirement that the students read anything other than the underlined words. Hard-to-teach students might find it easy, but they certainly would not benefit very much from it.

The task shown in Example 29 would be much improved if the students could show, by drawing arrows *within* the sentences, how word referents work. Having them draw lines between two columns at the bottom of the page casts a meaningful task in an extraneous form.

An enormous number of observations and suggestions can be made about instructional design. Comments on these few tasks are only an introduction to the topic.

16. *Workbooks should contain a finite number of tasks types and forms*. Special teacher-led instruction is sometimes needed the first two or three times a task form is used, but then less instruction is required. A consistent instruction form should then be maintained. Example 30 is page 10 of a workbook. Example 31 is the same form from another page of the workbook. Except for the title and the wording of the initial sentence

---

[6] Permission to reprint Example 26 was refused by Holt, Rinehart, and Winston.

Consonant Count

Read each sentence. Decide which consonant letter is used the most. Underline it each time

1. Rosa ran home around four o'clock.
2. "Mom, I am home," she said. "May I have some ham tonight?"
3. "If you still want ham after your father finishes fixing the fish, you can have it," said her mother.

4. My family lived along that road until last July.
5. Nan, who lives next door, will soon be nine.
6. My favorite part of Tina's costume is her top hat.
7. Up in my room is a pair of purple and pink party shoes.
8. Did you decide to wear the red dress?

EXAMPLE 27

91

Read each sentence. Write each underlined word under
the number of the sentence. The first one is done for you.
The letters across the top of the puzzle make a word.
Finally, write this word to complete the sentence below.

1. So Danny and his father
filled their <u>pockets</u> full of
walnuts and took them
home to dry.

2. Then Danny ran down the
hill to the <u>orchard</u>.

3. The <u>leaves</u> on some of the
trees were changing from
green to orange, red, and
yellow.

4. He saw that <u>apples</u> were
changing too.

5. "My bear was just a gray
squirrel getting <u>ready</u> for
winter," Danny said.

1	2	3	4	5
p				
o				
c				
k				
e				
t				
s				

The book was about a _____ bear.

EXAMPLE 28

What's What?

Read the story. Then match the words in dark print with the words they stand for.

Sir Wingate pointed to an inn. "Let's stop **there** for

the night," he said.

"I don't think it is open," said Sir Sidney.

"Sure it is," said Sir Wingate. "The lights are on. Can't you see **them**?"

"**I** think we should go to another inn," said Sir

Sidney.

"That's silly," said Sir Wingate. "I think **we** should

stay."

"Go!"

"Stay!"

After a while Sir Sidney saw the sun begin to rise. "OK," he said. "Let's stay."

Sir Wingate looked at him. "My good man," **he** said.

"It's perfectly clear that we should go."

1. there   the lights

2. them   the inn

3. I   Sir Sidney and Sir Wingate

4. we   Sir Sidney

5. he   Sir Wingate

EXAMPLE 29

The Right Word

Find the word in the box that makes each sentence correct.
Write the word on the line.

hundred	basement	afternoon	machine	interesting

1. Rudolf Rust is an **interesting** person.

2. He works in the **basement** of his house.

3. That's where he made a special time **machine**

4. This **afternoon** Rudolf took me for a ride.

5. We went one **hundred** years into the future.

EXAMPLE 30

The Right Word for the Job

Choose the word from the box that makes the sentence correct. Write the word on the line.

imitate	blowing	dark	direction
heard	lonely	older	beneath

1. Betty _____ the train whistle late at night.

2. It was like the _____ cry of an animal in the forest.

3. She went to the window wondering which _____ it was coming from.

4. She tried to _____ the whistle of the train.

5. In the _____ she couldn't see anything, but she heard the train getting closer.

6. The train rolled along, its whistle _____ in the night.

7. She thought, "Maybe when I'm _____ I can ride the train."

8. Then Betty crawled _____ the quilt and went back to sleep.

EXAMPLE 31

in the instruction, nothing has changed. This is a practice I applaud; if students can learn to work a task form, then they can concentrate on the task content. In this workbook, the advantages of these similar forms are somewhat compromised by the fact that these pages are 47 pages apart.

The repetition of task forms is *not* a common practice; in fact, it is quite uncommon. It is more usual to have *almost* as many task forms as there are pages of a level of a workbook. Two things can account for this: One is that there are as many different *contents* of tasks as there are pages in a workbook. The other is that there exists similarity of content, but little similarity of the task form in which that content fits.

The content listings from pages 49 to 78 of three workbook series gives some idea of the variety of content common to workbooks (see Examples 32, 33, and 34). The numbers in squares, circles, and wavy circles mark the number of times a task form is repeated. In the first program, three different forms were used twice. In the second, one form was used four times, two others twice. In the third program, no forms were repeated.

My conclusion is that in these three examples there is a veritable cafeteria of content, and therefore there is very little repetition of task form. Even so, when content is repeated, it is often in a different task form. My questions concern sufficiency and effectiveness: (a) Are there a sufficient number of tasks to provide for the massed practice that might enable hard-to-teach students to learn the content? (b) Do the almost continuously varying task forms make it more difficult or less difficult for students to learn the content? I suspect there is too little of too much and that continuous variety of both task form and task content contributes to the problems of hard-to-teach students.

EXAMPLE 32

Program A, pages 49–78

(49.) Practice with words with *ine*.
50. Practice with *oo*.
51. Choosing titles.
(52.) Word identification.
53. Using common syllables *a, be, un, ful, ly, ness*.
54. Vocabulary identification and use of *cl, bl, pl*.
55. Word referents.
56. Plural *ves* on words ending with *f*.
57. Following directions.
58. Alphabetical order.
59. Classifying words.
[60.] Practice with words with *ie*.

61. Compound words, comprehension.
62. Commas as a comprehension aid.
63. Noting details.
64. Syllables.
65. Puzzles.
66. Word identification.
67. Practice with words with *ash*.
68. Base words and endings.
69. Practice with words with *spr* and *str*.
70. Practice with *and*, comprehension.
71. Classifying words.
72. Contractions.
73. Sequencing.
74. Practice with words with *sw*.
75. Long and short *e* sounds, comprehension.
76. Multi-meaning words.
77. Practice with words with *ward*, comprehension.
78. Noting details.

EXAMPLE 33

Program B, pages 49–78

49. Words of the senses.
50. Doubling the final consonant.
51. Matching sentences to pictures.
52. Questions about story in reader.
53. Dropping the final *e* before *ed* and *ing*.
54. Literal and figurative language.
55. Questions about story in reader.
56. Puzzle.
57. Adding *ed* and *ing* to words that end in *y*.
58. Reading a chart.
59. Vocabulary, context clues.
60. Spelling of consonant phonemes.
61. Synonyms.
62. Questions about story in reader.
63. Matching sentences to pictures.
64. Commas in series and direct address.
65. Word meanings in a glossary.
66. Word identification.
67. Unit test.
68. Vowel sounds represented by *ou, u, oo*.
69. Comparatives.
70. Realism and fantasy, literal and figurative language.
71. Vowel sounds *uw, oo*.

72. Constructing direct address.
73. Quotation marks.
74. Follow directions.
75. Spellings with *ou, ow, oy, or.*
76. Syllable stress, dividing syllables.
77. Practice with *shall* and *will.*
78. Questions about story in reader.

EXAMPLE 34

Program C, pages 49–78

49. Word meaning.
50. Story ending.
51. Word pairs.
52. Cause and effect.
53. Following directions.
54. Vowel sounds.
55. Main idea and sequencing.
56. Outlining.
57. Vowels and compound words.
58. Alphabetizing.
59. Sequencing.
60. Vowel practice.
61. Phonetic spellings.
62. Main idea.
63. Comprehension questions.
64. Word identification.
65. Questions about stories from reader.
66. Writing dialogues.
67. Vocabulary.
68. Logic task.
69. Following a chart.
70. Finding details.
71. Words in context.
72. Similes and metaphors.
73. Predicates of sentences.
74. Sentence completion.
75. Poetry comprehension.
76. Sentence completion.
77. Sound identification.
78. Character description.

17. *The art that appears on workbook pages must be consistent with the prose of the task.* Pictures in workbooks are the subject of another book. But briefly, art that is confusing and inappropriate is bad, no matter how "artistic" its quality or how colorful it looks on a page. The art that appears in workbooks has been discussed in other places, and I am sure

that criticism of workbook art is not a new topic to publishers of basal programs. So, I confine myself to only a few examples.

Tasks that require students to pick a word, phrase, or sentence, to match a picture are found in many workbooks. Unless great care is taken with the art, such tasks are distressing. There are three items in the task in Example 35. There are probably 23 reasons for students to check wrong answers. Some of the problems originate in the art, some in the amount of inference the workbook designer had in mind. Item 1 is a very tiny picture of a farm with a barn. It shows a fence with what is perhaps corn next to it, and a tree with what are perhaps apples growing on it. To accommodate a long line of type, there has been a square cut from the illustration in the upper left-hand corner. The student is to check the answers the picture is "true of." (I note, but do not discuss, the difficulties inherent in the question "Which of these is true of this farm?") I would like to list some of the thoughts that *could* pass through a student's mind as he or she confronts this task. These are thoughts that a student might have who is acquainted with a farm, with the notion of "true," and with a strategy for thinking hard about each possible answer. (I will leave to your imagination the thoughts of a hard-to-teach student not fully acquainted with farms and *true,* nor equipped with such a sophisticated answering strategy.)

Here is the student's inner monologue: "This is a picture of a farm. Why do you suppose that square is cut out? Do you suppose there was a truck there? This looks like a good farm. 'New truck.' The farmer could have a new truck. My teacher is always telling us to visualize things when we read. I'll bet there was a truck there. I'll check truck. 'Apples to chew.' Are those apples on that tree? Maybe they're peaches; maybe it's just a different kind of leaf. Maybe my eyes are getting bad. Maybe I need glasses. Well, this looks like a trick to me. I'm not going to check 'apples to chew.' Anyway, who would chew apples on a tree? 'Corn grew.' Look at that stuff growing on the fence. That's not corn, those are like the hollyhocks in my grandmother's garden. I'm not going to check that one. 'Crew of apple pickers.' Well, I don't see any apple pickers, and if there's only one tree, that farmer is going to pick his own apples. I'm not going to check this one, but maybe apple here means apple there. I'm going to go back and check 'apples to chew.' I sure wish this artist drew better pictures."

This student will not have too much trouble with the second item, except perhaps to realize that whereas the first item gave him a lot of trouble, this one is ridiculously simple. When he reaches Item 3, his major problem will be with 'birds flew.' After all, the birds in the picture are flying. "Oh well," he says to himself, "It's a toss-up. If this is the old trick

Look at the picture. Then read the question
and check the answers.

Which of these is true of this farm?

__ new truck

__ apples to chew

__ corn grew

__ crew of apple pickers

Which of these is true of this park?

__ TV news

__ good stew

__ threw a ball

__ cats mew

Which of these is true of this street?

__ a few clouds

__ birds flew

__ crew of workers

__ new paint

EXAMPLE 35

question, I shouldn't check it; if they're just trying to make me read an *ew* word, I'd better check it." And since this student is a survivor, he checks "birds flew."

Surely there are better ways to construct tasks using *ew* words than this one. The art takes up a lot of room, yet each picture is tiny. Such inadequate art has a lot to do with making this task a guessing game.

Sometimes art would be better if it were not there at all. Example 36 also has three items. The students are told to underline "the sentence in the story that tells about all the story sentences," in other words, the main idea. I predict that for students accustomed to matching sentences to pictures, this task will be very confusing. My guess is that there will be a number of students who will try, for each item, to pick out the sentence that matches the picture. The pictures do not help students do the task; rather, they increase the probability of student error.

The hazards of using illustrations that serve as prompts for students to identify beginning, middle, or ending sounds are well known. One of my colleagues brought in this task. His child's teacher had marked it. A graduate student who was easily able to use the long vowel sound in the middle of each word in Example 37 as part of her identification procedure misidentified two pictures on this page (*car* for *jeep* and *crown* for *queen*). I still am bewildered by one of the pictures (so, perhaps, was the child who missed it). If one looks at the page from the point of view of a hard-to-teach student, less sure about the middle sound of any word, the possibilities for error are numerous: *toothpaste* tor *tube, lamb* for *sheep, rats* for *mice, worm* for *snake, horse* for *mule, ice* for *cube,* etc.

It is my opinion that this type of task should be abandoned by workbook developers. It is not likely that any set of pictures, no matter how clearly drawn, will be interpreted in the same way by their users. This task's potential for confusing students seems far greater than its possible benefit to them.

Finally, and these are very serious points, problems of perspective and proportion deserve careful attention. It seems likely that peculiar use of perspective and instances of real-life small objects drawn the same size as real-life big objects can cause confusion, especially for hard-to-teach students.

Equally careful attention should be given to the question of style. Workbooks as a means of exposing students to a variety of artistic styles may have value for art appreciation; however, it is not likely that all styles of art have equal pedagogical value. The primary purpose of workbook art must be always kept in mind. I see its primary purpose as that of facilitating students' understanding of something about reading. Art that is stylized beyond the real world reality of many students is not likely to achieve that purpose. Example 38 is only one of many examples of workbook art

Read each story. Underline the sentence in the story that tells about all the story sentences.

The boys and girls have pets.
Mike has some rabbits.
Kip has a cat.
Anna and her sister have a dog.

Snow fell on the houses.
It fell on the people.
It fell on the city streets.
Snow fell everywhere.

Mr. Fell likes to walk his dog.
Mr. Fell likes to walk dogs.
Mr. Fell likes to walk Bill's dog.
Mr. Fell likes to walk Kim's dog.

EXAMPLE 36

102

Long Sounds

EXAMPLE 37

103

that I judged to be pedagogically unsound. In addition to problems of proportion (the fly is as big as the microscope), there are problems of reality. Since students doing the task are supposed to be discerning reality from fantasy, I think the art should facilitate rather than obfuscate.

18. *Cute, nonfunctional, space- and time-comsuming tasks should be avoided.* In a sense both paper and time are money. Students spend only so much time in school, and they can deal with only so many pieces of paper. What is on each paper governs how a segment of student time is spent. How that times relates to reading should be a primary consideration. In Example 39 the students are asked to color the same number of circles as there are syllables in words. This task takes a long time to do, especially if the teacher is one to insist that each circle be completely colored. Furthermore, the teacher does not know (and this is in the realm of instructional design) why the student performing the task is right or wrong. A response mode that included marking the syllables would take the student much less time and provide the teacher with more information about the performance of the student.

In the workbooks I looked at there were many examples of inefficient use of time and space. These are task conditions that I suspect seriously affect the ultimate reading performance of hard-to-teach students.

19. *When appropriate, workbook tasks should be accompanied by brief explanations of purpose for both teachers and students.* Teachers should know why the task exists, and students should have some idea of what they are doing. Headings and other explanations for students should be in language the students are likely to understand.

The following task titles were selected at random from several workbooks. My description of what each task is about follows in parentheses. I do not think these titles convey much of a message to most of the hard-to-teach students doing the tasks. This lack of message means it is likely that these students do not have a clue about the purpose of the work in these tasks.

1. The Long and Short of It (for long and short vowels)
2. The Boy Roy (for practice with the *oi* sound)
3. That's Not a Ship (for a task with *sh* and *th* sounds)
4. Who or Which is? (for a task that involves only *which*)
5. Putting Down Roots (for practice with root words)
6. Contents Clues (for a table-of-contents task)
7. Pass the Word (for a dictionary task)
8. The Right Fit (a vocabulary/picture task)
9. Now Hear This (a vocabulary/picture task)
10. Hear! Hear! (initial and final sounds)
11. In Every Detail (picking out details)

For each group below mark an X through the picture or word that does not belong.

1. Fantasy

2. True
   Story

3. Science
   Article

4. Historical
   Fiction

5. Article   fantasy   6. Biography   birthplace
             information   schooling
             nonfiction   career
             captions   fairy godmother

EXAMPLE 38

SYLLABLES-PARTS IN WORDS

Read each word. Color the number of circles to tell how many syllables there are in each word.

○○○○ living	○○○○ clouds	
○○○○ Monday	○○○○ because	
○○○○ window	○○○○ apartment	
○○○○ another	○○○○ everyone	
○○○○ dropped	○○○○ mail	
○○○○ shades	○○○○ tea	
○○○○ sing	○○○○ Rumpelstiltskin	
○○○○ kettle	○○○○ name	
○○○○ whistle	○○○○ America	
○○○○ door	○○○○ grandfather	
○○○○ covered	○○○○ thanked	
○○○○ Walter	○○○○ father	
○○○○ open	○○○○ dinosaur	
○○○○ bed	○○○○ together	
○○○○ bedroom	○○○○ dump	

EXAMPLE 39

12. Your Fingers Do the Walking (a dictionary task)
13. It All Adds Up (reading the multiple choice questions)
14. Mainly the Idea. What's the Big Idea? Get the Idea? (for finding the main idea)

The list below contains a more straightforward set of titles. These were also randomly selected from workbooks.

1. Cause and Effect
2. Alphabetical Order
3. Compound Words
4. Fiction and Non-Fiction
5. Similes-Metaphors
6. Long Vowels
7. Consonants

These titles are not clever, not funny, but the message of each is clear. They *are* more efficient. The hard-to-teach students do not have to figure out the purpose of the task from a bizarre title or the context of the task.

20. *English major humor should be avoided.* How to test for the hit-rate of humor in workbooks is probably the subject of yet another extraneous doctoral dissertation, but I propose the following example (40) of what I call "English major" humor is not appreciated by too many students engaged in doing their workbook tasks.

Does this task represent an attempt to teach students that consonant clusters are somehow like grape clusters, or is this supposed to be a joke? I suspect that both the imagery and the joke pass right by most students as they laboriously copy the letters between the lines in each grape. The task would be instructionally much more viable if it required the students to circle consonant clusters as they appeared in words. At least there would be a chance that students would note how the clusters functioned in words. This suggestion fits into the guideline on instructional design and instructional design is probably not very compatible with English major humor. For the sake of all children, but especially for hard-to-teach children, I would urge workbook developers concentrate on tasks that have purpose for students.

CONCLUSION

After one of my colleagues read this paper, he said I should give an idea of the *proportion* of tasks in workbooks that do not adhere to the guidelines I have laid out. I have thought a lot about that suggestion and have decided

Look for tne Cónsonant Cluster

Underline the cluster of consonant letters in each word below.

sweet   border   raft   sender   sprain   skill   free

basket   street   best   green   fender   price   glass

Write the clusters of consonant letters in the cluster of grapes.
Do not write any cluster of letters more than once.

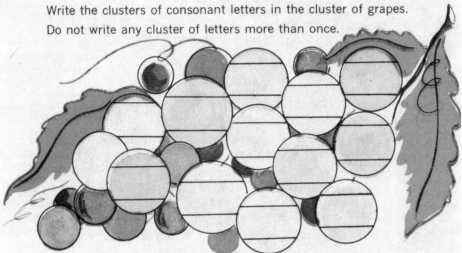

Underline the two consonant letters in the middle of each word
in the boxes below. Choose the word from each box to complete
each sentence and circle it.

| walnut |
| winter |

1. _ _ _ _ is the coldest time of the year.

| temper |
| tender |

2. The lion took _ _ _ _ care of her cubs.

| murmur |
| mongoose |

3. The children began to _ _ _ _ to each other.

| velvet |
| under |

4. He walked _ _ _ _ a ladder.

EXAMPLE 40

that such an attempt would be dangerous as well as presumptuous: dangerous because some people might not agree with my judgments and presumptuous because of the tentative nature of the guidelines. The guidelines are a list of suggestions based on my own classroom observation, readings of tasks, and curriculum-writing experience. They need to be thought about, evaluated, added to, and perhaps subtracted from. I leave it to you, the developers of workbook materials, to figure out the proportion of tasks in your workbook materials that adhere to those of the guidelines you think are important, and to add other guidelines as you examine your materials.

Another one of my colleagues asked if I had seen any tasks that called upon students to integrate their own and varying background knowledge and schemas into their workbook answers. My answer was that while there are many workbook tasks that assume the students working the tasks have a great deal of world knowledge, vocabulary not taught in the program, and good problem-solving strategies, none require students to integrate their own reactions into their workbook responses. The problem of designing tasks that will cause students to integrate their varying experiences into their responses is an interesting and not impossible challenge. The research in schema theory probably does have implications for workbook design. So does some of the other current research in reading. I suggest that workbook developers look at some of the research in comprehension, text structure, and readability to determine what has application to workbook tasks.

I would like to return to one of the guidelines, the one about workbook tasks providing a systematic and cumulative review of what is being taught in the program. Such a review would require an integration of what is in any given set of workbook tasks, not only with the lessons they are correlated with, but with the lessons that have preceded them. For this to be done properly means that workbooks must be carefully planned and developed with other parts of the basal program, and not as separate projects. Central to the notion of systematic and cumulative review are application tasks. Application tasks are either missing completely or occur infrequently in the workbooks I looked at. Application tasks would, for example, require students to operate on one passage with several of the comprehension concepts they have been taught, or, as another example, have students use a number of the structural analysis and phonics skills in one task. Students would read a paragraph, find the main ideas, the sequence of events, the important details, and review some of the vocabulary. Or they would underline a number of the letter combinations, base words, and affixes that occur in sentences they have just read. Wouldn't such tasks be more like the real challenges of learning to comprehend from text or of figuring out how letters, sounds, and parts of words add up to meaning, than simply inferring the details of three paragraphs or figuring out which *sp* word to fill in a blank?

I hope that a collaboration of practitioners, researchers, and program developers can improve workbooks. All of the hours students spend doing and practicing in their workbooks have to be considered a serious part of reading instruction. What is provided for them in those books should be given our serious consideration.

APPENDIX

Some Guidelines for Workbook Tasks

1. A sufficient proportion of workbook tasks should be relevant to the instruction that is going on in the rest of the unit or lesson.
2. Another portion of workbook tasks should provide for a systematic and cumulative review of what has already been taught.
3. Workbooks should reflect the most important (and workbook-appropriate) aspects of what is being taught in the reading program. Less important aspects should remain in the teacher's quide as voluntary activities.
4. Workbooks should contain, in a form that is readily accessible to students and teachers, extra tasks for students who need extra practice.
5. The vocabulary and concept level of workbook tasks should relate to that of the rest of the program and to the students using the program.
6. The language used in workbook tasks must be consistent with that used in the rest of the lesson, and in the rest of the workbook.
7. Instructions to students should be clear, unambiguous, and easy to follow; brevity is a virtue.
8. The layout of pages should combine attractiveness with utility.
9. Workbooks should contain enough content so that there is a chance a student will *learn* something and not simply be *exposed* to something.
10. Tasks that require students to make discriminations must be preceded by a sufficient number of tasks that provide practice on components of the discriminations.

11. The content of workbook tasks must be accurate and precise; workbook tasks must not present wrong information nor perpetuate misrules.
12. At least some workbook tasks should be fun and have an obvious payoff to them.
13. Most student response modes should be consistent from task to task.
14. Student response modes should be the closest possible to reading and writing.
15. The instructional design of individual tasks and of task sequences should be carefully planned.
16. Workbooks should contain only a finite number of task types and forms.
17. The art that appears on workbook pages must be consistent with the prose of the task.
18. Cute, nonfunctional, space- and time-consuming tasks should be avoided.
19. When appropriate, tasks should be accompanied by brief explanations of purpose for both teachers and students.
20. English major humor should be avoided.

REFERENCES

Carnine, D., & Silbert, J. *Direct instruction reading*. Columbus, Ohio: Merrill, 1979.

Durkin, D. Some questions about questionable instructional materials. *The Reading Teacher*, 1974, *9*, 13–17.

Heilman, A. W. *Principles and practices of teaching reading* (4th ed.). Columbus, Ohio: Merrill, 1979.

Spache, G. D., & Spache, E. B. *Reading in the elementary school*. Boston: Allyn & Bacon, 1973.

Zintz, M. V. *The reading process: The teacher and the learner* (2nd ed.). Dubuque, Iowa: Brown, 1975.

The workbook tasks used as examples in this paper are from the basal reading programs of the following publishers:

> The Economy Company, Oklahoma City, 1975
> Ginn and Company, Lexington, Mass., 1976
> Harper & Row, New York, 1976
> Holt, Rinehart & Winston, New York, 1977
> Houghton Mifflin Company, Boston, 1979
> Scott Foresman & Co., Glenview, Ill., 1981

The use of examples from these programs does not imply that other programs, not represented in the paper, are free of problem workbook tasks. Rather, the intent is that the points illustrated by the examples be applied by teachers and publishers to any workbook type materials being developed, considered, or used.

What Would Make
Workbooks Worthwhile?

Patricia M. Cunningham
Wake Forest University

In reacting to Jean Osborn's chapter, I am struck by the data suggesting that in the classes observed, *one-third* of the reading instructional time was spent working in workbooks. If these data can be generalized to most elementary classes, and I suspect that they can, then improving and increasing the comprehension instruction that takes place in workbooks must involve increasing the page space allotted to comprehension and improving the quality of what is on those pages.

The reasons for better workbooks are succinctly and poignantly described in Osborn's paper. She points out that while not every activity suggested in the teacher's manual is carried out, the stories get read and the workbook pages get done. She also notes that because the completed workbook pages are a consistent, observable indicator of what children can do on a day-to-day basis, teachers use performance in the workbook to evaluate children's progress.

Osborn makes explicit recommendations for improving workbooks. She argues that workbooks would work better if: (a) they had clear, concise directions and if these directions were consistent from level to level across similar tasks; (b) skills practice immediately followed the introduction of those skills by the teacher and sufficient practice were included; and (c) the reading level and interest level of the tasks were appropriate for the children at that particular stage of reading.

I would also agree with Osborn's recommendation about the "what" of better workbooks. She says that workbooks should emphasize the most important aspects of a reading lesson. But what are those aspects?

Working from the premises that all the workbook pages are going to get done by all the children in the reading group and that the teacher will make evaluations and instructional decisions based on the children's performance on those workbook pages, I would like to suggest that the most important aspects of reading are those that are universal. In this context, *universal* refers to those strategies that all good readers need to master. Activities that some children might profit from but that are not universally needed, as well as activities that are fun or enriching but not essential, could be included in the teacher's manual and on ditto masters. Teachers would choose to do these non-universal activities with the groups of children or individual children for whom they are needed and/or appropriate. Teachers could decide how much practice and review different children need by controlling the number of lessons taught and the number of ditto sheets used.

Assuming the acceptance of the principle that it would be beneficial for students if workbooks devoted most of their space to the most important, universal endeavors, I am now in the unenviable position of having to "stick my neck out" and suggest what these endeavors might be. I surveyed the huge and varied assortment of reading goals available in the literature and selected three that I believe are generally accepted by many reading authorities, have considerable support from empirical studies, and can be adapted to a workbook format. Since these goals are fairly well known, I will give only a brief explanation of each, and then I will provide some examples of how these ideas might be incorporated into workbook tasks.

1. *Comprehension occurs when readers access information they already know about the topic and relate what is known to what is being read* (Anderson, Reynolds, Schallert, & Goetz, 1977; Pearson, Hansen, & Gordon, 1979). It is generally understood and accepted that, as readers comprehend what they are reading, they relate the information gleaned from a page or passage to what they already know about a particular topic. Furthermore, they interpret what they read in a way that is consistent with what they already know. It would follow, then, that greater comprehension would result by providing students before reading with an activity that would bring to the front of their minds the knowledge they have about a topic and that simultaneously would help them discover some things they did not know or were unsure of about the topic. These two aspects of comprehension are labeled *schema access* and *purpose setting*.

Figure 1 is a workbook activity that, if completed before the reading of an expository selection on insects, would promote schema access and purpose setting. In Figure 1, an incomplete feature matrix is presented. The students' task is to add more insects and more features and then to

	GOOD FOR GARDENS	STING	LIVE IN COLONIES	EAT WOOD
BEES	+	+	+	−
LADYBUGS	+	−	−	−
APHIDS	−	−	−	−
TERMITES	−	−	+	+

FIG. 1. Schema Access/Purpose Setting—"Insects".

indicate with the appropriate symbols the features they believe characterize each insect. If students are unsure whether or not a particular insect
has a particular feature, a question mark can be entered.

Figure 2 is a schema-access, purpose-setting activity that might be
completed before students read a story about moving to a new school. In
both examples, the purpose of the activity is twofold. Prior knowledge is
consciously tapped so that it may be brought to bear upon the text, and
gaps in that knowledge are identified to help the reader set purposes for
reading.

2. *Texts have different structures; being able to follow the structure of*

HAVE YOU EVER MOVED TO A NEW SCHOOL?   YES   NO

WHO DO YOU KNOW WHO MOVED TO A NEW SCHOOL?

WHAT MIGHT SOME ADVANTAGES OF MOVING BE?

WHAT MIGHT SOME PROBLEMS BE?

FIG. 2. Schema Access/Purpose Setting—"Moving".

ACCORDING TO THE TEXT YOU HAVE JUST READ, SOME INSECTS ARE
BENEFICIAL, OTHERS ARE HARMFUL. COMPLETE THIS SUMMARY OF HARMFUL
AND BENEFICIAL INSECTS.

BENEFICIAL	HARMFUL
1. LADYBUGS WHY?	1. TERMITES WHY? THEY EAT WOOD
2. WHY? THEY POLLINATE FLOWERS AND PLANTS	2. WHY?
3. WHY?	3. WHY?

FIG. 3.   Following Text Structure—"Insects".

the text facilitates comprehension (Meyer, 1977; Meyer, Brandt, & Bluth,
1980; Stein & Glenn, 1977; Taylor, 1980).

Structure might be loosely defined as the way an author chooses to
present ideas or events so as to show the differential importance of and
relationships between these ideas and events. It is well known that stories
that have a beginning *(once upon a time)*, characters, setting, plot, and
resolution *(they all lived happily ever after)*, have different text structures
from the material contained in biology or economics textbooks. Further,
not all stories or informational texts have the same structure. Many researchers have tried to define the different story or expository structures
and to devise ways to provide students with practice in recognizing and
following these different structures. Researchers disagree about what the
different structures are and how they might best be taught, but there is
general agreement that readers with good comprehension can reconstruct
a story or exposition using the structure of the particular text.

Figure 3 presents a workbook activity designed to help students learn to
follow one type of structure represented by an informational selection on
insects. Imagine that the expository text was organized so that the major
idea (there are harmful and beneficial insects) was supported by information about particular insects, with explanations of why they are considered harmful or beneficial. The students read the text and then, with
books closed, complete the chart summarizing the characteristics of

harmful and beneficial insects. After completing the activity, the students could refer to the text to check their answers.

Figure 4 presents a workbook activity on text structure that helps students reconstruct the important events in a story. Our imaginary story on "Moving" is organized in such a way that there is a major problem (adjusting to a new school in the middle of sixth grade) and several smaller related problems. The students' text-structure activity requires that the problems, their attempted solutions, and an evaluation of these solutions be reconstructed after reading. Again, students would complete the activity without referring to the text and then, individually or in a group, check their responses with the text.

BILLY HAD TO CHANGE SCHOOLS IN THE MIDDLE OF SIXTH GRADE. AT HIS NEW SCHOOL, HE FACED A BIG PROBLEM OF ADJUSTING AND SEVERAL SMALLER, RELATED PROBLEMS. COMPLETE THIS SUMMARY OF PROBLEMS AND ATTEMPTED SOLUTIONS.

PROBLEM 1
BILLY WAS ALWAYS LATE BECAUSE HE COULDN'T UNLOCK HIS LOCKER.

ATTEMPTED SOLUTION
BILLY DIDN'T LOCK HIS LOCKER.

HOW WELL DID IT WORK?
NOT VERY, HIS JACKET WAS STOLEN.

PROBLEM 2
BILLY HAD NO ONE TO EAT LUNCH WITH.

ATTEMPTED SOLUTION

HOW WELL DID IT WORK?

PROBLEM 3

ATTEMPTED SOLUTION
HE CONVINCED HIS DAD TO LET HIM RIDE HIS BIKE TO SCHOOL.

HOW WELL DID IT WORK?

PROBLEM 4

ATTEMPTED SOLUTION

HOW WELL DID IT WORK?

FIG. 4.   Following Text Structure—"Moving"

YOU ARE ABOUT TO READ AN EXPOSITORY SELECTION ON INSECTS. LIST FOUR
QUESTIONS YOU HOPE WILL BE ANSWERED IN THE TEXT.

1.

2.

3.

4.

FIG. 5.   Control of Schema Access/Purpose Setting—"Insects".

3. *A variety of strategies is required for reading different texts for
different purposes. Being able to independently and automatically call up
and control the needed strategy facilitates comprehension* (Flavell, 1978;
Brown, 1980). The sheer ability to do something doesn't guarantee that it
will be done when necessary. Students need direction and guided practice
to help them learn the various strategies necessary for comprehension.
Gradually, however, the direction and guidance should be phased out
(faded), and students should independently and automatically realize
what strategy is called for and use it. The implication of this teaching and
fading procedure for workbook pages is that each successive workbook
page designed to teach a specific strategy should have less direction and
guidance than the preceding pages designed to teach that strategy. The
final workbook page should have minimal direction and guidance.

Figure 5 shows a schema-access/purpose-setting activity for an expository text on insects. In requires the students to do much more than did the
example in Figure 1. As students list the things they want to know about
insects, they are calling up their prior knowledge and setting purposes
based on gaps or contradictions in that prior knowledge.

SUMMARIZE THE IMPORTANT POINTS FROM THE TEXT YOU HAVE JUST READ ON
INSECTS.

SUMMARIZE THE MAIN EVENTS FROM THE STORY YOU HAVE JUST READ ON
MOVING.

FIG. 6.   Following Text Structure—Control. (a) "Insects"; (b) "Moving"

Figure 6 shows how students would demonstrate, with much less prompting than in the activities shown in Figures 3 and 4, that they could follow the structure of text.

In this paper, I have tried to respond to the omnipresence of workbooks by suggesting that if workbooks are occupying as much as one-third of reading instructional time, their pages should be devoted to the most important, universal activities associated with reading. I then discussed three findings from some of the current comprehension research that could be incorporated into workbook activities. They are not the only three aspects of reading that are universal, but rather are examplars of what might be included in workbooks.

Focusing workbooks on the strategies that all readers need to master would, I believe, result in four positive changes in reading instruction. (a) Children would spend approximately one-third of their reading instructional time engaged in comprehension and evaluation/appreciation activities. (b) These activities would be of value to all learners, since comprehension is an open system, one that is never mastered. Because of the complex interaction of familiar/unfamiliar subject matter, different text structures, and different strategies demanded by specific reading purposes, all readers can become better comprehenders. (c) Teachers would evaluate children's reading progress according to how well the children were moving toward the goals of reading comprehension and appreciation/evaluation rather than on how well children had mastered a set of random pages. And (d) teachers and children would be more apt to keep the goals of reading clearly in focus and not be as apt to "lose the forest for the trees."

I teach reading methods courses to undergraduate and graduate students, and I must admit that I do not spend one-third of my time talking about how to use workbooks. I do not know exactly how the money spent to develop a basal reading series is divided, but I doubt that one-third of the development budget is allotted to the workbooks. If workbooks are as important and integral to basal reading programs as their use would suggest, teacher trainers should spend more of their time helping teachers learn how to use them wisely, and publishing companies should allot to workbooks a reasonable share of the development dollar. Children are going to work in their workbooks; we must try to make these workbooks worthwhile.

REFERENCES

Anderson, R. C., Reynolds, R. E., Schallert, D. L., & Goetz, E. T. Frameworks for comprehending discourse. *American Education Research Journal,* 1977, *14,* 376–382.

Brown, A. L. Metacognitive development and reading. In R. J. Spiro, B. C. Bruce, & W. F.

Brewer (Eds.), *Theoretical issues in reading comprehension*. Hillsdale, N.J.: Lawrence Erlbaum Associates, 1980.

Flavell, J. H. Metacognitive development. In J. M. Scandura & C. J. Brainerd (Eds.), *Structural/process theories of complex human behavior*. Alphen a.d. Rijn, The Netherlands: Sijthoff and Noordhoff, 1978.

Meyer, B. J. F. The structure of prose: Effects on learning and memory and implications for educational practice. In R. C. Anderson, R. J. Spiro, & W. E. Montague (Eds.), *Schooling and the acquisition of knowledge*. Hillsdale, N.J.: Lawrence Erlbaum Associates, 1977.

Meyer, B. J. F., Brandt, D. M., & Bluth, G. J. Use of top-level structure in text: Key for reading comprehension of ninth-grade students. *Reading Research Quarterly*, 1980, *16*, 72–103.

Pearson, P. D., Hansen, J., & Gordon, C. The effect of background knowledge on young children's comprehension of explicit and implicit information. *Journal of Reading Behavior*, 1979, *11*, 201–210.

Stein, N. L., & Glenn, C. G. An analysis of story comprehension in elementary school children. In R. Freedle (Ed.), *Multidisciplinary perspectives in discourse comprehension*. Norwood, N.J.: Ablex, 1977.

Taylor, B. M. Children's memory for expository text after reading. *Reading Research Quarterly*, 1980, *15*, 399–411.

4 Readability—Appraising Text Difficulty

Alice Davison
Center for the Study of Reading
University of Illinois at Urbana-Champaign

DEFINING THE ISSUES

In this chapter I discuss the general topic of assessing the difficulty of a *text* (and I use this term to refer to any passage of connected written discourse). I speak primarily from a critical point of view about the role of readability formulas in doing the job of assessing the reading difficulty of a text. I concentrate on the use of readability formulas in a job which should be related centrally to the writing of text books. This job is the assessment of reading difficulty coupled with the *diagnosis* of the sources of difficulty.

If a particular text passage is to be part of a book or series of materials intended for readers of a particular level of reading ability, then a standard procedure might be to see what the text's level of difficulty is, as measured by two or three of the commonly used readability formulas—and it is a good idea to take an average of the results, sinice there is always the possibility of an error of a grade or two in the results of any one formula. Then if the text turns out to be too hard, by these measures, one of two possible steps could be taken: (a) The text would be discarded in favor of another comparable text with the appropriate content and lower score of readability. In this case, readability formulas are used in their original purpose of ranking a group of similar books or texts out of books, relative to one another. But there is another possibility: (b) Since well-written texts with exactly the right subject matter are not always in abundant supply, the text which seems to be too hard might be revised to remove the sources of the difficulty so that the text is easier to read and is suitable for readers at the designated level of reading ability.

The central question then is, what feature of the text should be changed to make it easier? Here we see the need for some measure which is both *evaluative*—gives predictions of the level of reading difficulty; and *diagnostic*—a measure which says what *causes* the text to be difficult, on the assumption that if some or all of these features of the text are changed, the reading difficulty of the text will be lowered.

Readability formulas were originally conceived of as evaluative measures, and their proponents reiterate that this is the purpose they should be used for. But if a text is being written or revised so that it matches a particular level of ability in its intended readers, it is rather inescapable that readability formulas will influence the changes made, if only because it is usually desirable to try to guarantee that a text has a particular level of difficulty. Tacitly or not, formulas are used to diagnose what causes difficulty in reading. In fact, a participant at the 1979 National Reading Conference expressed surprise that this was an issue of current interest. She and her colleagues had used formulas for years in writing mathematics textbooks.

In this chapter, I demonstrate that if readability formulas *are* used in this way, they can only give wrong answers to the question of what changes should be made in a text to make it easier. I argue that changes should be made in texts because of inherent difficulty, or problems of ambiguity, etc., in that text, and not *just* to influence the score which the text will get via readability formulas. Any changes which are made have to be subject to the judgment of the writer or editor, which will include knowledge of language, literary style, etc., and ability to express ideas in the best way which communicates the content and logical relations of the text.

The method that has been used to demonstrate the influence of readability formulas comes from a study by Robert Kantor, myself, and other linguists at the Center for the Study of Reading (Davison, Kantor, Hannah, Hermon, Lutz, & Salzillo, 1980). We compared two versions of four texts, a freely written original in most cases, and a revision or adaptation, which was supposed to be easier to read. The original texts ranged from about Grade 6.5 to Grade 12, while the adaptations ranged from Grade 5 to Grade 8. Thus, we were able to see the changes made in the text by comparing the corresponding parts of the "before" and "after" versions. While some of our points are based originally on a particular kind of reading material, subsequent searching in both text and trade books for children has convinced us that the style of writing which we believe results from relying on readability formulas is quite widespread and is certainly not confined to the materials we studied originally. The reading materials from which these texts were taken have also been changed somewhat in content, so that more diversity is found, but there do not seem to be changes in ways of treating the language of the texts.

The kinds of changes we studied, and their probable causes, are illustrated below in (1) and (2). The first sample is a sentence with hard words like *curative,* which must be paraphrased semantically, and proper names like *Hippocrates,* so that the full understanding of the sentence depends on knowledge of the identity and importance of a historical figure. The background knowledge is also spelled out in the adapted version. Note that the adapted version is considerably longer, if much clearer, than the original, which is part of a feature article that appeared in the New York Times magazine some years ago.

1. (original)

Hippocrates recommended milk to his patients as a *curative*
    1   2   3
beverage.
    4

(adaptation)

One of the most famous Greek doctors told his patients to drink
                           1   2   2   4
milk to cure illness.
      3   3

In the second sample, a long sentence is broken up into separate parts, with a little tidying up, condensation, and elimination of redundant material. Some words are also paraphrased.

2. (original)

I had kept my nerve pretty well *till* dawn, just as the faint light was coming, *when* we looked out *and* saw the water whirling against the bay window.

(adaptation)

But we all kept our courage up. As the faint light of dawn was coming, we looked out. The water was whirling by.
                       (we saw)

Required inferences are given in parentheses below the sentence.

These changes are not surprising if one keeps in mind that readability formulas measure sentence length and the complexity, unfamiliarity, or length of vocabulary items—see (3):

3. Readability formulas (sample of types)

   a. Dale and Chall

      Comprehension = .1579 (percent words not on Dale-Chall list of 3000 common words) + .0496 (words/ sentences) + 3.6365.

   b. Gunning

      Readability index = .4 (mean sentence length + % words over 2 syllables).

   c. Fry

      Grade level = intersection of values for sentence length and word length measured in syllables on the Fry Readability Graph; factors are weighted differently for earlier vs. later grades.

Clearly the changes made here, whatever their intrinsic worth, also do their bit to lower the vocabulary score (1) and sentence length (2). But note also that simplifications may be contradictory: Paraphrasing lexical items may considerably *lengthen* the sentence and add subordinate clauses to it, as in (1), while the objective in (2) is to *shorten* sentences, to break up coordinate clauses, and to eliminate subordinate constructions.

Aside from the possible logical contradiction in taking readability formulas to their extreme conclusion as guides to making changes in texts, I present some evidence here which *strongly* suggests that making changes in texts solely in accordance with readability formulas will have several really harmful effects. Changes of the type described above may very seriously distort the logical relations between the parts of the text, sentences, or paragraphs; they may disrupt the presentation of ideas, and make it impossible for the meaning of the original text to be presented in the adapted text. In some cases meaning is simply eliminated; in some cases it is left to the reader to make the correct inferences without many cues as to what the right inference is. The less information is expressed explicitly in the words and syntactic structures of the text, the more load is placed on the ability to make inferences and to use background information. While adults and skilled readers may be able to do this adequately, it is unlikely that all younger inexperienced readers can.

I begin by giving some examples of the kinds of deleterious changes motivated by readability formulas, along with some examples from the same sources of changes which *do not* follow from readability formulas, but *do* make the contents of the original clearer or easier to read. I also point to some features of texts which are important for ease or difficulty of reading and to which readability formulas cannot possibly be sensitive. (This is also largely true of other formula-like measure of linguistic variables in texts.)

CLAUSE SPLITTING

As we see in (2), one consequence of sentence shortening is that conjunctions are taken out as clauses are made into independent sentences. Many conjunctions which specify logical and other semantic relations between clauses are also markers of subordinate constructions, and so cannot stay if their complement clauses are made into main clauses. Although synonyms can be used, often the clause connectors are just deleted. In (2), the conjunctions of time are in some sense redundant, though the deletion of *till* in the revised version of (2) does not convey *loss* of confidence when dawn began to break, and leaves it up to the reader to *infer* that the narrator saw the waters whirling by. This is a fairly common example of the meaning of conjunctions being duplicated by normal inferences of connection and relevance.

But in other cases, the loss of connectives is not so harmless. In (4), the conjunction which indicates "means" and marks a subjectless subordinate clause is not kept in the revised version.

4.   (original)

If given a chance before another fire comes, the tree will heal its own wounds *by* ϕ grow*ing* bark over the burned part.

(adaptation)

If given a chance before another fire comes, the tree will heal its own wounds.   *It* will grow new bark over the burned part.
         (means)
         (and next)

Clearly the original sentence is not unclear or ambiguous; it is just fairly long. Making the means clause a separate clause serves to shorten average sentence length. While it is *possible* to infer the correct meaning, it is equally possible to make the wrong inference, especially if the reader does not know much about how trees work. The following sentence could simply express some event which takes place next, after the tree heals its wounds.

In (5), we see a purpose clause, expressed by a subjectless infinitive construction, replaced by a separate sentence, again to break up a fairly long sentence with a parenthetical clause in the middle of it.

5. (original)

"I'm going down to the contract," said Jack, "*to see* that every-thing is alright."

(adaptation)

"I'm going down to the building project," Jack said. "*I have to see* if everything is all right."   (obligation = purpose?)

While the motivation of breaking up this long sentence may not necessar-ily be reprehensible, the effect is to replace an unambiguous purpose clause be an expression of obligation, which is not the same thing at all. From obligation, one *might* infer purpose, but there is nothing in the sentence which says that this inference must be made. Since the character Jack in this narrative risks his life in a flood to go back to the project, it is more appropriate to express his motivation as his own purpose rather than external obligation. While one could reconstruct the exact meaning of this sentence from the whole narrative, it seems strange to make mean-ing *less* explicit in the process of simplification, since more cognitive work is required to construct the meaning of the text.

On the other hand, there are changes which are made in adaptations which run counter to the trend of splitting up sentences with loss of connectives. For example, the change made in (6) actually improves the text.

6. (original)

We had water to drink after that. We set out basins and caught
                              (because)   (consequently)
raindrops.

(adaptation)

We set out basins *to* ϕ catch the raindrops *so that* we would have water to drink.

In the original, the unconjoined sequence of two sentences must be re-lated by the inference that the first sentence describes the result of the events described in the second sentence. The revision reverses the order of the sentences so that they reflect the order in which the events oc-curred. Many studies have shown that both adults and children prefer to have clauses mentioned in "natural" order, that is, the order in which the events took place (Linde, 1976; Osgood & Sridhar, 1978; Pearson, 1974–75). In the adapted version, the original two separate sentences are con-nected by an explicit subordinating connective which expresses result and purpose relations between the clauses. Here the reader is saved a great deal of interpretive work.

INFERENCES

Causal and other relations between parts of a sentence often depend on specific pieces of information. If this information is deleted, then the correct inference is less clearly determined. For example, in (7), two original sentences contain reduced relative clauses, which express subordinate or background information, and may impose some barriers to language processing of the sentence because the reader must interrupt work on the main clause, keeping the first part in temporary memory.

7. (original)

> Angler fishes, *among the most unusual of luminescent fishes,* have fingerlike extensions which dangle in front of their mouths. Fishes *attracted to these lights* are easily caught and eaten.

(adaptation)

> Angler fishes (   ) have fingerlike lights which they dangle in front of their large gaping mouths. Fishes *in the dark* are easily caught
> (they can't see?)
> and eaten.

The first of the subordinate constructions is deleted without much effect, since it only contains some justification for the great interest of angler fishes. But the second subordinate construction explains why the angler fish is successful in luring other fish into its mouth. Without this information, all sorts of wrong inferences are possible: that the non-angler fish cannot see their way in the dark, or cannot see the angler fish, etc.

In some cases the adaptor has anticipated the need to fill in for younger readers some information which might be obvious to adults. For example, in (8), the adaptor has carefully added *when it froze,* obviously not counting on the ability of readers to infer that only skim milk in frozen form would be used in a skating rink.

8. (original)

> In Toronto, a suburban ice-skating rink was flooded with 250 *surplus* gallons of it [= skim milk]. Skaters found that it chipped less easily than frozen water.

(adaptation)

> An ice-skating rink was flooded with it. Skaters found that *when it froze* it chipped less easily than *frozen* water.

One might be able to infer *retrospectively* that it was frozen after reading the part at the end of the sentence about comparing skim milk to frozen water. But this means false starts and going back and reinterpreting previously interpreted material. The adaptor *added* length to the sentence, but may have actually facilitated the reader's job of interpreting the sentence, since the added information rules out a blind alley in interpretation. (Of course, the deletion of the presumably unfamiliar word *surplus* may make the reader wonder why milk is being used in this unusual and apparently wasteful way.)

One of the deceptive factors in adaptation is the fact that, if the reader pays attention to the text and has a certain amount of background knowledge and inferencing ability, it is *possible* to communicate the "same" message with simpler words and syntax. Inferences often parallel or duplicate semantic and syntactic relations. But it is far from clear that relying on inferences to communicate what is left out in the name of simplification actually makes the reader's job easier, or if it does, whether the message of the text comes through without distortion. It is possible—and in some cases *probable*—that a text may be simplified to the point of being readable at a particular level as measured by readability formulas without being *comprehensible*. Simplification would therefore have defeated its own purpose.

In (9) is given the first paragraph of a book for children on the American Civil War. This paragraph comes from a fairly old trade book chosen as an extreme example of simplification leading to incoherence, and of the amount of inferencing work which is necessary when explicit information is left out.

9. [1]Before the Civil War the Negroes in the South were slaves. [2]Many
   (And after?)   (But not in the North?)
   people in the North thought that this was wrong and formed a party to
                              = ? Slavery in South only?
                                  Slavery in general?

   prevent the spread of slavery. [3]When this party elected Abraham
   (But if slavery in the South is wrong?)   (Not the whole country?)

   Lincoln President of the United States, people in the slave states

   became very angry. [4]They thought Lincoln and his party
           (At Lincoln? At the party?)   (Reason?)

   were going to take their slaves away, and then they would be unable
           (Spread of slavery?)

   to grow cottom,   which was almost the only
       (Another issue: How related to slavery?)

   thing their farms produced.
       (What about farms in the North; how are they different?)

The events immediately preceding the Civil War and the causes that led up to it are given in one paragraph of 79 words in 13 clauses, 6 main clauses, and 7 subordinate clauses. The message is quite complex, while the language of the paragraph is supposed to be very simple—at least it sounds simplified to an adult. Although the sentences themselves are fairly long, there is only one adverbial subordinate clause, marked by *when,* and two coordinating conjunctions, *and* and *and then.* There are clearly marked subordinate clauses, beginning with *that, to,* and relative pronouns. An adult who knew American history would probably say that the paragraph says nothing actually *wrong,* except perhaps that a political party elects a president. All the relations within the paragraph can be inferred, either from using background knowledge plus the contents of the paragraph, or by eliminating all the inferences which are contradictory and picking the interpretation which fits all of the sentences together.

Yet the paragraph itself is disconnected to the point of incoherence, and it is not clear how it would be interpreted by someone without much background knowledge. I have tried to reconstruct some of the misleading messages that might be inferred along the way. For example, the reference of *this* in (2) is quite unclear until the fourth sentence is reached, and the phrase *spread of slavery* contradicts the content of the fourth sentence, which refers to *existing* slavery. Finally, the relation of slaves to cotton is left completely vague, and it is not made clear that there were both moral and economic aspects to the institution of slavery. The differences between Northern and Southern farms and economy is not made clear, allowing the reader to wonder exactly what the conflict was about. No doubt it would be possible, as an exercise, to rewrite this paragraph, perhaps in shorter sentences, so that the intended message is expressed clearly. One of the obvious changes to make is in the organization and sequence of ideas, and I return shortly to this theme. What I want to emphasize here is that simplifying words and syntax does not necessarily simplify the task of the reader, and often increases the demands of the text, beyond low-level decoding tasks.

TOPIC, BACKGROUND INFORMATION, AND FOCUS

I made the uncontroversial claim in the last section that subordinate clauses often express background information, information which is subordinate to the main topic of the discourse. Thus the syntactic relations of the sentence give some information about the author's characterization of various pieces of information in the text. What happens if the syntactic structures in a long or complex sentence get changed? I want to show here some examples of how the message gets distorted and receives different emphasis when the syntactic form in which the message is expressed gets changed in the process of adaptation or editing. It has been shown in many studies, such as Gourlay and Catlin (1978), Haviland and Clark (1974), Perfetti and Goldman (1975), and Perfetti and Lesgold (1977) that it makes a difference in comprehension, in written or spoken language, whether thematic material comes after an appropriate context which introduces it, or whether there is no such context, or the context is separated by irrelevant material from the thematically marked material (sentence topic for example).

Two important notions for describing discourse properties of sentences are *focus* and *topic*. The main emphasis of a sentence or focus is often on the last large chunk. The focus in (10) in its original form would therefore seem to be on the creature leaving a luminous trail *as it moves about*.

10. (original)

This small *sand-dwelling* animal *emerges* at night *and* secretes a luminous *mucus* as it moves about.

(adaptation)

This small animal, which lies in the sand, comes out at night. As it moves about, it secretes a luminous substance.

In the adaptation, the sentence is split into two sentences, with the subordinate adverbial clause moved to the front, where it merely expresses background information which is taken as given. Hence, there are two focuses, *comes out at night* and *secretes a luminous substance,* each of which receive equal emphasis. The effect communicated is certainly not the same, and not as coherent, as in the longer original, which subordinated a lot of background information about the luminous worms to the main point of the luminous trails.

Somewhat more serious damage can be seen in two versions of a recent sixth-grade science text, in (11).

11. (First edition) Topic: Visible and invisible creatures in lakes

You probably saw lily pads, grass, reeds, and water weeds *growing in the shallow water near the shore.* And maybe there were water striders gliding over the surface of the lake, *and* small fishes darting among the shadows of the lily pads.

(Second edition)

You probably saw lily pads, grass reeds and water weeds. *These plants* grow in the shallow water near the shore. There may have been water striders gliding over the surface of the lake. Did you see small fishes darting in the shadows of the lily pads?

The point of the introductory passage, of which this is a part, is to focus attention first on creatures that can be seen, and then on microorganisms that *cannot* be seen without a microscope. Clearly someone has been at work shortening sentences, by splitting coordinate sentences such as the last one, and by making subordinate construction into independent sentences. The subordinate phrase, a reduced relative clause, in the first sentence gives some background information about the location of certain plants. As the original reads, the description of the pond emphasizes the things one sees here and there. The overall topic is a class of large things which can be seen, though each of these things is not particularly important in itself, nor is its location of crucial importance. With the creation of an independent sentence for the subordinate construction, the sequence of topic in the paragraph is distorted. It appears that *these plants* are in fact a topic in their own right, and the information about where they grow seems to define a new topic of things near the shore. Then the next sentence about water striders has no obvious connection to what goes before. It appeared to at least one adult reader that the emphasis of the revised form was on the location of various items. In the original, it was clear that the first sentence was part of a series of parallel sentences giving instances of lake creatures and plants, and that location was less important background information.

The moral here is that subordinate clauses promoted to main clauses introduce their own sentence topics. If this metamorphosis takes place without regard to the logical connections of sentence topics in a paragraph, the result can be the introduction of incoherence, sentence disconnectedness, and topic shifts, rather than simplification.

The same sort of changes, done with care, can improve a text, as (12) shows.

12. (original)

In World War II, Japanese naval officers *during* blackout action near an enemy moistened the powder in the palm of their hands *and* read their navigation charts in the dim light it produced.

(adaptation)

During World War II Japanese naval officers used this powder. *When they were close to the enemy* during *blackout* night action, they moistened the powder in the palm of their hands. They could read their navigation charts in the dim blue light that it gave.

Here the text expresses some fairly complex information about a very unusual kind of substance, about which no one would very likely have any background information. Hence the adaptor took particular care to explain the setting by adding some information *(close to the enemy)* and by placing background information in subordinate clauses at the beginning of the sentence. The split of the coordinate construction allows two distinct focuses on two salient facts. The division into separate sentences in this case is appropriate to the information which the author and adaptor wanted to communicate.

In (13), we have an original version of a paragraph which packs 9 clauses or large phrases into three long sentences.

13. (original)

[a]Motor launches take visitors [b]into such a lagoon on the southern coast of Puerto Rico [c]*where on dark nights there is* a dramatic display of bioluminescence. [d]Curving lines of light fall from the bow [e]as the launch enters the lagoon, and [f]a trail of light is left in the boat's wake.

In the lagoon, [g]*which has one of the greatest concentrations of bioluminescence in the world,* [h]it appears as though a huge floodlight were burning under the launch, and [i]the bow seems to be plowing into a wall of fire.

(adaptation)

[b]On the southern coast of Puerto Rico is a lagoon [g]*that has one of the greatest amounts of bioluminescense in the world.* [c]*On dark nights, it creates a very dramatic display.* [e]As the motor launch enters the lagoon, [d]curving lines of light fall from the bow. [f]A trail of light is left in the boat's wake. [h]It appears as though a huge floodlight were burning under the launch, and [i]the bow seems to be plowing into a wall of fire.

The adaptor wanted to shorten the sentences by splitting up some of the clauses into separate sentences. But the result, while it has nearly the same clause units in five sentences, has also been reorganized in a very clear way, so that the sentence divisions do not create incoherence. The subordinate clauses (c) and (g) have not been made into main clauses, which interrupt the flow of ideas; that is, the description of a trip in a motor launch illustrating the curious features of the lagoon. Instead, since they express background information, they have been placed early in the paragraph so that they represent prior information and previous context which in relation to the sentences which follow. Their position in the paragraph is the analog of subordinate clause function, and so clause (c) has the same value in the adaptation as in the original, even though it is no longer a subordinate clause. The changes which the adaptor made here show awareness of text structure and overall logical organization, factors not measured by traditional readability formulas. Clearly, the success of this adaptation is *not* due to reliance on readability formulas.

POINT OF VIEW AND EVIDENCE

One pattern of change which we noted in the study of adaptations was motivated primarily by a wish to shorten the sentence by deleting what seems to be an extraneous part of it. As illustrated in (14–17), what gets deleted are adverbs like *apparently, supposedly,* etc. and main clauses with verbs of perception, belief, or report in them.

14. (original)

    A railroad freight agent has figured that it would require at least 40 modern flat cars to haul just the trunk alone.

    (adaptation)

    And at least forty freight cars would be needed to haul away just its trunk.

15. (original)

    The Romans *were said by Pliny to* rub bread soaked in asses' milk on their faces to make them fairer and prevent the growth of beards.

    (adaptation)

    The Romans rubbed bread soaked in asses' milk on their faces. *They thought that* this would make their skin paler. *They also thought* it would keep their beards from growing!

16. (original)

    Nero's wife, Queen Poppea, took a daily bath in it [= milk] and *supposedly* had 500 beasts on tap for the purpose.

    (adaptation)

    She kept five hundred animals to make sure of having enough milk each day.

17. (original)

    Apparently, too, most of these fish can control when they flash their lights in the dark waters where they live.

    (adaptation)

    Most of these fish can control the flashing of their lights.

The function of these constructions is to express the author's view of the reliability of the statements expressed. In (14), the author shows in the original version that the statement is indeed reliable, since it is based on the word of an expert in freight. In the revised form, the statement is attributed without qualification to the author, who appears omniscient. In (15), the situation is more complicated, since the sentence expresses a report of a belief. We might believe Pliny, who was a contemporary witness, while not accepting the beliefs of his time, that milk is good for suppressing beards. The adaptor takes the tack that it is all right to suppress attribution of true propositions, since they are true anyway and will appear to come from the author. Only when beliefs are bizarre or erroneous are they attributed to other people. But this strategy is misleading, since many statements are probably true, though based on incomplete or subjective evidence. Learning to judge the reliability of statements depending on their source, who says them, and what qualifications the sources have is an important skill which is part of the competence of an adult reader. Thus, expressions like these, and other things such as adverbs *supposedly*, etc. have more real importance in the communication of ideas than they might appear to. While their elimination does moderately reduce sentence length and complexity, their absence deprives the unskilled reader of exposure to something very important, something which basal readers in the later grades recognize as important, and something which is introduced as a drill in practice materials. It comes under the heading of distinguishing fact from opinion, and if it is important, as it clearly is, why should opportunities for learning it be routinely eliminated?

In one of the texts I have quoted from, the narrative of flood survivors, what has also been eliminated are references to the *narrator's* perceptions. These may be inferred, since the narrator is telling about the events witnessed at first hand. But again the story is given in the adaptation the tone of an omniscient author not necessarily present. One would think that references to the narrator's thoughts and feelings at a particular *moment* in the narrative would help the reader identify with the story more and make it more vivid and easily comprehended.

This assumption is part of some characterizations of readability. That is, people *like* to read and have less trouble reading texts which make reference to them, or which they can identify with easily (cf. Flesch, 1949, 1951). On this assumption, many history texts for school and pleasure reading try to dramatize or personalize historical events by telling them through the eyes of a particular individual. But this method has its limitations if what the author wants to communicate is primarily historical knowledge, rather than an interesting story which slips in some historical facts as background; as one of my colleagues has pointed out to me, fiction is an excellent way of presenting historical facts in a vivid way.

To look at point-of-view phenomena a little more closely, I extended our study by looking at different treatments of the same historical events. I chose as a difficult test case some books about the War of 1812, which was a particularly incoherent war, taking place over a wide stretch of territory for often unclear and possibly conflicting motives. (The texts involved were all trade books, but the point will apply to history texts as well.) One book which stuck to a summary of events from an objective point of view stated right at the beginning that the war was a fairly strange war, as wars go, and listed some reasons why. While the book did not always make all of the subparts clear or show all the relations between the parts, it at least told the reader what to expect and gave a clear overall framework to place the episodes in. Other, presumably more readable books described the war through the eyes of various individuals. But this method practically guarantees that the reader will have trouble understanding important facts and piecing together all the parts. No single individual really had an overview of what was going on. So the narrative of people involved in the conflicts of the Midwesterners with the Indians would have no obvious connection with a war conducted on the Great Lakes or the Atlantic coast between the United States and Great Britain. The lesson I want to draw here is that readability is a relative matter, that what makes some aspects of a text readable may not, in the end, serve the overall purpose of allowing a young reader to interpret and remember the content of a text.

The major point I want to make in this chapter is that readability is a relative rather than an absolute effect. In part, the readability of the means of communication, the language and organization of the sentences, is relative to the goals of communicating a message. The amount of simplication which a text will be able to undergo is also relative to how much of its content is to be preserved, and the more content must be preserved, the more a text must be paraphrased—and lengthened—or carefully reorganized so that content is expressed in alternative ways. In fact, readability formulas are pretty useless in telling a writer how to do this, as I hope the sorry examples discussed here have shown. The more successful changes have come from the writers themselves, acting as writers who are aware of text organization, stylistic nuance, and possible ambiguities both implicit and explicit. What I have just said is not novel and has been said many times before, but here are reasons for judging readability formulas as rather useless in defining texts which are readable. Tom Anderson's presentation makes the same point in a different way. He shows that the absence of clear, organizing information and expressions of time and cause may make a text uninterpretable. Exactly those indications of logical relations are the things which readability formulas encourage writers to delete. At best, the need to shorten sentences distracts a writer from other important considerations, such as discourse organization and the inferences the reader must make. Yet these factors may make the difference between a comprehensible text and one which is not.

What I am arguing for here is basically subjective judgment about a large number of text features which are subtle and often unquantifiable and relative rather than absolute. I do not want to condemn out of hand all objective measures simply because they are objective. Clearly it would be very nice to have alternatives to readability formulas which did a better job. Researchers have proposed such alternatives, at least programmatic ones: Some, such as Endicott (1973), Reddin (1970), Schmidt (1977), and Selden (1977), give different weights to constructions of different difficulty. Others, such as Fagan (1971), Richek (1976), and von Glaserfeld (1970–71), count subordinate clauses, or left branching structures, or relations which are not indicated with clear, explicit, overt markers. There are formulas based on taxonomies of "hard" constructions, such as those of Botel and Granowsky (1972), Dawkins (1975), and Henry (1977). There are methods, which are themselves pretty subjective and also laborious, for gauging the coherence and complexity of sentences in a text (Kintsch & Vipond, 1979), and other studies (Gourlay & Catlin, 1978) which note the relationship between sentences of overlapping reference. While some are sensitive to discourse notions such as topic, focus, and background information, others are sensitive to number of items referred to and redundancy in the sequence of sentences, or to syntactic complexity of sentences without reference to the organization and sequencing of the information presented.

Each of these gets at some aspect of texts which may contribute to ease or difficulty of reading, though none, to my knowledge, tries to cover all the possible sources of difficulty. What is really needed is a successful cognitive model of language processing which is sensitive to the different loads of semantic, syntactic, and inferential processing. These relations probably change as a child matures, is able to comprehend complex syntax in all contexts rather than just some, and is capable of processing larger chunks of sentences at once. Perfetti and Lesgold (1977) note that while children's short-term memory for items which are processed together may not increase with age, short-term memory's ability to function increases, so that information is processed faster and more efficiently and encoded in long-term memory. It is also the case that absolute sentence length is not so important (Glazer, 1974), provided that clause boundaries are clearly indicated and clause constituents are not interrupted by sub-constituents.

Complex sentences should therefore be harder to process because they make greater demands on short-term memory than simple clauses or sequences of conjoined clauses. Yet there is a trade-off: One of the functions of harder constructions, such as ones with subordinate constructions, is to make a message more compact, and its internal logical relations more explicit. But there is a trade-off between what a reader can process and how efficiently the message is expressed. There is some evidence (Pearson, 1974–75) that provided they can handle the syntactic structures, children prefer the more explicit and compact form of a message, where causal relations are concerned, or where focus on attributes is involved in relative clauses. (See discussion in Huggins, 1977.) There is also reported evidence that the omission of logical connectives affects comprehension (Irwin, Marshall, & Glock, 1978–79, cited in Irwin & Davis, 1980, who argue for an eclectic approach to assessing readability.)

What I have against readability formulas is not based on a preference for subjective measures, though I am arguing that *informed* subjective judgment is the best replacement now available in children's texts, and the best corrective for the abuses of language. This subjective judgment might profit, however, by information about what goes on in psychological and linguistic research, on human cognition and ability to process language, on children's acquisition of their language and ability to understand spoken and written language. In the last 50 years much research has been done on this subject, and this period has seen major theories come and go as more and more sophisticated information about language, thought, and reading has been accumulated.

Readability formulas were originally conceived in the 1920s and 1930s. The ones in common use today were refined in the 1950s, and some work has been done, for instance by Bormuth (1966), on different means of measuring reading comprehension independently of the formulas, and on showing correlations with other variables, such as degree of subordination. But the developments in research about readability formulas have taken place in a manner virtually independent of research on the central issues of how the human mind processes language. The use of readability formulas can only be stabs in the dark as predictions, and totally uninformative as guides to writing because they do not and cannot define causes of difficulty.

In conclusion, readability formulas have a generally negative and harmful effect on the writing and revising of texts to be used as reading materials. Yet the tradition behind readability formulas, their simplicity—or simple-mindedness—and their cheapness recommend them to many people. It is really a serious dilemma for people who want to create texts of high quality which are soundly organized and coherent, and who at the same time want to respond to people who demand readability scores instead of relying on experience and judgment. It is to be hoped that much can be done to educate the public about the actual and appropriate values of readability formulas and their serious limitations.

REFERENCES

Bormuth, J. R. Readability: A new approach. *Reading Research Quarterly*, 1966, *1*, 79–132.

Botel, M., & Granowsky, A. A formula for measuring syntactic complexity: A directional approach. *Elementary English*, 1972, *49*, 513–516.

Davison, A., Kantor, R. N., Hannah, J., Hermon, G., Lutz, R., & Salzillo, R. *Limitations of readability formulas in guiding adaptations of texts* (Tech. Rep. No. 162). Urbana: University of Illinois, Center for the Study of Reading, March 1980. (ERIC Document Reproduction Service No. ED 184 090)

Dawkins, J. *Syntax and readability*. Newark, Del.: International Reading Association, 1975.

Endicott, A. L. A proposed scale for syntactic complexity. *Research in the Teaching of English*, 1973, *7*, 5–12.

Fagan, W. T. *The relationship between reading difficulty and the number and type of sentence transformations*. Paper presented at the annual meeting of the International Reading Association, Atlantic City, New Jersey, April 1971.

Flesch, R. *The art of readable writing*. New York: Harper, 1949.

Flesch, R. *How to test readability*. New York: Harper, 1951.

Glazer, S. M. Is sentence length a valid measure of difficulty in readability formulas? *The Reading Teacher*, 1974, *27*, 264–268.

Gourlay, J., & Catlin, J. Children's comprehension of grammatical structures in context. *Journal of Psycholinguistic Research*, 1978, *7*, 419–434.

Haviland, S. E., & Clark, H. H. What's new: Acquiring new information in sentence perception. *Journal of Verbal Learning and Verbal Behavior*, 1974, *13*, 512–521.

Henry, G. *The relation between linguistic factors of written style identified by principal components analysis and reading comprehension as measured by cloze tests*. Liege Belgium: University of Liege, 1977. (ERIC Document Reproduction Service No. ED 151 730)

Huggins, A. W. F. *Syntactic aspects of reading comprehension* (Tech. Rep. No. 33). Urbana: University of Illinois, Center for the Study of Reading, April 1977. (ERIC Document Reproduction Service No. ED 142 972)

Irwin, J. W., & Davis, C. A. Assessing readability: The checklist approach. *Journal of Reading*, 1980, *24*, 124–130.

Kintsch, W., & Vipond, D. Reading comprehension and readability in educational practice and psychological theory. In L. G. Nillson (Ed.), *Memory processes*. Hillsdale, N.J.: Lawrence Erlbaum Associates, 1979.

Linde, C. Constraints on the ordering of *if* clauses. *Berkeley Linguistics Society*, 1976, *2*, 280–285.

Osgood, C. O., & Sridhar, S. N. *Unambiguous signalling of naturalness in clause ordering: A language universal?* Unpublished manuscript, University of Illinois, 1978.

Pearson, P. D. The effects of grammatical complexity on children's comprehension, recall, and conception of certain semantic relations. *Reading Research Quarterly*, 1974–75, *10*, 155–192.

Perfetti, C., & Goldman, S. Discourse functions of thematization and topicalization. *Journal of Psycholinguistic Research*, 1975, *4*, 257–271.

Perfetti, C., & Lesgold, A. M. Discourse comprehension and sources of individual differences. In M. Just & P. Carpenter (Eds.), *Cognitive processes in comprehension*. Hillsdale, N.J.: Lawrence Erlbaum Associates, 1977.

Reddin, E. Syntactical structure and reading comprehension. *The Reading Teacher*, 1970, *23*, 467–469.

Richek, M. A. Effect of sentence complexity on the reading comprehension of syntactic structures. *Journal of Educational Psychology*, 1976, *68*, 800–806.

Schmidt, E. L. *What makes reading difficult: The complexity of structures*. Paper presented at the annual meeting of the National Reading Conference, New Orleans, December 1977.

Selden, R. *Sentence structure and readability: The influence of frequency-based expectancies of syntactic structure on the comprehensibility of text*. Unpublished doctoral dissertation, University of Virginia, 1977.

von Glaserfeld, E. The problem of syntactic complexity. *Journal of Reading Behavior*, 1970–71, *3*, 1–14.

Readability as a Solution
Adds to the Problem

Walter H. MacGinitie
University of Victoria

Readability formulas have been badly tarnished, and my own commentary will not restore their luster. At the outset, then, it is appropriate to remember that readability formulas have served a number of worthwhile purposes. From a research perspective, it is interesting to try to determine what text characteristics are found difficult under particular circumstances by particular people. From a practical perspective, formulas have provided an objective basis for insisting that information written in specialized language be made more accessible to the average citizen. It was largely through the influence of readability formulas that agricultural bulletins were made more readable for the farmer, that Army regulations were rewritten so that at least some soldiers could understand them, and, most recently, that many legal documents have been made more comprehensible to those few among us who are still not lawyers. Readability formulas may even have helped make some written materials more appropriate for the children who read them. Of this last I am not sure, for in their general application to children's reading materials, the formulas have not been used to limit arcane and specialized forms of written language but to limit the range of children's written language experience.

There are two practices that on balance threaten to make the use of readability formulas more harmful than helpful. These practices are the use of the formulas as a basis for modifying or creating children's texts and the use of readability scores as a legislated basis for deciding the suitability of texts for a particular grade.[1] Alice Davison and Georgia

---

[1]Developers of readability formulas have long cautioned against such practices. See, for example, the discussion of the use of readability formulas in Dale and Chall (1956).

Green have illustrated the problems created by these practices; I would like to describe the logical inappropriateness of these practices.

There are three important points to be considered if we are to understand what we are doing when we apply readability studies to modify or limit the texts that students read. The first of these is that a naturally occurring relationship is not, by itself, a sound basis for intervention. The second is that what students find difficult to read is influenced by what students have read and what they have been taught. The third is that many students have not had the reading experience or the reading instruction we assume they have had.

A naturally occurring relationship is not a sound basis for intervention. We all know that a correlation does not necessarily represent causation. We know that one cannot induce fall weather by painting the maple leaves red. We should not be surprised, then, if shortening some sentences does not make the text easier to read. The difficulty with applying readability findings to modify text actually goes a bit beyond this well-known problem. We try to induce fall weather by painting *pine needles* red. We apply readability criteria to topics, ideas, and structures where they have not yet been shown to have a relationship to text difficulty. Schools should not demand indiscriminate application of readability criteria, and publishers should not vie to be the first not to know what they are doing in trying to meet an uninformed demand.

The fact is, we have little understanding of the effects of a uniform, ubiquitous application of readability criteria, for what students find difficult to read is influenced by what they have read and what they have been taught (Chall, 1977). It is meaningless to say a text is difficult; it is difficult *for someone.* Whether a text is difficult depends on the reader as well as upon the text. Whether a reader finds a text difficult is influenced by the reader's experience. Students are able to read easily those words, constructions, and organizations that they have had a lot of experience reading. When readability formulas are used to govern the characteristics of the texts that students read, they govern the students' reading experience and influence what will be readable.

Any applied readability criterion will eventually determine what students find difficult to read. One must recognize this fact in order to understand the significance of recommending that a particular text characteristic be avoided because it is difficult. Once it is generally avoided, most students will certainly find it difficult.

Most work on readability assumes that reading (or listening) difficulty is a function of various characteristics of text and of a group of readers with more or less immutable reactions to those characteristics. There are two ways to make text easier for many students to read. One is to eliminate text characteristics that cause many students difficulty. The other is to give students help and experience in understanding text that has those characteristics. There are also two ways to make text difficult for many students to read. One is to include text characteristics that cause many students difficulty. The other is to insulate students from help and experience in reading text with various characteristics.

I recently showed a group of experienced elementary teachers some written material that I thought had been made both puerile *and* more difficult by the author's effort to keep the sentences very short. I showed how I thought the material could be rewritten to make the ideas easier to understand by allowing the sentences to be longer and by using sentence structure to specify relationships. The teachers felt strongly, however, that the short-sentence version would be easier for their young students to understand, precisely because the students were accustomed to reading that sort of text. Whether the teachers were right about the relative difficulty could be determined by experiment, but the result would be of no consequence, for the teachers were certainly right in pointing out that the students' experience would strongly influence the relative difficulty of the two versions of the text. The experiment would not be a measure of anything we might wish to call the inherent difficulty of the two versions.

Educators and publishers seem bent on conducting a gigantic, poorly designed experiment to make text difficult for students by insulating them from experiences with a variety of types of text. Consider how one might conduct an experiment to see if it is possible to make text with certain characteristics difficult for students to understand. One logical way to conduct such an experiment would be to control the characteristics of the material read by the experimental group while allowing the control group to read materials with a wide variety of characteristics. The text characteristics that educators and publishers have chosen to try to make difficult are any sentence structures that usually require sentences of some length and words that are long or uncommon. The experiment is not well designed because the words and structures are only loosely defined and controlled, and there is no control group. Measures of change over time cannot replace the control group, since there are many other concomitant changes in education and society that are also influencing how easily students can read various materials. Besides, there is even pressure now for tests to be designed to measure only the experience of the experimental group.

One could expect to gain general agreement that certain writings are more felicitous than others, and one could have no quarrel with the hope that most materials for students will be well written and appropriate; but to judge that materials are well written or appropriate *only* if they avoid certain vocabulary, or certain constructions, or long sentences is another matter. It is empty to assert and dangerous to legislate that good or appropriate writing will uniformly contain or exclude specific lexical or structural characteristics.

In one study at the Teachers College Research Institute for the Study of Learning Disabilities, we have been working with a small group of intermediate-grade students who often fail to test their initial hypotheses about the main idea of a paragraph and who persevere in applying their initial interpretation (MacGinitie, Kimmel, & Maria, 1980). These children have great difficulty understanding paragraphs that have any of several structures we have loosely and informally classed as "inductive paragraph structures." Our present recommendation is not that materials for these children be rewritten to avoid inductive structures but that the children be helped to recognize and understand text that is so structured. The work that John Bransford describes will be a useful guide in devising appropriate learning experiences. There is a good chance that these children can be helped to understand text that is inductively structured, for, like most students, they have previously received little or no instruction on their specific text comprehension problems.

And this is the third and most important point to understand about recommendations for restricting text characteristics. Students have not had the reading experience or the reading instruction we assume they have had. That they have not had the instruction is beginning to be documented. Durkin (1979) has illustrated that teachers are likely to ask many questions of students as checks on the students' understanding of text, but that they seldom give instruction to help students who have not understood. It is not surprising that teachers follow this pattern, for this pattern is set for them by the teachers' manuals for the students' textbooks. In these manuals, there is almost no guidance for the teacher as to how to help students use the text to figure out the message. This lack has been a focus of a second study by Dolores Durkin (1981), which she has described in this volume. How to help the student use the text to figure out the message—how to help the student who does not understand a particular segment of text—is a topic notably lacking, also, in most reading methods courses in teacher training programs.

When students do not understand a segment of text, they are not likely to receive instruction in reading. Instead, they are likely to receive instruction in whatever the text is about. The experience they gain is not reading experience, but experience in listening to their teachers' explanations.

Ruth MacGinitie and I have studied this phenomenon recently while giving inservice teacher training. We have worked with teachers of all grade levels and all subject matter areas to help them learn how to help students understand text. We have shown the teachers various sentence structures, cohesive ties, paragraph structures, metaphorical usages, punctuation conventions, and other features of the texts they are using that are important cues to meaning. We have worked with the teachers to help them develop questions that will reveal whether students understand the text that involves these features. We have *tried* to help teachers develop question sequences, explanations, analogies, diagrams, and general teaching strategies that will help students understand the text and learn from the text. In this last we have not been very successful. The teachers understand the language cues we show them, they are able to locate possible difficulties in the text, they learn to find useful cues to meaning, and they learn how to develop questions that will reveal whether students are using the cues and understanding the text. However, when they actually encounter a student who does not understand the text, the teachers explain the content; they do not help the student understand the text. (An example of this distinction is shown in Appendix A.)

Most of the teachers we have worked with are excellent teachers. Their intuitions as to which aspects of the text will be difficult are excellent, and the leading questions, analogies, and other devices they use to make the content clear to the students are very effective. But the distinction between helping with the content and helping with the text is difficult for teachers to differentiate in practice. When a student needs help in understanding text, it is very difficult for a concerned teacher not to step in and explain the content. This is particularly true, of course, in content area reading, even in the early grades.

Our observations of this phenomenon in many circumstances led Ruth to a generalization that I have dubbed *Ruth's Law:* Ruth's Law is that the more obvious or painful the student's lack of comprehension, the more likely that the teacher will explain the content rather than the text. When students cannot do the problems at the end of a section of text in the math book, for example, it will be very obvious from the idle pencils, the raised hands, and the fidgeting that they have not understood the text. It will be very unlikely, therefore, that the teacher will, in this circumstance, try to help the students understand the text. Similarly, a student who does not understand the written instructions for a science experiment presents a painfully obvious problem, and the teacher is proportionally likely to give the student personal directions. After some experience, teachers learn implicitly which kinds of written materials, when not understood, will produce the most obvious classroom problems, and they often give up assigning such materials altogether. The result is that many students have very little experience reading important types of material.

We have not found content area teachers, even at the secondary level, rejecting the idea that they should teach reading. They readily accept the premise that one of their objectives should be for the students to learn how to read material in their content area, and are willing to devote some time to this objective. They want their students to be independent readers and learners; their training and practice have simply not encompassed that objective. For example, when they try to think how they might help a student understand a paragraph, their first impluse is to rewrite the paragraph to make it easier for the student.

There are, of course, exceptions to the picture I have given. We have observed some literature lessons, in particular, that were superb examples of how students can be helped to understand written text. Yet the occasional elementary-grade teacher who teaches reading comprehension effectively during reading period is likely to switch to an explain-the-content mode during science.

One can observe a number of teaching practices related to this tendency to explain content and ignore what the students have read. Teachers often ask students to read material in class or as homework. If the material is read in class, seldom are the students allowed enough time to read it carefully. We do not seem to believe that students can be learning when we are not telling them something. Whether material is read in class or at home, the same content is usually explained subsequently by the teacher. Students who have difficulty reading the material soon learn that the same content will all be covered later by the teacher. Students who *could* read and understand may learn not to bother.

The obvious long-term course of what Ruth and I have observed is that many students do very little reading in the content areas throughout their school careers. Students who encounter difficulty with new and characteristic language forms in science or history—forms that are unfamiliar in students' oral language experience—get no help in understanding those new forms. They fall farther and farther behind those other students whose backgrounds or abilities, and motivations, allow them to work out an interpretation of the new forms and to become familiar with them. The end result is well known: A large group of students who cannot readily learn by reading and for whom many characteristics of written language are difficult. They have not had the experience or the instruction in reading we assume they have had.

The problem is not with the quality of teaching we have seen: The problem is with the focus of the teaching; seldom is the focus on understanding text. The teachers are simply responding to the same urge that makes us all itch to take over when we see someone fumbling to open a lock or untie a knot. The problem lies in the training the teachers have had and in the teachers' manuals they use. In any one school the failure to help students read cannot be corrected by one awakened teacher. There must be a concerted effort throughout all the grades to help students understand written text and to make students reasonably responsible for understanding written text.

I will recapitulate the three points one must consider in order to understand how flimsy the basis is for legislating readability restrictions on text characteristics.

1. A natural correlation does not mean that intervening to change one variable will predictably influence the other. A text may possess characteristics that are awkward in many circumstances, yet are apt, or even customary, for expressing a particular message.

2. The materials that are currently being read determine, in large part, current reading abilities and readability findings. What a reader has frequently read in a particular context will be easy to understand; what a reader has seldom read in a particular context will be difficult to understand. Legislated restrictions on specific characteristics of text will themselves guarantee that those characteristics will remain difficult for most students.

3. The reading experience and instruction that students receive are less than we assume. Experience and instruction are limited by current readability restrictions. More importantly, experience and instruction are limited by a variety of teaching practices that stem ultimately from inadequacies in teacher training and inadequacies in guidelines for the use of published materials.

I am not saying that we should assign novels by Henry James to classes of third graders. Individual students should read materials that are generally appropriate for them and should be helped to understand forms that are difficult for them. Legislation of specific restrictions on text characteristics, however, is a presumptuous folly—presumptuous because we have not thought through the effect of what we are doing, folly because such legislation will work against its own goals.

REFERENCES

Boning, R. A. *Specific skills series*. New York: Barnell-Loft, 1976.

Chall, J. S., with Conrad, S. S., & Harris, S. H. *An analysis of textbooks in relation to declining SAT scores*. New York: College Entrance Examination Board, 1977.

Dale, E., & Chall, J. S. Developing readable materials. In N. B. Henry (Ed.) *Adult reading*, 55th Yearbook of the National Society for the Study of Education, Part II. Chicago: University of Chicago Press, 1956.

Durkin, D. What classroom observations reveal about reading comprehension instruction. *Reading Research Quarterly*, 1979, *14*, 481–533.

Durkin, D. Reading comprehension instruction in five basal reader series. *Reading Research Quarterly*, 1981, *16*, 515–544.

MacGinitie, W. H., Kimmel, S., & Maria, K. The role of cognitive strategies in certain reading comprehension disabilities. *The Forum*, 1980, 6(4), 10–13.

APPENDIX A:
Illustrations of Helping Students Understand
the Content and Helping them Understand the Text

Suppose that a small group of students in Grade 5 has read the following paragraph in a lesson about birds:

Usually the bones of birds' wings are hollow. This gives the bones strength without weight. The surface of the wing is curved. The fact that the front edge of the wing is thicker than the rear edge also makes for easier flight. (Boning, 1976, Level D, Unit 2).

The teacher has asked the students why the surface of a bird's wing is curved—what difference the curvature makes—and it is clear that the students do not know; they do not see the relation of the third sentence to the rest of the paragraph. The teacher might then proceed somewhat as follows:

TEACHER: How many of you have ever flown a kite? (All the students raise their hands.)

TEACHER: What is there about a kite that makes it able to fly? (None of the students answers.)

TEACHER: Suppose the kite were made out of a board. Would it fly?

STUDENT: No.

TEACHER: Why not?

STUDENT: It's too heavy.

TEACHER: So what is one of the things about a kite that makes it able to fly?

STUDENT: It's light.

TEACHER: So being light makes it possible for the kite to fly. That's one thing that makes it possible for a bird to fly, too. A bird is light because its wing and leg bones are hollow. After you have made the kite, do you change its shape in any way to make it fly better?

STUDENT: You put a tail on it.

TEACHER: Do you do anything else to it?

STUDENT: You bend it. You tie a string across the back to make it curved.

TEACHER: Good. A bird's wings are curved too. They are curved in a different way but the curve in a bird's wings makes it easier for the bird to fly. So being light, and having the right shape to the wing helps a bird to fly. The paragraph tells us one other thing that helps a bird to fly. Have you ever noticed the shape of an airplane wing? Is it thicker at the front edge of the wing—towards the nose of the plane—or is it thicker at the rear edge—the edge toward the tail?

STUDENT: It's thicker at the front edge.

TEACHER: Well, a bird's wing is thicker at the front edge, too. That also helps the bird to fly. So we have learned three things about the way birds are built that help them fly: a bird is light, because its wing and leg bones are hollow; a bird's wing is curved; and the front edge of a bird's wing is thicker than the rear edge.

These Grade 5 students now probably have a fairly good understanding of the main points that were made in the paragraph. What the teacher has done, however, is to help the students understand the content of the paragraph without helping them in any way to see how the language of the paragraph could help them construct that understanding. In other words, the teacher has given them no help in learning how to read.

Now that the students have an understanding of the content of the paragraph, the teacher might ask the students to read the paragraph again to see how the paragraph presented the information. Or the teacher might actually assist the students in relating their new knowledge to the way that knowledge is communicated by the paragraph. However, teachers seldom ask students to refer again to the paragraph after the content has been discussed. If they would do so, that step in itself might be very instructive for some of the students.

The alternative to helping students understand the content apart from the text is helping the students use the text to gain the information. In the following example, the teacher helps the students work with the text. The teacher does supplement the text with additional information and examples, but primarily to help the students confirm their understanding of the text.

The students have read the same text as in the first example and indicate a similar lack of understanding—they do not understand that the curve in a bird's wing makes it easier for the bird to fly.

TEACHER: Read the last sentence.

STUDENT: "The fact that the front edge of the wing is thicker than the rear edge also makes for easier flight."

TEACHER: What does it say makes it easier for a bird to fly?

STUDENT: The front edge of the wing is thicker than the rear edge.

TEACHER: Have you ever noticed the shape of an airplane wing? Is it thicker at the front edge of the wing—towards the nose of the plane? Or is it thicker at the rear edge—the edge towards the tail?

STUDENT: It's thicker at the front edge.

TEACHER: That makes it easier for the airplane to fly, just as it makes it easier for a bird to fly. Now, when the sentence says, "The fact that the front edge of the wing is thicker than the rear edge *also* makes for easier flight," why does it say "also?" (None of the students raises a hand.) If I said "Patty *also* made Bill angry," what would "also" mean?

STUDENT: That somebody else made Bill angry, too.

TEACHER: So when it says, "The fact that the front edge of the wing is thicker than the rear edge *also* makes for easier flight," what does "also" mean?

STUDENT: That something else makes for easier flight, too.

TEACHER: Good. What else makes for easier flight? (None of the students raises a hand.) Well, if I said "Patty *also* made Bill angry," would I be about to tell you who the other person was, or would you already know?

STUDENT: We'd already know.

TEACHER: So the paragraph is talking as if you already know what else makes for easier flight. Look at the sentence just before the one with the *also*. That sentence will tell something else that makes it easier for birds to fly. What does the sentence say?

STUDENT: "The surface of the wing is curved."

TEACHER: Okay, so the front of the wing being thicker than the back is one thing that makes it easier for birds to fly. What is something else that does?

STUDENT: The wings are curved.

TEACHER: That's right. The top of an airplane wing is curved too. (The teacher draws a cross section of an airplane wing on the chalkboard.) This curved shape helps an airplane to fly, just as the curved shape of a bird's wing helps a bird to fly. What else does the paragraph tell about that might make it easier for birds to fly?

STUDENT: Their bones are hollow.

STUDENT: How would that help birds to fly? (None of the students raises a hand.) Read the second sentence.

STUDENT: "This gives the bones strength without weight."

TEACHER: *What* gives the bones strength without weight?

STUDENT: The bones are hollow.

TEACHER: Good. Since the wing bones are hollow, they are strong without being heavy. Why would that be important for a bird?

STUDENT: Well, the bones have got to be strong or they'd break, and if the bird was too heavy, it couldn't fly.

TEACHER: Look again at the paragraph, now. What three things does it tell about that make it easier for a bird to fly?

STUDENT: Their bones are light and strong.

STUDENT: Their wings have a curved shape, like an airplane wing.

STUDENT: Their wings are thicker at the front than they are at the back.

In the above example, the teacher used a similar structure with familiar content ("Patty *also* made Bill angry") as an analogue to help students understand a more difficult sentence with less familiar content. This is often a helpful device. Throughout the example the teacher has focused the students' attention on what "the paragraph says" and has thus helped them learn how to solve a problem presented by difficult text. Notice that the teacher did not try to analyze *everything* about the text.

In particular, the teacher did not discuss the two possible interpretations of *also* in the last sentence. The teacher decided to help the students focus on the appropriate interpretation rather than asking them to choose between that interpretation and the alternative ("also makes for easier *flight*"). We know that too much analysis can kill the enjoyment of literature, and, similarly, incessant analysis of subject matter text can be stultifying. Thus, the teacher will continue to help the students directly with content on many occasions, choosing to help them work out an interpretation of the text primarily when the text is difficult yet important or representative of modes of expression that are frequently encountered in the particular text or subject matter area. If students had consistently received such help in constructing the meanings of texts from the primary grades onward, many of them would need much less such help in the intermediate and secondary grades.

5 A New Point of View on Children's Stories

Bertram Bruce
Bolt Beranek and Newman, Inc.
and
Center for the Study of Reading
University of Illinois at Urbana-Champaign

Whatever else one expects of education, two goals of reading instruction stand out. One is that a child develop a healthy appreciation for what reading can mean, including, one hopes, an enjoyment of reading for its own sake. Paired with this goal of developing positive attitudes is a second goal of developing in the reader the skills for reading, ultimately for reading with care and critical insight.

The task of selecting, designing, adapting, editing, or writing texts for children is immensely important in the process of attaining these educational goals. Work of Durkin (1978–79; this volume) and others, as well as simple classroom observation, shows that published materials influence teachers, students, and most classroom activities. But, unfortunately, there are few solid principles, or even good definitions of the issues, on which to base decisions about text selection. Complicating this is the fact that what we do know about the reading process says that small differences in texts may have significant effects on comprehension and enjoyment. This is especially true when we consider the relation of text characteristics to the reader's prior knowledge, values, and expectations (see Adams & Bruce, 1982).

A simple model for the effects of some text characteristics on the reader is shown in Figure 1. On the right side of the figure are shown two possible end states of the educational process, both of them undesirable: (a) a negative attitude toward reading in general, and (b) failure to learn the skills essential for reading. These end states could be produced, via one or more intermediate states (shown in dashed boxes), by the use of texts with certain undesirable charactristics. Among these, there are five that

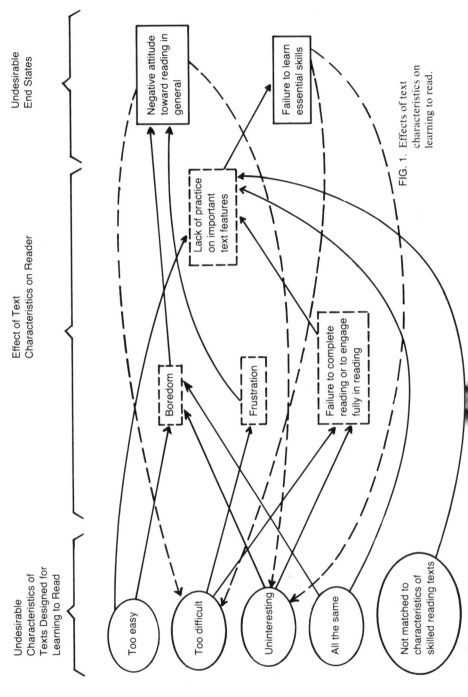

FIG. 1. Effects of text characteristics on learning to read.

154

warrant special attention. Texts may be *too easy* or *too difficult*. Even if they are at the right level of difficulty they may be uninteresting. If at the right level and interesting, there can still be problems if the texts children read are *all the same*. Finally, texts at the right level, which are interesting and diverse, may still be inappropriate if they are *not matched to the texts that skilled readers read*. Some interrelations of these characteristics and effects on the reader are shown in the figure. Solid arrows represent a causal relation between a text characteristic and an effect on the reader; dashed arrows represent the reciprocal influence that undesirable states in the reader have on text characteristics. The latter illustrates that text characteristics are, in fact, characteristics of the reader and text in interaction.

The connections made between text characteristics and effects on the reader in the figure show that the nature of the texts that children encounter while learning to read plays a major role in the development of their attitudes about reading and their reading skills. Texts that are too difficult may cause unnecessary problems at the time and generate frustration with reading that results in more general difficulties later on. Texts that are too easy may bore a child, thus producing negative attitudes about reading that again lead to future difficulties. Moreover, easy texts may not expose children to many of the text features they must learn in order to become skilled readers. Characteristics of a text that contribute to interest and enjoyment likewise affect general attitudes about reading and, thereby, both current and future ability to read and comprehend. In sum, enjoyment and difficulty, each important in and of themselves, also affect each other.

The problem is not solved, however, by ensuring that texts are all interesting and at the right difficulty level. If the texts are all the same, the collection of texts may become boring, again leading to negative attitudes. Finally, if the range of texts used for learning to read fails to match the text that skilled readers are expected to read, then the child may simply not learn all the essential skills. To take an extreme case, if we expect skilled readers to learn to interpret poetry, we would not give them only science books.

To compound matters, attempts by publishers, teachers, and parents to select (or design) texts to match a child's reading level are fallible, since we have no solid means for assessing either a child's reading comprehension abilities or text difficulty, not even considering the problem of interaction between text and child, or long-range effects of teaching practices. And attempts to match texts to children via selection or adaptation of texts can introduce new and unexpected sources of difficulties (Bruce & Rubin, in press; Bruce, Rubin, & Starr, 1981; Davison, Kantor, Hannah, Hermon, Lutz, & Salzillo, 1980; Steinberg & Bruce, 1980).

Clearly, a better understanding of the properties of texts that contribute to a reader's difficulties and/or enjoyment is in order. This would facilitate the matching of texts to readers with varying skills, knowledge, and interests, and, perhaps just as important, show where well-intended mismatches have occurred. Knowing more about texts would also help in teaching, for example, in adjusting the balance between reading activities such as reading to children, sustained silent reading, and reading aloud. It could also help in identifying causes of specific reading difficulties and perhaps suggest strategies for reading which can be explicitly taught.

This chapter presents a brief overview of the theoretical perspective underlying our work on text analysis, emphasizing our work on stories for children in Grades 1 through 5. The presentation is example-based; for more precise formulations of the concepts see Bruce (1980a; 1980b; 1981), Bruce and Newman (1978), Newman (1980), and Steinberg and Bruce (1980). Three factors, drawn from a theoretical model, which plausibly influence involvement of the reader with a story and story comprehension difficulty, are discussed: conflict, inside view, and point of view. These factors imply techniques for classifying and evaluating texts. The paper presents the results of an exploratory coding of a sample of basal reader stories and children's trade books. Briefly, the coding reveals a distribution of types of conflict, inside view, and point of view that may tend to increase the distance from the text that a reader feels and may provide inadequate preparation for the full range of stories (and other texts) that a skilled reader is likely to encounter. This has important implications for text selection and for ways to teach story understanding.

CONFLICT

Some form of conflict may be an essential ingredient for good stories (Bettelheim, 1976; Bruce, 1978). Consider, for instance, this excerpt from *Helga's Dowry* (de Paola, 1972). Helga, a troll, is trying to increase her dowry so that she can marry Lars. She has just struck a bargain: If she can chop and split the trees on a plot of land within a week, the land will become hers.

> "Oh what luck to find a greedy man.
> And now I'll chop as fast as I can.
> I'll swing my Troll axe so sharp and fine,
> And that mountain pasture will soon be mine!"
> warbled Helga.
>
> She chopped and chopped. But the forest seemed to
> grow larger every day that Helga worked.

"I'd almost think there was Trollery afoot," said
Helga, pausing to catch her breath.

"There is!" said a tree with a laugh that shook all
its branches.

"Plain Inge!" said Helga.

"I see you're out here trying to earn a dowry,"
bellowed Inge, who had turned herself into a tree.

"A dowry earned is as good as a dowry given," shouted
back Helga.

"I'll make sure there's no dowry earned," yelled Tree-Inge.
"Besides, our wedding is tomorrow. Lars couldn't wait!"

That did it. Helga was furious!

"I'll turn you into kindling wood!" cried Helga, who
promptly turned herself into a boulder!

Rolling down the mountainside, Boulder-Helga headed for
Tree-Inge. But Tree-Inge just moved aside. Madder than ever,
Boulder-Helga rolled up the mountainside to get a better start.

But when she came tumbling down again, Tree-Inge moved
aside once more.

All day, the battle raged. The air was filled with
flying timber.

Then suddenly it was quiet.

Helga changed back into herself again and Tree-Inge
shook with laughter.

"Giving up?" she asked.

"You'll see," answered Helga, walking off to the rich
man's house.

Although this is just an excerpt, one can see aspects of larger plot
elements—Lars' abandonment of Helga, the competition between Helga
and Inge, Helga's determination and resourcefulness. In particular, one
can see various conflicts. First, Helga has an *environmental conflict* with
respect to her goal to have the trees chopped down. But the story would
be impoverished if this were its only conflict. In fact, Helga also has an
obvious *interpersonal conflict* with Inge because of their competing goals
to win Lars. Other related interpersonal conflicts are between Lars and
Helga and between Helga and the greedy rich man. In other stories there
are also *internal conflicts* in which a single character struggles to resolve
incompatible goals within himself or herself.

Conflict is a major source of complexity for stories. As we can see in
the Helga example, understanding of conflict implies understanding
characters' goals, how their goals interrelate, and how plans to achieve
those goals mesh or clash. Another important observation is that the
characters' actions are not just physical movements, but *social* actions
(Bruce, 1975, 1980b) designed to have effects on other characters: Inge

gloats, Helga threatens, Inge gloats again, Helga tricks, and so on. Most of their actions are conditioned by their respective beliefs about the world, about each other, and about each others' beliefs. The act of interpretation of their actions depends upon beliefs about their beliefs. Such belief-based interpretation is sometimes needed in the case of environmental conflict, often for interpersonal conflict, and always for internal conflict. Not surprisingly, inferences about beliefs and interactions of plans can become quite complex (see Newman, 1980).

The fact that readers must infer beliefs, or, in other words, come to understand a character's model of the world, in order to understand social interaction among characters, is one reason why conflict often induces greater involvement with the characters. This, in turn, makes the conflicts more important to the reader, and thus the story itself becomes more engaging.

INSIDE VIEW

In the conflict example just discussed, we saw how the need to understand characters' beliefs, which is vital to conflict development, has the side effects of complicating the reader's task and facilitating involvement with the characters. We learn of these beliefs through a variety of devices, including inferences, from a character's utterances or other actions, inferences from what other characters say or do, and direct or indirect quotation of thoughts. *Inside view* encompasses the latter device as well as direct statements about a character's values and feelings.

The extent to which an author lets us see inside a character in this way affects to a great extent how much we are able to empathize with the character. It also adds to the processing load for reading because it permits, and then requires, the reader to keep track of multiple, often conflicting, views of the world.

To make some of these distinctions more concrete, consider the following excerpt from a *George and Martha* story (Marshall, 1974) called "Split Pea Soup:"

Martha was very fond of making split pea soup. Sometimes she made it all day long. Pots and pots of split pea soup.

If there was one thing that George was *not* fond of, it was split pea soup. As a matter of fact, George hated split pea soup more than anything else in the world. But it was so hard to tell Martha.

One day after George had eaten ten bowls of Martha's soup, he said to himself, "I just can't stand another bowl. Not even another spoonful."

So, while Martha was out in the kitchen, George carefully
poured the rest of his soup into his loafers under the table.
"Now she will think I have eaten it."
But Martha was watching from the kitchen.

George and Martha are the main characters in this story (as in all the
George and Martha stories). What is especially interesting in this excerpt
is that the perspective alternates between them. (This is made even
clearer by the pictures that accompany the text.) A consequence of the
shifting perspective is that it is plausible to have an inside view of each
character. We see Martha's fondness for making split pea soup as well as
George's dislike of eating it.

The amount of inside view in a story can vary greatly, from none at all
to that found in stories such as *Ramona the Brave* (Cleary, 1975), that are
essentially narrated (cf. Booth, 1961) by a character's thoughts. High
inside view undoubtedly increases the possibility for strong involvement
of the reader with a character. It is reasonable to suspect that different
amounts of inside view have different effects on enjoyment and difficulty,
and that the diversity of exposure will have consequences for the development of comprehensive skills.

POINT OF VIEW

The fact that the amount of inside view varies is but one example of a
more general phenomenon of stories: The reader is not permitted to see
everything that pertains to the events of the story (even in the case of the
so-called "omniscient" perspective). Instead, the reader sees the story
world as it might be perceived from a particular *point of view*.

A Formal Model for Point of View

Traditional classifications of point of view have provided only a handful of
categories. One such classification suggests that the primary distinguishing feature is person (first, second, or third). Another provides for
omniscient, limited omniscient, objective, and first person accounts (see
Perrine, 1966). The problem with any of these traditional classification
schemes is that they cannot encompass more than a few of the major
dimensions along which narration varies (see Booth, 1961, for a summary).

For example, the so-called "omniscient" point of view is sometimes
used to describe a story in which events are described from the spatial
perspective of more than one character. It is also applied in cases where

TABLE 1
Point of View Types

| Engagement | *Person* | |
	First	*Third*
Yes	Engaged Narrator	In-Effect Narrator
No	Unengaged Narrator	Observer

either the overall amount of inside view is high, or where an inside view for more than one character is given. These features do not always coincide. A more fruitful approach may be to identify the relevant features or dimensions first, as Booth, Chatman (1978), and others have begun to do, and then select subsets of those dimensions for specific purposes.

Consider, for the moment, just two of the distinctions pertinent to narration: *person,* and an aspect of rhetorical form that we call *engagement* (see Table 1). A story can be told using the syntactic form of first person ("I," "me," etc.) or third person ("he," "she," etc.), ignoring at this time the less common use of second person. Regardless of the person, a story may be told by a narrator who is engaged or not in the events of the story.

For the case of first person stories, engagement is the crisp distinction between stories such as *Huckleberry Finn* (Twain, 1961), in which the narrator (Huck) describes events in his life, and stories of the Uncle Remus type, in which the narrator (Uncle Remus) describes events that do not affect him directly.

For the case of the third person stories, the narrator may be an unengaged observer, the *implied author,* who relates actions but does not participate in them. There is also an important case of third person narration, identified by Booth (1961), in which we see the world so much through one character's eyes that the story is, in effect, narrated by that character. We call this form, *in-effect narration.* Thus, we can have a third person story with engaged narration.

The distinctions of person and engagement thus define four story types. These have different structural characteristics in terms of our formal model. The model, which is developed and discussed in Bruce (1981), essentially begins with an examination of what we mean by the word "narrator." This indicates that stories may be narrated at more than one level. For example, if Huck narrates his story, then there must be an author (the *implied author*) who has created Huck the narrator. The implied author talks to an *implied reader* and the narrator, Huck, talks to an *implied implied reader.* Adding the real author to the model, we get these levels of communication:

Real author	$\longrightarrow$	Real reader
Implied author	$\longrightarrow$	Implied reader
Huck*	$\longrightarrow$	Implied implied reader

(The asterisk indicates the engagement of Huck in the story he tells.)

Multiple levels of rhetorical structure add variety and increase the range of possibilities for text interpretation. Do they make stories more difficult to comprehend? Possibly, although a countervailing force is that the provision of additional narrators gives a reader more possibilities for engagement, thus facilitating comprehension.

For the purpose of discussion, we show in each example below the multiple levels of rhetorical structure. We have also used these structures as a framework for coding stories. However, the results reported here are only on the two types of person and the two types of engagement.

Observer

The simplest of the four point-of-view types that we consider here is the *observer* account. In this type, the one who tells the story is not engaged in the events of the story, and the syntactic form is third person. For example, look at the following excerpt from *The Three Billy Goats Gruff* (M. Brown, 1957):

> Once upon a time there were three billy goats who were to go up to the hillside to make themselves fat, and the name of all three was "Gruff."
>
> On the way up was a bridge over a river they had to cross, and under the bridge lived a great ugly troll with eyes as big as saucers and a nose as long as a poker.
>
> So first of all came the youngest Billy Goat Gruff to cross the bridge. "Trip, trap! trip, trap!" went the bridge.

Using the notation introduced above, we can diagram the rhetorical structure as follows:

| Real author | $\longrightarrow$ | Real reader |
| Implied author | $\longrightarrow$ | Implied reader |

Observer accounts are prevalent in children's stories—well over half of the stories we have analyzed—and understandably so since the form is relatively simple. But this simplicity may be misleading, especially when the observer account is coupled with a low inside view. In *The Three Billy Goats Gruff*, we are not told of the thoughts of the billy goats, and none of them are narrators. As a result, we do not know the motives of the first two goats when they tell the troll to wait for a bigger goat. Some readers think the little goats know what end awaits the troll while others think the goats are just saving themselves. Ambiguities such as this may lead to different interpretations of the entire plot of a story.

The Three Billy Goats Gruff is obviously a successful story, but it employs a point-of-view type (observer) and an amount of inside view (none) that does not always succeed. When the storyteller is neither identifiable as a person outside of the story nor as a character engaged in the story, the story itself becomes abstract in a way that increases what has been called "distance" for the reader. This may make the story less engaging and less interesting, and ultimately more difficult to read.

Unengaged Narrator

A second point-of-view type, called *unengaged narration,* is also told by one not engaged in the events of the story. Here, however, the story is told in first person. The storyteller is made explicit, so we get an additional level of communication. For example, consider *Winnie-the-Pooh* (Milne, 1926):

> Sometimes Winnie-the-Pooh likes a game of some sort
> when he comes downstairs, and sometimes he likes
> to sit quietly in front of the fire and listen to a story.
> This evening—
> "What about a story?" said Christopher Robin.
> "*What* about a story?" I said.
> "Could you very sweetly tell Winnie-the-Pooh one?"
> "I suppose I could," I said. "What sort of stories does
>   he like?"
> "About himself. Because he's that sort of Bear."
> "Oh, I see."
> "So could you very sweetly?"
> "I'll try," I said.
> So I tried.
> Once upon a time, a very long time ago now, about last Friday,
> Winnie-the-Pooh lived in a forest all by himself under
> the name of Sanders.

A character, identified here as "Father" narrates the first part of *Winnie-the-Pooh* in first person, but then, beginning with the familiar "Once upon a time . . . ," he becomes an unengaged narrator for a story about Winnie-the-Pooh and his friends. The rhetorical structure for unengaged narration is similar to that of observer accounts, the principal difference being an additional level of communication:

Real author	⟶	Real reader
Implied author	⟶	Implied reader
Father	⟶	Christopher Robin

Engaged Narrator

A case of correspondence between person and rhetorical form is the following excerpt, told in first person and exhibiting engaged narration. Written in a child's version of Sam Spade style, it is from *Nate the Great* (Sharmat, 1972). Note that this rhetorical form fosters a high inside view, since we see everything through the narrator's thoughts:

> I went to Annie's house. Annie has brown hair and
> brown eyes. And she smiles a lot. I would like Annie if
> I liked girls.
> She was eating breakfast. Pancakes. "I like
> pancakes," I said. It was a good breakfast. "Tell me
> about your picture," I said.
> "I painted a picture of my dog, Fang," Annie said. "I
> put it on my desk to dry. Then it was gone. It happened
> yesterday."

In the *Nate the Great* example, we have an implied author and a created narrator (Nate). We also have the hint of a third narrator, namely, Annie, who tells, to Nate, her story of losing her picture. Adding Annie to our model, we would have four levels of communication; the basic story, however, has just three:

Real author	⟶	Real reader
Implied author	⟶	Implied reader
Nate*	⟶	Implied implied reader

In-Effect Narrator

The final point-of-view type to be considered here is *in-effect narration*. Although it uses the syntactic third person, it effectively creates a narrator out of the thoughts of one character. In terms of a traditional point-of-view classification scheme, in-effect narration can be seen as the extreme form of limited omniscience, that is, everything is presented from the spatial perspective of one character and there is a high inside view, but only for that one character. For example, consider the following excerpt from *Ramona the Brave:*

> Ramona hoped their mother would be home from her
> errand, whatever it was. She couldn't wait to tell what
> had happened and how she had defended her big sister.
> Her mother would be so proud, and so would her father
> when he came home from work and heard the story. "Good
> for you, Ramona," he would say. "That's the old fight!"
> Brave little Ramona.

Notice that the passage does not relate any specific actions, but rather that Ramona "hoped" and "couldn't wait," that her mother "would be proud," and her father "would say." The author has tried to give us a view of Ramona's thoughts just as she might give us a view of the house where Ramona lives.

The rhetorical structure for in-effect narration is the same as that for engaged narration:

Real author   ⟶   Real reader
Implied author   ⟶   Implied reader
Ramona*   ⟶   Implied implied reader

A LOOK AT STORIES FOR CHILDREN

Previous Work

Factors such as conflict, inside view, and point of view are important both in a theory of stories and in a theory of skilled reading. Do they matter for children learning to read? Are children sensitive to the distinctions? Do children's texts vary significantly in terms of the factors? Since our theories of skilled reading are still in their nascent stages, it is difficult to answer these questions, and it might be considered premature to do so. On the other hand, there are some intriguing findings that suggest further exploration will be productive.

First, recent work of Green and Laff (1980) has shown that children as young as 5 years old are sensitive to subtle differences in literary style, being able, for instance, to distinguish the rhymes of Virginia Kahl from those of Dr. Seuss. Brewer and Hay (1981) have reported similar results on sensitivity to point-of-view differences. They found that even 3–year–olds could make correct judgments about the age (adult vs. child) and sex of the narrator of a story that was read to them.

Second, a previous story survey (Steinberg & Bruce, 1980) points to major differences in the diversity of conflict types and rhetorical structures in several important categories of texts. Specifically, the range in low-level (Grades 1–3) basal reader stories is much restricted relative to that of either upper-level (Grades 4–5) basals or trade books. Moreover, there are types not uncommon in adult texts that are found rarely, if at all, in even the upper-level trade books.

Third, the study just mentioned also looked at the relationship between higher-level features of stories and readers' preferences. There was a statistically significant correlation between the amount of inside view and reader preference. The results are significant even when calculated separately for upper-level or lower-level texts. This result is for adult ratings of inside view and preference, and needs to be compared to children's preference ratings. Nevertheless, it suggests that inside view and other rhetorical devices may be of general importance for creating and maintaining reader interest.

Fourth, recent work on narrative structure in the oral and written traditions of various cultures, e.g., Hawaiian talk-stories (Watson-Gegeo & Boggs, 1977), Athabaskan stories (Scollon & Scollon, 1980), and Black folk tales and oral narratives (Labov, 1973; Smitherman, 1977), has shown major differences among these cultures in rhetorical style, narrative conventions, and story content. These differences are not yet well understood, but it is likely that they have consequences for children learning to read. The few cases where cultural differences of this sort have been taken into account in teaching reading have yielded positive results (e.g., Au, 1980).

Fifth, there is a growing body of rhetorical theory (Applebee, 1978; Booth, 1961; Bruce, 1981; Chatman, 1978; Holland, 1968; Iser, 1974; Rosenblatt, 1978) that is helping to make traditional distinctions more precise and more amenable to use in analyzing stories. These theories also point to the importance of rhetorical features in the act of reading.

Sixth, the legitimate concern with readability of texts for children has been shown to be ill-served by the readability formula approach (Davison, et al., 1980). If our concern goes beyond decoding and so-called "literal comprehension," we should consider features that contribute to conceptual complexity as well as those that may affect lexical and syntactic load. Perhaps, in addition, we should consider readability (in its most limited sense) in the context of other issues such as reader involvement, which may be affected by types of conflict, inside view, and point of view.

Methodology

The sample of our study of the variation in conflict, inside view, and point of view in children's stories comprised 200 texts. These were drawn randomly from four groups, three leading basal reading series, which I refer to as Basal A, Basal B, and Basal C, and a collection of trade books. The trade books were drawn from several published lists; most (62%) were on lists called "Children's Choices" that are compiled on the basis of children's preferences by the International Reading Association together with the Children's Book Council and published each fall in *The Reading Teacher*.[1] Each group was thus represented by 50 books. The sets of 50 were subdivided by grade level, 10 from each of Grades 1 through 5.

---

[1]A comparison among different types of trade books was not a major aim of this study. However, it is interesting to note that books from the Children's Choices lists were more likely to have interpersonal and internal conflicts, had higher amounts of inside view, and were more likely to have engaged narration.

The stories were analyzed in terms of a number of features, including author commentary, number of rhetorical levels, focus characters versus point-of-view characters, and rhetorical form. below, I describe just those categories that relate to conflict, inside view, and point of view.

For conflict, each story was rated on a scale of 0–3 for the overall intensity of environmental, interpersonal, and internal conflicts. A rating of 0 meant that there was no conflict of that type; 3 meant there was conflict of that type and that it was significant for the characters and the story. A story with no conflicts of any type would get a rating of three 0's.

For inside view, a similar scale was used to indicate essentially no insight into any character's thoughts and feelings at one extreme to a deep view of one or more characters at the other extreme. To describe the point-of-view coding scheme in full would require a discussion beyond the scope of this paper (but see Bruce, 1981). Essentially, however, stories in the sample were classified by person and engagement, that is, into one of the four point-of-view types described above.

Results

Results from this survey are consistent with others we have done (e.g., Steinberg & Bruce, 1980) in highlighting major differences across grade level and text category that may have important effects on learning to read. I mention a handful of these, pointing out where further research is needed.

First, we calculated the distribution of conflict types for the four story groups in our sample (Table 2). Stories with no conflicts were almost entirely in the lower-level basal categories. When there were conflicts in lower-level basal stories, the environmental type was the most common. Otherwise, interpersonal conflicts were the most common. This somewhat unusual distribution of conflict types in basal stories cannot optimally prepare children for understanding conflict forms encountered in reading other texts, and may even lead to difficulties.

Examination of inside view for the stories in our sample reveals an increase in the incidence of high inside view in the upper-level stories (Table 3). This was even more pronounced for the basal stories in the sample. This abrupt shift in a key story feature such as inside view is an important finding to investigate further, for it points to a possible explanation for some of the difficulty children encounter in the transition from lower- to upper-primary level reading.

In terms of point of view (Table 4), there are again results that point to the need for further studies. The most common type among the basal stories is the observer account. Other types, which predominate in the trade books, are found rarely, if at all, in the basals. In particular, the

TABLE 2
Percentages of Stories with Different Types of Conflict

Text Group	Conflict Types				
	None[a]	E only[b]	P but no I[c]	P and I[d]	I but not P[e]
Basal A					
Grades 1–3	30	43.3	23.3	3.3	0
Grades 4–5	0	40.0	25.0	15.0	20.0
Basal B					
Grades 1–3	36.7	30.0	23.3	10.0	0
Grades 4–5	5.0	20.0	55.0	10.0	10.0
Basal C					
Grades 1–3	6.7	33.3	33.3	10.0	16.7
Grades 4–5	0	10.0	40.0	40.0	10.0
Trades					
Grades 1–3	0	13.3	46.7	16.7	23.3
Grades 4–5	0	15.0	40.0	40.0	5.0

[a] None = no conflict
[b] only = only environmental conflict
[c] but not I = interpersonal but not internal conflict
[d] P and I = interpersonal and internal conflict
[e] but not P = internal but not interpersonal conflict

engaged participant type and the in-effect narration, both types which would seem to promote involvement of the reader, are less prevalent in the basals, especially at the lower levels. Research is needed here to determine the effects of the different point-of-view types.

Although there are a number of inferences one might draw after examining stories from individual aspects such as conflict, inside view, or point of view, it may be even more revealing to consider these aspects in combination. One combination, in particular, seems worth studying.

There are stories that have no conflict of any kind (a rating of 0 for each type) or only environmental conflict. Many people would say that such stories have no conflict; for the moment, let us refer to them as "low-conflict" stories. Some of these low-conflict stories also have at most low inside views (0 or 1 on our rating scale). Of the low-conflict stories with low inside view, some have an observer account point of view, that is, no identifiable narrator and no in-effect narration.

The kind of story just sketched would seem to lack many of the features that contribute to involvement of the reader. Without conflict it is more difficult to have the buildup of suspense and its resolution that Brewer and Lichtenstein (1981) identify as crucial to ratings of storyhood. Without an inside view the reader is left with tenuous references about a character's thoughts and feelings, and thus may have difficulty in empathizing with that character. With only observer accounts the reader cannot resort to

TABLE 3
Average Amount of Inside View

Text Group	Grades	
	1–3	*4–5*
Basal A	.8	2.05
Basal B	.4	1.25
Basal C	.93	1.95
Trades	1.3	1.9

Rating scale:
none	0
low	1
medium	2
high	3

identifying with or interacting with the narrator. In sum, although we might not want to reject this kind of story outright, it is unpromising as a candidate for engaging a reader, particularly a young reader. Moreover, such a story provides few anchor points for the reader to use in constructing an interpretation. Thus, although it is less complex than some other story types, it may be harder to comprehend. Finally, such a story fails to give children the opportunity to exercise the skills they need for comprehending stories that do have conflict, vents in characters' minds, or complex rhetorical structures.

If one were given the task of designing or selecting books for children, the type of story discussed above would not appear ideal. At the very

TABLE 4
Percentages of Stories Told from
Different Points of View

Text Group	Unengaged		Engaged	
	Observer	*Unengaged Narrator*	*In-effect Narrator*	*Engaged Narrator*
Basal A				
Grades 1–3	96.7	0	0	3.3
Grades 4–5	75.0	5.0	5.0	15.0
Basal B				
Grades 1–3	93.3	6.7	0	0
Grades 4–5	65.0	0	20.0	15.0
Basal C				
Grades 1–3	83.3	0	6.7	10.0
Grades 4–5	75.0	0	10.0	15.0
Trades				
Grades 1–3	63.3	0	10.0	26.7
Grades 4–5	40.0	5.0	20.0	35.0

TABLE 5
Percentages of Stories with (1) Low Conflict,
(2) Low Inside View, and (3) Observer Point of View

	Grades	
Text Group	1–3	4–5
Basal A	63.3	10.0
Basal B	66.7	15.0
Basal C	26.7	10.0
Trades	13.3	15.0

least, it should be represented by no more than a small fraction of the children's library. A look at our coding results shows that this is not the case for basal readers in our sample (Table 5).

For the upper-level books, the low-conflict, low-inside-view, observer account stories constitute 10–15% of the samples. The same holds for the lower-level trade books. For the lower-level basals, however, the percentages range from 26.7 to 66.7, with a mean of 52.2% (versus 10% for the trades). Thus, over half of the stories in the readers in the first three grades have the combination of little or no conflict, low inside view *and* no identifiable narrator. This percentage seems high, especially since the existence of stories with conflict, inside view or more complex rhetorical structures in both low-level trades and the basals shows that it is possible to have such stories at the beginning reader's ability level.

EDUCATIONAL IMPLICATIONS

It is unusual for analyses of literature for children to consider rhetorical elements such as author-reader distance, commentary, point of view, or inside view, or details of character-to-character interaction. This is unfortunate, first, because there are a number of reasons to think that these features are important for comprehension and enjoyment, and second, because there is now evidence that categories of texts vary systematically in terms of these "higher-level story features." Clearly, more research is needed, but our results thus far already have a number of implications for educational practices.

Reading Aloud to Children

The positive relationship between reading aloud to children and their subsequent reading ability has been demonstrated in a number of studies (Chomsky, 1972; Durkin, 1966; McCormick, 1977). The results reported here provide an additional theoretical justification for these largely empirical findings. Namely, in order to develop the skills necessary to comprehend complex content and rhetorical structures, a reader may need to be exposed to them. Thus, reading aloud to children, in addition to fulfilling its frequently asserted motivating function, may also be supplying the only opportunity for many children, specifically those who do not have access to books outside of school, to develop the skills they need to become good readers.

Questions to Ask

The factors identified in this chapter highlight areas that may cause difficulties for children in reading and skills that need to be learned. These areas are often neglected, or at most, handled in a haphazard way when stories are discussed. A recognition of their contribution to story complexity together with our emerging taxonomy of conflict types, point-of-view types, and so on, should lead to more productive comprehension questions to ask of readers as well as specific concepts to teach.

Cultural Match

A third issue is improving the match of texts to readers with nonmainstream cultural backgrounds. Often, such readers are those having the most difficulty in comprehension, and their difficulties understanding texts might be due to mismatched expectations arising from cultural differences. Smitherman (1977) has argued that in Black folk tales, to take one example, there is a high incidence of commentary by the author and other distinctive rhetorical structures. These features reflect an oral literary tradition that developed partly as a consequence of the fact that reading and writing for slaves was against the law. There is little evidence that the characteristics of these black folk tales, which are reflected in church language and street language, to name just two areas, are taken into account in designing texts for children to read. Further study of stories from different cultures and subcultures may reveal other distinct patterns. As a first step in improving the cultural match, we should at least diversify the diet of stories given to children.

Reader Involvement

The issue of reader involvement has been touched on at several places in this chapter. It clearly plays an important role not only in a child's affective response to reading but also in his or her ultimate ability to read with comprehension. Another aspect of reader involvement should not be underrated: More engaging stories may interest adults (parents, teachers, and so on) more; their interest or disinterest will be communicated to children. It is not surprising that many of the enduring children's stories, e.g., "Hansel and Gretel," can be shown to have complexities that allow multiple levels of interpretation (see Bettelheim, 1976; Bruce & Newman, 1978; also, Newman, 1980, for a similar analysis of Sesame Street skits).

Text Design and Selection

Finally, we come to the issues of most concern to publishers and to those who select texts for children to read. The data presented and reviewed here do not provide recipes for text design or selection, but they do suggest some considerations that should become part of the process. There are four of these.

First, if we want the stories designed for learning-to-read to match the stories that skilled readers are expected to be able to read (and that some children read independently), then we should either expand the range of story types within basals or supplement them with trade books. Second, if we want to maintain basal stories as they are and not supplement them, then we should be aware that children will not be exposed to many of the story types that they will surely encounter during the transition to skilled reading. The subsequent encounters may then require special attention from teachers. Third, if we want basal stories to be more engaging for children, then we should probably move in the direction of the trade book stories in our sample, i.e., more interpersonal and internal conflict, greater inside views, and more engaged narration. Also, there should be a greater variety of story characteristics in the basals. Fourth, and finally, we should be aware of a text's characteristics with respect to features such as conflict, inside view and rhetorical structure. This awareness should influence how the text is presented, what questions are asked of the student, and what difficulties or responses we expect.

CONCLUSION

Textbooks, including basal reading series, have always, and perhaps even more in recent years (Bowler, 1978; Thompson, 1980), been scrutinized by groups with moral, political, religious, or occasionally, educational agendas to fulfill. In addition, the increasing use of readability formulas has added new linguistic constraints to the textbook design and editing process. The accumulation of such constraints makes it increasingly difficult to achieve primary educational goals, such as development of positive attitudes about reading, and learning the essential skills for reading. Texts that meet all the constraints may ultimately fail in terms of their primary purpose. The research reported here supports this gloomy forecast.

One could interpret this research and our recommendations as the attempt to impose one or more set of constraints. That is, publishers now have to worry about point of view types as well as about such things as not denigrating Paul Revere, not using street talk, or not mentioning divorce (Clark, 1981). That interpretation would be wrong. Rather than adding constraints of a new order, these analyses suggest that the relatively less constrained trade books may come closer to meeting what should be the primary goals for the basals. Of course, basal series are what most children read today. What we should do is to ensure that when choices about the design or selection of a passage for a series are made, we not lose sight of its educational purpose.

Our studies of children's stories are highlighting features that may account for reader involvement with characters and the author, for reader enjoyment, and for difficulty in comprehension. These features have traditionally been viewed as being in the domain of literary analysis rather than that of reading research, though they have direct implications for reading. We believe it is useful to continue this exploration, and plan to expand our survey of children's texts. We also plan experiments to investigate directly the effect of the textual features we have defined on children's comprehension and involvement with reading.

REFERENCES

Adams, M. J., & Bruce, B. C. Background knowledge and reading comprehension. In J. Langer and M. T. Smith-Burke (Eds.), *Reader meets author/Bridging the gap: A psycholinguistic and sociolinguistic perspective.* Newark, Del.: International Reading Association, 1982.

Applebee, A. N. *The child's concept of story.* Chicago: University of Chicago Press, 1978.

Au, K. H. *A test of the social organizational hypothesis: Relationships between participation structures and learning to read.* Unpublished doctoral dissertation, University of Illinois, 1980.

Bettelheim, B. *The uses of enchantment: The meaning and importance of fairy tales.* New York: Knopf, 1976.

Booth, W. C. *The rhetoric of fiction.* Chicago: University of Chicago Press, 1961.

Bowler, M. The making of a textbook. *Learning,* March 1978, 38–42.

Brewer, W. F., & Hay, A. *Children's understanding of the author's point of view in stories.* Paper presented at the meeting of the Society for Research in Child Development, Boston, April 1981.

Brewer, W. F., & Lichtenstein, E. H. Event schemas, story schemas, and story grammars. In A. D. Baddeley & J. D. Long (Eds.), *Attention and performance IX.* Hillsdale, N.J.: Lawrence Erlbaum Associates, 1981.

Bruce, B. C. *Belief systems and language understanding.* BBN Report No. 2973. Cambridge, Mass.: Bolt Beranek and Newman Inc., January 1975.

Bruce, B. C. What makes a good story? *Language Arts,* 1978, *55,* 460–466.

Bruce, B. C. Analysis of interacting plans as a guide to the understanding of story structure. *Poetics,* 1980, *9,* 295–311. (a)

Bruce, B. C. Plans and social actions. In R. Spiro, B. Bruce, & W. Brewer (Eds.), *Theoretical issues in reading comprehension.* Hillsdale, N.J.: Lawrence Erlbaum Associates, 1980. (b)

Bruce, B. C. A social interaction model of reading. *Discourse Processes,* 1981, *4,* 273–311.

Bruce, B. C., & Newman, D. Interacting plans. *Cognitive Science,* 1978, *2,* 195–233.

Bruce, B. C., & Rubin, A. Strategies for controlling hypothesis formation in reading. To appear in J. Flood (Ed.), *Understanding reading comprehension.* Newark, Del.: International Reading Association, in press.

Bruce, B. C., Rubin, A., & Starr, K. L. Why readability formulas fail. *IEEE Transactions on Professional Communication,* 1981, *PC-24,* 50–52.

Chatman, S. *Story and discourse.* Ithaca, N.Y.: Cornell University Press, 1978.

Chomsky, C. Stages in language development and reading exposure. *Harvard Educational Review,* 1972, *42,* 1–33.

Clark, B. Woman to protest certain textbooks. *Dallas Morning News,* February 15, 1981.

Davison, A., Kantor, R. N., Hannah, J., Herman, G., Lutz, R., & Salzillo, R. *Limitations of readability formulas in guiding adaptations of texts* (Tech. Rep. No. 162). Urbana: University of Illinois, Center for the Study of Reading, March 1980. (ERIC Document Reproduction Service No. ED 184 090)

Durkin, D. *Children who read early.* New York: Teachers College Press, 1966.

Durkin, D. What classroom observations reveal about reading comprehension instruction. *Reading Research Quarterly,* 1978–79, *14,* 481–533.

Green, G. M., & Laff, M. O. *Five-year-olds' recognition of authorship by literary style* (Tech. Rep. No. 181). Urbana: University of Illinois, Center for the Study of Reading, September 1980. (ERIC Document Reproduction Service No. ED 193 615)

Holland, N. *The dynamics of literary response.* New York: Norton, 1968.

Iser, W. *The implied reader.* Baltimore: Johns Hopkins University Press, 1974.

Labov, W. *Language in the inner city.* Philadelphia: University of Pennsylvania Press, 1973.

McCormick, S. Should you read aloud *to* your children. *Language Arts,* 1977, *54,* 139–143, 163.

Newman, D. *Children's understanding of strategic interaction.* Unpublished doctoral dissertation, University of California at San Diego, 1980.

Perrine, L. *Story and structure.* New York: Harcourt, Brace & World, 1966.

Rosenblatt, L. M. *The reader, the text, the poem.* Carbondale: Southern Illinois University Press, 1978.

Scollon, R., & Scollon, S. B. K. Literacy as focused interaction. *The Quarterly Newsletter of the Laboratory of Comparative and Human Cognition,* 1980, *2,* 26–29.

Smitherman, G. *Talkin and testifyin.* Boston: Houghton Mifflin, 1977.

Steinberg, C., & Bruce, B. C. *Higher-level features in children's stories: Rhetorical structure and conflict* (Reading Education Report No. 18). Urbana: University of Illinois, Center for the Study of Reading, October 1980.

Thompson, H. The most censored books in America. *Parents' Choice,* 1980, *3,* 4.

Watson-Gegeo, K. A., & Boggs, S. T. From verbal play to talk story: The role of routines in speech events among Hawaiian children. In S. Ervin-Tripp & C. Mitchell-Kerman (Eds.), *Child discourse.* New York: Academic Press, 1977.

LITERARY REFERENCES

Brown, M. *The Three Billy Goats Gruff.* New York: Harcourt Brace Jovanovich, 1957.

Cleary, B. *Ramona the brave.* New York: Morrow, 1975.

de Paola, T. *Helga's dowry.* New York: Harcourt Brace Jovanovich, 1972.

Marshall, J. *George and Martha.* Boston: Houghton Mifflin, 1974.

Milne, A. A. *Winnie-the-Pooh.* London: Methuen, 1926.

Sharmat, M. W. *Nate the great.* New York: Dell, 1972.

Twain, M. *The adventures of Huckleberry Finn.* New York: Norton, 1961.

On the Appropriateness of Adaptations in Primary-Level Basal Readers: Reaction to Remarks by Bertram Bruce

Georgia M. Green
Center for the Study of Reading
University of Illinois at Urbana-Champaign

I begin my comments on the subject of differences in content and literary structure between basals and trade books by saying that I find Bruce's chapter provocative because I have been led, via a rather different route to very similar conclusions. I address my remarks to the implications of some of them for the appropriateness of adaptations in primary-level basal readers.

When trade books are adapted to appear as selections in basal readers, and sentence length, passage length, and vocabulary complexity are reduced, very often what gets left out (along with anything that might have moved the reader to appreciate the author's wordcraft) is precisely the details that contribute to story complexity and character development. Because of this, important factors are absent that could have contributed to reader involvement (and consequent interest and motivation).

My interest was originally in the language of basal reader stories, rather than the content. I discovered that in 1908, Huey (1908/1968) had criticized the available primers for being unnatural, inane, and disconnected.[1] His criticism is as appropriate today as it was then. Despite periodic controversies, the language of primary-level basals remains stilted and unnatural. This is due at least partially, no doubt, to pressures

---

[1] "Next to the beauty of [the illustrations in] the primers, the most striking thing about at least three fourths of them is the inanity and disjointedness of their reading content, especially in the earlier parts. No trouble has been taken to write what the child would naturally say about the subject in hand, nor indeed, usually, to say *anything* connectedly or continuously, as even an adult would naturally talk about the subject (Huey 1908/1968, p. 279).

for conformity within the basal reader publishing industry, particularly pressures for conformity to readability formulae (often mounted by powerful forces on the fringes of educational research and practice: textbook adoption committees). However, it has never been made clear whether the limitations codified in the readability formulae were necessary and helpful, or whether, on the other hand, they might not have the effect of making text more difficult to interpret (as Davison, Kantor, Hannah, Hermon, Lutz, & Salzillo, 1980, indicate) and less rewarding to attempt. They certainly seem to in example (1), an excerpt from a beginning-level book with an average sentence length of 3.1 words, and a Fry Score at the low end of Grade 1:

1. Tap, tap, tap. See me work. I make good things.
   See the red ones. See the blue ones. See the yellow ones.
   No, no, no. I do not want red ones. I do not want blue
   ones. I want green ones.
   No, no, no. I do not want big ones. I want little ones.
   No, no, no. I do not want little ones. I want big ones.
   Oh, my. Oh, my. No one wants my things. I will go to
   bed. I will work in the morning.
   [This book is a version of "The Shoemaker and the Elves"
   with a total vocabulary of 80 words. *Elves* and *shoemaker* and even *shoes*
   are not among them.]

The selection in example (2), from a basal's version of Aesop's fable about the hare and the tortoise (average sentence length: 5.15 words) is no more coherent, and neither one strikes me as half as interesting as watching reruns of *Sesame Street* for the fifth time.

2. Rabbit said, "I can run. I can run fast. You can't run fast."
   Turtle said, "Look Rabbit. See the park. You and I will run.
   We'll run to the park."
   Rabbit said, "I want to stop. I'll stop here. I can run, but
   Turtle can't. I can get to the park fast."
   Turtle said, "I can't run fast. But I will not stop. Rabbit
   can't see me. I'll get to the park."

Preliminary research at the Center for the Study of Reading (Green & Laff, 1980), indicates that some 5–year–olds can tell the difference between stories by Beatrix Potter and stories by Margaret Wise Brown, on the basis of linguistic and stylistic properties (Green, 1982b). It seems highly likely that 6– and 7–year–olds are able to detect the differences between such stories on the one hand, and on the other, stories like the one quoted in (2). If they can, and if they prefer the stylistic complexities of popular trade books, as basic principles of attention theory would suggest (in general, complex activities are preferred to simple ones), then requiring them to read the colorless, artificial prose seems pointless at best; at worst, it wastes valuable time that could be spent in more profitable ways and risks boring the children and conveying to them that there is nothing interesting to be learned in books, or even in school. I do not deny that some vocabulary control and repetition might be helpful in the very first stages of reading instruction, and I am not suggesting that children jump into *War and Peace* as soon as they know the letters of the alphabet. What I am questioning is whether such artificial requirements on texts have to be imposed in as heavy-handed a manner as they sometimes are.

To put it another way, the use of bona fide children's literature in beginning reading programs might motivate children who are now not being motivated to learn to read. For children who come to first grade with little experience with books, learning to read may not be very attractive, especially if their encounters with text lead them to believe that all that is in store for them if they do learn to read is dull little stories (or worse, non-stories with no inside view and no conflict) in increasingly smaller print. Children who come to first grade motivated to learn to read will probably learn to read regardless of what method and materials are used, although they may become restless and "turned off" when they perceive the enormous gap between what their parents read to them at home and what they are expected to read in school. But it is the children who come to first grade with little prior knowledge of the wonders of books for whom motivation is a critical factor. If the materials are to bear the burden of motivating them, then the early materials will have to be intrinsically worth reading—i.e., enjoyable—because it is likely that these children will find little reason to work to learn to read if the only pay-off is approval from the teacher. Learning to read is its own reward when one knows that there are many things one will want to read. If a child does not know this, and not all teachers will take the time to help them discover it by reading to them, learning to read may be no particular thrill, and the child may feel it is not worth the bother. In fact, the strategy of "simplifying" text according to readability formulae in order to encourage poor readers may actually be counterproductive in that children who read only basal-edited texts may find them so difficult to interpret, as a direct result of the supposed simplifications, or so pointless, or both, that they lose whatever internal motivation they might have had to learn to read or to learn to read better. Might more children learn to read better if their reading instruction texts consisted of genuine, uncut, unaltered works of children's literature?

After all, the assumption that graded readers need to be edited to meet norms arbitrarily established over 50 years ago depends on the assumption that children who can *tell* stories with an average sentence length of 12.1 words and a Fry Score of Grade 3,[2] who beg to listen to stories like *Mrs. Piggle-Wiggle*[3] and *The Wizard of Oz,* with average sentence lengths of 31 and 22, and Fry Scores of Grade 7 and 8, respectively, must require simplified, shortened stories with shortened sentences and reduced vocabulary even after they have learned the basic principles for interpreting print. This assumption is not unique to the textbook publishing industry, or even to the educational establishment. When an ordinary grandmother learned that a granddaughter with whom she has enjoyed serious and sophisticated conversations was learning to read, she wrote to the child:

> 3. I am glad that you are learning to read. Now I can write a
> letter to you.
> We have lots of snow. Do you have a sled? Sam likes to play
> in the snow. She likes to chase the rabbits and squirrels in
> the snow.
> She can run fast. They can run faster. Can your cat run fast
> and chase a rabbit?

To return to the question: Might more children learn to read better if their texts consisted of bona fide children's literature? Several studies suggest that this might indeed be the case. Schlager's recent (1978) analysis of the circulation, over a three-year period, of 52 Newbery Award books showed that 7- to 12-year-olds strongly preferred books written from the perspective of 7- to 12-year-olds. This means that for a book to be successful with this group, the attitudes and actions of the main characters, whatever their age—or species[4]—must "invite the child's identification with them, and so generate interest in the unfolding of the story" (1978, p. 141). This entails that the stories contain whatever rhetorical devices are necessary to tell them from an identifiable point of view, and no doubt accounts at least in part for the immense popularity of such

---

[2] As determined from a sampling of the stories told by 5-year-olds and transcribed in Pitcher and Prelinger (1963).

[3] At age 3, my daughter asked me to teach her to read so that she could read *Mrs. Piggle-Wiggle* by herself. Now 6, she says *Mrs. Piggle-Wiggle* (Fry Score Grade 7–8) is easier than Laura Ingalls Wilder's *Little House in the Big Woods* (Fry Score Grade 5) "because it [*Little House* . . .] has too many words I don't know," but she loves to read them both. (Note for formula fans: This disparity is probably a function of the Fry formula's dependence on syllable counts; the words she does not know are mainly monosyllabic or disyllabic names for unfamiliar objects.)

[4] According to Schlager's claim, a book about an adult rat would be as interesting as a book about a fifth grader, as long as the rat had the perspective on the world that a 7- to 12-year-old has.

writers as Beverly Cleary, Judy Blume, and Norma Klein, who have made a hallmark of this.

Research bearing directly on the value of regular exposure to bona fide literature for the development of reading skills is reported by Cohen (1980). She directed a large-scale experiment in which 155 second graders listened every day for an entire school year to stories selected for the naturalness and vividness of the language used, and their potential for allowing for emotional identification with characters' aspirations, fears, and other feelings and adventures. A group of 130 students in different schools from the experimental group constituted a control group. Teachers in the control group proceeded as usual, with stories an occasional treat, if read at all, and not chosen according to the specific criteria for the experimental group. All students were in "homogeneously grouped classes at the top, middle, and bottom of the second grade. These placements were determined a priori by the teachers and school administrators according to levels of reading and reading readiness achieved by the children at the end of first grade" (Cohen, 1980, p. 9). The populations studied included a range of 30–45% Puerto Rican children, 40–55% Black children, and the rest White. Compared to the control group, the experimental group showed increases in vocabulary size, word knowledge, reading comprehension, and vocabulary quality. If this is not convincing evidence of the value of regular exposure to bona fide literature, nothing will be. And, for reasons already mentioned, I see no reason not to expect similar results when the children do the reading themselves.

When I began voicing the heretical thought a few years ago that children might learn better from unaltered texts than from adaptations, the reaction I got was: "Seven– and eight–year–olds already have enough trouble learning to read. Besides, they probably wouldn't notice the difference. Leave well enough alone!" Since I suspected that some of the difficulty they encountered in learning to read was actually an effect of the use of the readability formulae governing the text-writing and adaptation process, I concentrated on the second issue: Would children be able to distinguish literary styles in a way that would suggest that they could tell the difference between bona fide literary works and adaptations of them? I arranged a small-scale experiment. Over a two-week period, thirteen children listened, in a naturalistic setting, to two works by each of five children's authors. When they listened to tapes of a third work by each of the five authors, six of the ten children who completed the interviews were able to correctly identify the authorship of three or more of the five stories.

To do this, they had to be able to make distinctions among the prose of Beatrix Potter, Margaret Wise Brown, and Bill Peet, and between the verse of Virginia Kahl and Dr. Seuss, distinctions that depend on rather subtle linguistic cues, as the following extracts suggest.

4. "If you are a gardener and find me," said the little bunny,
"I will be a bird and fly away from you."
"If you become a bird and fly away from me," said his mother,
"I will be a tree that you come home to."
(Margaret Wise Brown, *The Runaway Bunny*)

Peter gave himself up for lost, and shed big tears; but his sobs
were overheard by some friendly sparrows, who flew to him in
great excitement, and implored him to exert himself. (Beatrix
Potter, *The Tale of Peter Rabbit*)

"Where in blazes did you come from?!!" she shrieked, giving the
boulder a vicious kick. (Bill Peet, *Big Bad Bruce*)

5. But I'm also in charge of the brown Bar-ba-Loots
Who played in the shade in their Bar-ba-loot suits
and happily lived, eating Truffula fruits.
NOW . . . Thanks to your hacking my trees to the ground,
there's not enough Truffula fruit to go 'round.
And my poor Bar-ba-loots are all getting the crummies
because they have gas, and no food in their tummies.
(Dr. Seuss, *The Lorax.* Random House, 1972)

And everyone cried, "There's been an error;
That beast is never a cause for terror.
He'd never harm us; he's kind and true.
We must protect him; What shall we do?"
At last they announced, after due reflection,
"We'll send the men off in the wrong direction."
(Virginia Kahl, *How Do You Hide a Monster?* Scribners, 1971)

To identify unfamiliar passages by these authors on the basis of style, the
children had to make judgments, whether they were aware of it or not,
about such aspects of literary style as the repetition and lyrical rhyth-
micity of Margaret Wise Brown's sentences, the Victorian words and
phrases *(shed, in great excitement, implored, exert)* of Beatrix Potter, and
Bill Peet's violent language *(where in blazes)* and characters (whose actions are reported with such terms as *shrieked* and *vicious kick).* Discrimination between the two verse passages is perhaps more subtle, as both
have the same meter. Nevertheless, such cues as Dr. Seuss' made up
species (Bar-ba-loots, Truffula) and compound nouns *(Bar-ba-loot suits),*
and colloquial language *(whack, smacker, crummies, tummies),* as opposed to Virginia Kahl's more restrained syntax *(cause for terror, after
due reflection)* and recherché vocabulary *(error, true* for "faithful," *reflection* for "thought," *due* for "sufficient") make this not too difficult a task.

Although these children were kindergarteners, most of whom could not
read, I did not conclude from the fact that six out of ten of them could

make fine stylistic discriminations, that the general population of beginning readers could necessarily tell the difference between the literary selections in (4) and (5) on the one hand, and basal prose like that in (2), (6), and (7), on the other.

6. Nancy and Nick started to play together.
   They got very noisy and then heard a tap.
   "That's Mrs. Muffle," Nancy said. She lives
   under us. We are too noisy."
   "I had better go home," Nick said. "I wish
   I could go back and play in the little town
   where I lived. We could make noise there,"
   he said as he ran up the steps.

(Fry Score 2, Average sentence length: 9.1 words)
[Adapted from the following section of *Noisy Nancy and Nick,* by Lou Ann Gaeddert. Doubleday, 1970. Fry Score 3, Average sentence length: 9.8 words.]

Nancy and Nick built a huge tower with Nancy's blocks.
They sat and looked at it for a while. Then Nancy got
her dump truck and zoomed it into the base
of the tower. Blocks crashed to the floor.
"Let's do it again," shouted Nick.
They were building a new tower when they heard a
bang on the floor.
"What's that?" asked Nick.
That's the lady downstairs," explained Nancy. "We're
too noisy. We can't knock our tower down this time."
"I'd better go upstairs," whispered Nick as he tiptoed
to the door. "I wish I could go home and play with
my friends in Ohio. We didn't have to be quiet there."
Nick turned and ran up the stairs, but Nancy saw that
there were tears in his eyes.

7. Every morning was the same for Little Hippo. All the
   big hippos would wait for him to get up. They wanted
   to take care of him.
   After Little Hippo was up, he was never by himself.
   Someone was always around to take care of him.
   If Little Hippo wanted food, Big Charles would see
   that he got it.
   "Little Hippo wants some food," Big Charles would call.
   "Bring it over here."
   The big hippos would do just that. Then they would
   wait for Little Hippo to eat.

(Fry Score 2, Average sentence length: 7.0 words)
[Adapted from the following section of *The Secret Hiding Place,* by
Rainey Bennett. Cleveland: Collins-World, 1960.
Fry Score 2, Average sentence length: 7.3 words.]

Little Hippo was the pet of the herd. Every morning the
big hippos waited for him to wake up so they could take
care of him. "Shush," they whispered. "Little Hippo is
sleeping. "Quiet, all!" said Big Charles.
And every morning the big hippos pushed and bumped each other,
hurrying to bring Little Hippo his breakfast of
lily pads and corn. Big Charles said, "Put the lily
pads here and the corn there." Then they all settled
down to watch Little Hippo eat.

Still, I felt encouraged to go on to test the question directly: Would
second graders be more interested in reading unedited works by established children's authors, despite the fact that by readability formula standards the texts might be above their level, or would they prefer their meat
pre-cut, so to speak? And if they prefer original works to adaptations, do
they understand them as well?

Unhappily, I have no results to report yet, as I am still in the process of
testing materials to use in an experiment that ought to settle the question.
Second graders will be asked to read two versions of the same story, and
then be interviewed about their preferences. They will also be asked to
read a third text, which will be a version of a different story. This third
text will be either the trade book original or the basal adaptation. The
students will be tested for comprehension on the third text. If it turns out
that they prefer the supposedly more difficult original versions, and do as
well or better on the comprehension measurements on the originals, I will
regard that as prima facie direct evidence that the emperor has no
clothes—that it is time to dethrone the tyrants of Short Sentences and
Limited Vocabulary. (Davison et al. 1980, have already demonstrated
that these will not always have the effect of increasing reading ease pre-
dicted by readability formulae.)

A section of the text analysis group at the Center for the Study of
Reading has been reading adaptations from second-grade basal readers
and comparing them to the trade books they are adapted from. It has been
a real revelation. For a variety of reasons, finding materials suitable for
this experiment has turned out to be much harder than we imagined it
would be, despite the fact that, in general, roughly 50–80% of the selections in second-grade basals seem to be adaptations of trade materials.
Sometimes the changes seemed insignificant—deletion of a descriptive
adverb here, an elaborating sentence there, as in (8).

8. [From *Nothing Much Happened Today,* by Mary Blount Christian. Reading, Mass.: Addison-Wesley, 1973]

Mother gasped. "Cat? Cat?
We don't have a cat."
"I guess you could say
it was a visiting cat,"
Stephen explained.
"It came through the window."
"The window?" Mother shrieked.
That cat broke the glass?"
Stephen shook his head.
"Nope. The window was open.
We had to let the smoke out."
Mother grabbed her forehead.
"Smoke! What smoke?"
"The smoke from the oven
when the cake batter
spilled over," Elizabeth volunteered.
Mother waved her arms.
"Why were you baking a cake?"
"For the school bake sale,"
Alan reminded her.

As adapted:

Mrs. Mayberry gasped, "Cat? Cat? We don't have
a cat!"
"You might say it was a visiting cat," Steven
explained. "It came through the window that we
opened to let the smoke out."
Mrs. Mayberry held her head. "Smoke! What
smoke?"
"The smoke from the stove when the cake spilled
over," Elizabeth offered.
Mrs. Mayberry waved her arms. "Why were you
making a cake?"
For the school bake sale," Alan reminded her.

(In this adaptation, such deletions actually had the effect of increasing the average sentence length from 6.1 to 8.1 words per sentence, as the sentences that were left out tended to be significantly shorter than the ones left in.) But more often than not, we perceived the changes as making the stories duller as well as shorter.

We were surprised to learn that many of the basals include adaptations of "Easy Reader" trade books—books that are marketed as being written with controlled vocabulary and sentence length. Sometimes adaptations of these already highly constrained texts are only trivially different from the originals, but in other cases, as illustrated in (9), adaptation consists primarily of deletion of all sentences not affecting the action of a story.

9. "The Case of the Sinking Pond," Chapter 4 of *Detective Mole*, by Robert Quackenbush. Lothrop, Lee and Shepard, 1976:

Detective Mole got a call from
Mrs. Duck.
He grabbed his magnifying glass
and ran to the pond.
"Detective Mole at your service,"
he said.
He was talking to a water lily.
Mrs. Duck swam toward him.
"Here I am," she said.
"Sorry about that," Detective Mole
said. "My sunglasses were fogged."
He asked Mrs. Duck to tell him
her problems.
"My pond is slowly sinking,"
she said. "My feet drag
on the bottom as I swim.
I'm sure someone is stealing
the water. If this keeps up,
my poor ducklings will never
learn their water tricks."
Detective Mole took his detective
manual from his pocket.
"This reminds me of the famous
DISAPPEARING MINERAL
WATER MYSTERY," he said.
He searched the edge of the pond
with his magnifying glass.
He found some hoof prints.
They went across Mrs. Duck's
back yard and out the gate.
"Aha!" he said. "I think I have
solved this case."
Mrs. Duck and her ducklings
followed the trail of hoof prints
with Detective Mole.
The prints led them to Mr. and
Mrs. Horse's back yard.
Mrs. Horse was pouring a bucket
of pond water into some empty
bottles.

Detective Mole quietly slipped
up behind her.
"Caught in the act!" he said.
Mrs. Horse jumped in surprise.
She dropped the bucket and
the bottles.
Mrs. Duck was very angry.
"Why are you taking the water
from my pond?" she demanded.
Mrs. Horse explained that she
didn't think Mrs. Duck would mind.
"The pond water has such
good minerals," she said.
"And Mr. Horse has been drinking
too much root beer. So I am
filling his empty root beer
bottles with your good water.
I want my husband to drink
mineral water instead of
root bear. It is so much
better for him."
"Humph!" said Mrs. Duck.
"Your idea is not better for me.
My pond is sinking!"
Mrs. Horse said, "Dear me.
I didn't know that. Please
forgive me."
They had always been good friends,
so Mrs. Duck forgave her.
"Besides, it will rain soon,"
she said. "The pond will fill up again."
"I couldn't bottle much more
of the water anyway," Mrs. Horse
said. "Almost all of my metal
bottle caps have disappeared.
It is a real mystery. I can't
imagine what happened to them."
Detective Mole thumbed through
his detective manual.
"My manual says there is
something about this that
doesn't hold water," he said.
"I'll check it out."

As adapted:

Detective Mole got a call from Mrs. Duck. He grabbed
his magnifying glass. Then he ran to the pond.

"Detective Mole at your service," he said. But he was
talking to a water lily. He couldn't see very well,
even with his magnifying glass.
Mrs. Duck swam toward Detective Mole. "Here I am,"
she said.
Detective Mole asked Mrs. Duck to tell him her problem.
"The water in my pond is slowly sinking," said Mrs.
Duck. "My feet touch the bottom when I swim. I'm sure
someone is stealing the water. If this keeps up, my
ducklings will never learn to swim."
Detective Mole searched the edge of the pond. He
found some footprints. The footprints went across
Mrs. Duck's backyard and out the gate.
"Aha!" he said. "I think I've solved this case."
Mrs. Duck and her ducklings followed the footprints
with Detective Mole. The footprints led them to Mr. and
Mrs. Horse's backyard. They found Mrs. Horse pouring
a can of water into some empty bottles.
Detective Mole quietly walked up behind Mrs. Horse.
"I caught you!" he said.
Mrs. Horse jumped in surprise. She dropped the can
and the bottles.
Mrs. Duck was very angry. "Why are you taking water from
my pond?" she asked.
"The pond water is so good to drink," Mrs. Horse said.
"That's why I'm filling these empty bottles with your
pond water. I didn't think you would mind."
"Well!" said Mrs. Duck. "I do mind! My pond is sinking!"
Mrs. Horse said, "Oh, I didn't know that. Please
forgive me."
They had always been good friends, so Mrs. Duck forgave
Mrs. Horse.
"Besides it will rain soon," said Detective Mole. "The
raindrops will fill your pond again."

This affects the length of the text, though not the average sentence length
or the readability score. Deletion of sentences judged extraneous does,
however, have a pronounced effect on what a reader can infer about the
motives and plans of a character, and thus affects the extent to which a
text is a story, by reducing the text to an unrelated sequence of events.
What gets deleted are the very elements that Bruce has identified as being
present in lower concentration in basals than in trade books. We have
been tempted to include differences of this sort in our preferences research, but so far have resisted, as our intent has been to investigate
differences of language, not content. We did ask one 6–year–old which of

the versions of "The Case of the Sinking Pond" she preferred. She answered, in no uncertain terms, that she liked the original better because "Mrs. Horse got the water for important reasons" while in the other "she just got it to drink." Also, the child "didn't like Detective Mole being nearsighted" in the basal and added that she didn't like the basal as much because "Mrs. Duck talks back to Mrs. Horse, and that's not nice." Queried about this, she said that "Well! I do mind!" is a "mean way of talking" but "Humph! Your idea is not better for me" is just "grouchy." But the large-scale differences in content entailed by editing that removes information about attitudes and motives are a different question from "mere" differences in language, as are questions of paragraphing conventions, typography, and other matters of graphic design that might also affect preferences and comprehension.

If our hypothesis is confirmed, and it turns out that children do prefer stories that do not condescend to them, and (perhaps for the same reason) comprehend them without significant difficulty, then it will strengthen the arguments against providing children with a reading diet of supposedly simplified texts rich in the poly-unnaturalness of primer language, and poor in the meat of conflict and participant perspective that make reading a good text as interesting as watching a good drama.

An additional argument against the regular use of such texts resides in the fact that in depending on watered-down, style-leveled adaptations, the educational system fails to expose children, from a very early age, to new words and a wide variety of rhetorical devices and literary styles. This makes it that much more difficult to teach appreciation and imitation of style, and even literal comprehension, in later stages of education. Indeed, a child who is not exposed to the wealth of literary usages and devices, and to a variety of writing styles in school, and who does not independently read much may be seriously handicapped in simply interpreting texts written in styles at variance with the prose of the basal readers that have been his primary model of written text. Not only is it potentially boring to read materials with little or no syntactic or lexical challenge and even less stylistic variation, but having only materials like that to read also deprives children of an opportunity to learn in a natural way the complexities of syntactic and lexical manipulation (Green, 1982a) that constitute style and contribute ubiquitously to the task of interpreting text as intended by the author. If children are not exposed to unfamiliar words and syntactic constructions because they are "too hard," how are they supposed to ever learn to deal with them?

Indeed, a number of people (e.g., Johnson, 1979, p. 41) have pointed out advantages of not meddling with the vocabulary in a text and letting children encounter unfamiliar words in their natural, meaningful contexts. When a word they do not know prevents them from understanding *some-*

thing they have an interest in, they are not shy about asking. Leaving vocabulary management to the children lets them learn new words encountered in reading in exactly the same way they have been managing for five or six or seven years to learn new words they encounter in speech. It also enables them to practice doing what they will have to do when they come across unfamiliar words and phrases in their independent reading for the rest of their lives. When they are adults, there will be no one to "prepare the vocabulary" for them; they will have to depend on their own abilities to make inferences from the context. Of course, some children may need to be encouraged to ask about what they do not understand, taught that it's okay to volunteer that you don't know something, okay to interrupt to ask for clarification. Fine; it seems to me that in general, beyond the scope of reading instruction strategies, teaching children how to be responsible for their own education ought to be a prime goal of public schooling.

What, then, are the prospects for basal readers? What has been said so far about the inferiority of adaptations to original, bona fide children's literature might seem to imply that the whole idea of basal readers should be scrapped and replaced in reading curricula with a selection of unaltered, unabridged children's books. That is certainly one possible alternative; high quality, inexpensive reproductions of highly acclaimed children's books at all levels of difficulty are already available. But that is not the only possibility. If you can't beat 'em, you can join 'em. Instead of publishing adaptations of trade books, the providers of basal reading series could follow the lead of one publisher and reprint the trade books in their entirety, as most now do for poetry selections. That way they can even capitalize on the reputations of the works they are reprinting, instead of having to hide that information in small print on the acknowledgments page. They can even continue to publish the teacher's manuals and workbooks, and regularly include expanded sections on the author, the style, and critical interpretation even in the primary grades.

"But what about textbook adoption committees?" you ask. "All those people, *demanding* that our books meet those arbitrary readability formulae before we can even get a license to sell our books!" Well, that is a problem, but it may not be insurmountable. First of all, if a properly scaled study is carried out that confirms our hypothesis, and shows that more children learn to read, and learn earlier and better, using original texts with literary merit than children using adaptations that strip the texts of their drama and poetry, and inadvertently make them harder to understand, then it should not be hard to sell a package of such texts to educators responsible for choosing curricular materials. More than a few are already unhappy with the lack of literary value in the selections in available basals.

Second, for the couple of years that it will take to convince adoption committees and legislatures of the folly of depending on rigid, ignorant, insensitive, and arbitrary formulae to choose what schoolbooks their children will use (and I would think that a joint effort by researchers, publishers, and professional organizations like the International Reading Association would have a good chance of success in this), it should be possible to publish for those states where conformity to readability formulae is required by law, special editions of the same texts, adapted to meet their criteria. It would not be new for a publisher to provide a special edition of its series for a single state in order to meet the criteria set by or for that state's adoption committee. If after a while, schools using the unadapted versions were enjoying gains in reading scores and increased enthusiasm for reading, that might be enough to cause adoption committees and legislatures to revise their requirements.

But specially adapted editions would not even be necessary to meet the demands for adherence to readability formulae. I am not suggesting that texts should not be graded for difficulty, only that they should not be graded so hard. Vocabulary control, phonetic similarity, and repetition need not be artificially manipulated; they can be sought within carefully selected complete texts with inherent literary value. An experienced teacher's judgment of what a group can read and enjoy shouldn't be overruled by some arbitrary interpretation of an artificial formula.

I would like to close, utopian idealist that I am, with a few comments on what kind of criteria might replace the simplistic and arbitrary formulae for use in selecting texts for inclusion in a reading curriculum. One criterion ought to be, as Huey (1908/1968) implied, naturalness. This means getting away from such characteristics of "primer language" as excessive local repetition as in *"Look," said Mike. "Look, look. Come and look. Come and look at Ann,"* or as in the story cited in (2). Repetition within a story can be aesthetically pleasing, as in Margaret Wise Brown's *Goodnight Moon* (which has a total vocabulary of only 54 words). And repetition probably has a stronger reinforcement effect if it is cyclic within a story, as in Brown's *Runaway Bunny,* or spread out over several stories than if it is concentrated in the space of one or two pages. Repetition and vocabulary can probably be controlled in primary-level readers as easily by the selection of texts as by adaptation.

Adopting naturalness as a criterion also means getting away from the preponderance of short sentences with no subordinate clauses, with only one or two verb tenses, and with excessive use of verb conjunction *(He ran and ran and ran)* to indicate intensity or duration. In addition, and perhaps most significantly, it means avoiding the use of illustrations to convey information that is not explicit in the text, as in (1) and (2). Illustrations are fine as long as they are redundant or, perhaps better, merely decorative. But when interpreting the illustrations is necessary in order to make sense out of the text, they interfere with the natural development of an internal competence for recognizing coherent text. This in turn may have serious consequences for the development of inferential comprehension, and consequently, for comprehension of expository prose.

Of course, making naturalness of prose an important criterion in selecting texts does not mean limiting the texts to those that use language the way the children themselves do.[5] First of all, for several obvious reasons, one would not want texts containing, except for effect, a high proportion of sentences that went on and on conjoining clause after clause with *and*, as Hunt (1965) says children tend to use. Second, it is well known that even from the earliest stages of language acquisition, children understand more linguistic forms than they use. Their "passive vocabularies" are greater than their active vocabularies, and even if they read *ocean liner* as "ocean linner," they may still infer its correct meaning in context. Finally, as must also be obvious, if their exposure is limited to material containing only forms they have already demonstrated mastery of, it follows that instruction can never be responsible for expanding that mastery and increasing their knowledge of words and constructions, rhetorical strategies and styles.

I suppose all this sounds like a very radical proposal, and I know radicalism is no longer in vogue, but the potential benefits seem to me so great that I cannot help but think that the idea of abandoning adaptations deserves serious consideration. The current (and perhaps intuitive) procedures for "simplifying" texts result in making the texts unnatural, more difficult to understand, and less interesting than the originals. Far from motivating children who are struggling to learn to read, they appear to decrease the pay-off for learning to read, by making reading appear too difficult and too boring to be worth the effort. When children are having difficulty with texts that they know are supposed to have been made easy for them, this can generate feelings of inherent worthlessness and cause children to view themselves as failures and to stop trying. But if it is the texts that are at fault, and not the children, then it is time to provide beginning readers with inherently enjoyable texts, rather than just promising eventual gratification in knowing how to read; it is time to give them a different *kind* of text.

---

[5] As Reid (1970, p. 35) suggests in recommending use of more transitive verbs and indirect quotation instead of the ubiquitous literary convention *"Quote," said XX,* so that the language of the primers will be more like that of first graders according to Strickland's (1962) characterization of it.

REFERENCES

Cohen, D. M. The effect of literature on vocabulary and reading achievement. *The world of words, Folio II.* New York: Bank Street College of Education, 1980, Pp. 8–15.

Davison, A., Kantor, R. N., Hannah, J., Hermon, G., Lutz, R., & Salzillo, R. *Limitations of readability formulas in guiding adaptations of texts* (Tech. Rep. 162). Urbana: University of Illinois, Center for the Study of Reading, March 1980. (ERIC Document Reproduction Service No. ED 184 090)

Green, G. Linguistics and the pragmatics of language use. *Poetics,* 1982a, *11,* Pp. 45–76.

Green, G. Competence for implicit text analysis: Literary style discrimination in five-year-olds. In D. Tannen (Ed.), *Analyzing discourse: Text and task.* Georgetown University Roundtable on Languages and Linguistics 1981, 142–163 Washington, D.C.: Georgetown University Press, 1982b.

Green, G., & Laff, M. *Five-year-olds' recognition of authorship by literary style* (Tech. Rep. No. 181). Urbana: University of Illinois, Center for the Study of Reading, September 1980. (ERIC Document Reproduction Service No. ED 193 615)

Huey, E. B. *The psychology and pedagogy of reading.* Cambridge, Mass.: M.I.T. Press, 1968. (Originally published 1908.)

Hunt, K. W. *Grammatical structures written at three grade levels* (NCTE Research Report No. 3). Urbana, Ill.: National Council of Teachers of English, 1965.

Johnson, T. D. Presenting literature to children. *Children's Literature in Education,* 1979, *10,* 35–43.

Pitcher, E. G., & Prelinger, E. *Children tell stories.* New York: International Universities Press, 1963.

Reid, J. Sentence structure in reading primers. *Research in Education,* 1970, *3,* 23–37.

Schlager, N. Predicting children's choices in literature: A developmental approach. *Children's Literature in Education,* 1978, *10,* 136–142.

Strickland, R. The language of elementary school children: Its relationship to the language of reading textbooks and the quality of reading of selected children. *Bulletin of the School of Education,* Indiana University, *38*(4), 1962.

6 Content Area Textbooks

Thomas H. Anderson
Bonnie B. Armbruster
Center for the Study of Reading
University of Illinois at Urbana Champaign

Why some students are not proficient in learning from content area textbooks is a question that has challenged us for several years. In seeking an answer to this question, we have proceeded along two fronts—one focused on the student and one on the text. We began with the student, investigating studying strategies that students can use to help them learn from texts. In pursuing this research, we examined many of the materials that students were being asked to study. We began to suspect that the textbooks themselves might be contributing to comprehension and learning problems since we often had difficulty finding texts suitable for teaching students the basics of studying. This difficulty prompted us to begin an investigation of texts in an effort to identify the aspects of text that seemed to impede learning.

Our research with both students and texts has been encouraging. First, we have identified some helpful studying strategies that students can be taught to use. Second, we have identified aspects of texts that can pose comprehension and learning difficulties. It is this second area that is discussed in this chapter.

A fundamental premise is that the primary purpose of content area textbooks is to provide information. We recognize that textbook authors may have other purposes, such as entertainment (in order to interest or motivate the student) and persuasion (in order to convince the student of a particular point of view). Nonetheless, we assume that the primary aim of a textbook is to *inform* the student about the content area.

A second premise is that textbook authors should abide by a "cooperative principle" of text similar to Grice's (1975) "cooperative principle" of conversation. The four maxims of Grice's principle are based on the speaker's contribution to a conversation.

1. *Quantity:* Make your contribution as informative as required but no more informative than required.
2. *Quality:* Try to make your contribution one that is true.
3. *Relation:* Be relevant.
4. *Manner:* Be perspicuous, by avoiding ambiguity, obscurity of expression, and unnecessary prolixity.

In keeping with the Gricean cooperative principle, we have formulated a somewhat overlapping set of maxims that focus on the author's contribution to a text-based exchange of information. (These maxims are in some cases also implicit in rhetoric, the art of discourse.)

1. *Structure:* Choose a discourse structure that best conveys the informative purpose.
2. *Coherence:* Make the relationships among ideas clear enough so that there is a logical connection or "flow of meaning" from one idea to the next. (This rule overlaps with Grice's Manner rule.)
3. *Unity:* Address one purpose at a time; do not stray from the purpose by including irrelevant and distracting information. (This maxim combines Grice's Quantity and Relation rules.)
4. *Audience Appropriateness:* Make sure that the text fits the knowledge base of the reader. (This maxim is related to Grice's Quantity and Manner rules, and perhaps to the Relation rule.)

We believe that when an author follows these maxims, he or she has produced "considerate" text—text designed to enable the reader to gather appropriate information with minimal cognitive effort: "Inconsiderate" text requires the reader to put forth extra effort in order to compensate for the author's failure to have applied the maxims. Note that an inconsiderate text is not necessarily incomprehensible, but it does require more effort, skill, strategy, and prior knowledge to comprehend.

The primary purpose of this chapter is to share our analytical tools for determining the relative considerateness of texts. We identify some aspects of text that can cause comprehension problems, suggest how authors might avoid those problems, and provide an instrument for evaluating the considerateness of a text.

Before we proceed, two caveats are in order. First, our suggestions are directed primarily at textbook prose. We do not address other factors affecting the quality of textbooks, such as the teacher's manuals, student activities and exercises, and graphic art. Second, our suggestions do not constitute a complete guide to writing or evaluating text. Not enough is known about reader variables, text variables, and the complexities of reader and text interactions to produce such a guide. However, we think our concerns about structure, unity, coherence, and audience appropriateness are valid. In this chapter we present research evidence about the importance of each of these characteristics and make suggestions for evaluating and writing text with respect to each one. Finally, we present a master checklist encompassing all of the suggestions.

STRUCTURE

Definition

Very simply, structure refers to the system of arrangement of ideas in text and the nature of the relationships connecting the ideas. The structure of text is determined by the author's purpose. This purpose can be thought of as a question the author is addressing. In other words, the form of text follows its function.

We have found it useful to think of the structure or form of content area text in terms of *text units* and *text frames,* terms that are defined below.

The Text Unit. In many disciplines authors appear to be guided by a few basic purposes or questions. Table 1 presents some of these general purposes or questions and the name of the text structure corresponding to each. Table 2 illustrates these structures. The text structures corresponding to these general purposes constitute the basic structural components or building blocks of content area text. We call these basic building blocks text units. Each text unit is typified by certain kinds of relationships, expressed as words (usually connectives) and phrases. Table 3 presents some of the words and phrases commonly associated with each text unit.

Text Frame. Like the text unit, the text frame contains information that responds to a question (usually implicit). The structure of a text frame is different from that of a text unit in that the frame's structure is shaped in large part by the thinking patterns that are typical of the discipline (content area) being represented in the text. For example, biologists deal with the generic concepts of systems, structures, and processes. Sociologists work with concepts of cultures, groups, and societies. Physical geographers think in terms of climate, landforms, and geological proc-

TABLE 1
Types of General Author Purposes of the
Corresponding Text Structures

Examples of Author Purposes or Questions		*Structure*
Imperative Form	Interrogative Form	
Define *A*.	What is *A?*	
Describe *A*.	Who is *A?*	Description
List the features/ characteristics/traits of *A*.	Where is *A?*	
Trace the development of *A*.	When did *A* occur (in relationship to other events)?	Temporal Sequences
Give the steps in *A*.		
Explain *A*.	Why did *A* happen?	
Explain the cause(s) of *A*.	How did *A* happen?	
Explain the effect(s) of *A*.	What are the causes/ reasons for/effects/ outcomes/results of *A?*	Explanation
Draw a conclusion about *A*.		
Predict what will happen to *A*.	What will be the effects/outcomes/results of *A?*	
Hypothesize about the cause of *A*.		
Compare and contrast *A* and *B*.	How are *A* and *B* alike and/or different?	Compare/contrast
List the similarities and differences between *A* and *B*.		
Define and give examples of *A*.	What is *A*, and what are some examples of *A?*	Definition/Examples
Explain the development of a problem and the solution(s) to the problem.	How did *A* get to be a problem and what is (are) its solutions?	Problem/Solution

esses. One obvious purpose of content area text authors is to communicate specific instances of the generic concepts of their discipline. For example, the author of a biology textbook who wants to inform the reader about the digestive system has as a purpose the answer to the question, "What is the digestive system?"

Each of the generic concepts of a discipline has a set of features or attributes that are typically associated with the discipline. For example, typical features of biological systems are *location, component parts,* and *function.* In communicating a specific instance of a generic concept, then, the author responds to implicit questions about the associated features:

TABLE 2
Examples of Basic Text Structures

Description

The gaucho was a fierce-looking character. His hair was long and his face was bearded. The sun and wind made his skin dark and tough. His teeth gleamed white and his dark eyes shone. There was no mistaking the special clothes he wore. His narrow-brimmed felt hat was fastened under his chin with a rawhide cord. He wore a loose-fitting jacket and a scarf tied around his neck. His pants were baggy and some-times had lace at the bottom of the legs. His wide leather belt was ornamented with silver coins kept brightly polished. On his feet were boots made from untanned skin taken from a colt's leg. The end of the boot was opened so that the gaucho's toes could grasp the buttons at the end of the straps that hung from his saddle.

Fincher, E. B. *In a race with time: An introduction to Latin America.* New York: Macmillan, 1972, p. 245.

Temporal Sequence

Sod houses were usually built on a slight rise or hillside to escape flooding. First, a floor space was leveled out with spades. This was wet and tamped down until solid. The next step was to cut bricks from the sod. Then the bricks were laid to make the walls. When the walls were about three feet high, simple wooden frames for the doors and windows were put in place. Finally, the roof, made with cedar beams and sod bricks, was put on.

Racing Stripes. Glenview, Ill.: Scott, Foresman & Co., 1978.

Explanation

Action of Frost
In cold or mountainous regions, rocks are often subjected to the action of freezing water because of daily changes in the temperature. During the day, when the tem-perature is above the freezing point of water (0°C), rainwater or melted snow or ice trickles into cracks in the rocks. During the night, when the temperature falls near the freezing point of water, the trapped water expands as it changes into ice.

As freezing water expands, the expanding ice pushes against the sides of the cracks with tremendous force, splitting the rocks apart. In this way, large masses of rock, especially the exposed rocks on the tops of mountains, are broken into smaller pieces. Frost often has the same effect on the paved streets of our cities. During the winter, water trapped in cracks in the pavement freezes into ice. The ice may expand enough to crack and loosen the pavement. Potholes develop from such cracks.

Contemporary Science Book 1. New York: Amsco School Publications, Inc., 1977, pp. 282–283.

(Continued)

197

TABLE 2 *(Continued)*
Examples of Basic Text Structures

Definition-Example

Fungi
Like the algae, the fungi are simple in structure and lack roots, stems, and leaves. Unlike the algae, fungi lack chlorophyll and cannot make their own food. Examples of fungi are *bacteria, yeasts, molds* and *mushrooms.*
(The text goes on to define bacteria, yeasts, molds, and mushrooms.)

Lesser, M.S. *Life Science.* New York: Amsco School Publications, Inc., 1967, p. 177.

Comparison-Contrast

There is a likeness in location between the central valley of Chile and the central valley of California. These two valleys are alike in other ways. Both have thousands of acres of excellent agricultural land. Soil washed down from the mountains has, in both countries, built deep, fertile valley land. Both central valleys have a mild climate. In both, water is available for irrigation. Under these favorable circumstances, a wide variety of agricultural products can be grown. Both California and Chile are known for the table grapes, raisins, and wine produced in their vineyards. Melons, citrus fruits, and other subtropical products are widely grown. Thus the central valley of Chile, like the similar valley in California, can support a large farm population.

Even the location of cities in relation to the farmland invites comparison between Chile and California. Toward either end of the central valleys in both countries are areas where commerce and industry are highly developed. Santiago, Chile, is somewhat similar to San Francisco, California, in its location. Concepcion, Chile, is somewhat similar in location to Los Angeles, California.

Fincher, E. B. *In a race with time: An introduction to Latin America.* New York: Macmillan, 1972, p. 225.

Problem-Solution

A coffee boom followed the sugar boom and the gold boom. When the Brazilians discovered that the coffee tree, a native of Africa, flourished in the red soil of the South, coffee trees were planted by the thousands. Later on, they were planted by the millions. Fortunes were made in "brown gold," as coffee was known.

But so much coffee was produced that the people of the world could not use all of it. Coffee was stored in warehouses, coffee was burned, coffee was dumped into the sea. This was done in an effort to keep the price from falling to the point where all the planters would be ruined. To make the problem yet more serious, other Latin American nations extended their coffee plantations, and African countries also began to have coffee plantations.

The Brazilian government took steps to save the situation. Planters were encouraged to destroy many of their coffee trees and grow other crops. The amount of coffee put on the market in any one year was regulated. Meanwhile, Brazil sought an agreement between the nations that exported coffee and the nations that imported it. The object was to limit the supply of coffee so that it would not be sold at too low a price.

Fincher, E. B. *In a Race with Time: An Introduction to Latin America.* New York: Macmillan, 1972, p. 304.

TABLE 3
Text Units and Commonly Associated Words and Phrases

Description		
(This text unit is often not associated with particular words and phrases. There may be mention of characteristics, properties, features, traits, and functions, but they are not specifically signaled.)		(to be) (to have) is a property of is a feature of is a characteristic of is a part of
Temporal Sequence/ Process	then, and then before after next follows earlier later finally	previously prior subsequently precedes afterwards first, second, third (dates)
Explanation	causes affects leads to in order to so that produces therefore	because enables since as a result (of) consequently thus for this reason
Compare/contrast	is similar to similarly like likewise in the same way is different from on the one hand	on the other hand however but although instead yet while
Definition/Examples	is defined as means that is named is called is labeled is referred to as that is for example	for instance type of kind of example of e.g. such as includes including
Problem/Solution	the problem is . . . the solution is . . .	
(This text unit is often not associated with particular words and phrases. There may be mention of *problems* or *difficulties* and their *solutions* or *cures,* but often the problems and solutions are not specifically signaled.)		

"Where is the digestive system located?" "What are its component parts?" "What is the function of the digestive system?"

The kind of text that informs the reader about an instance of a generic concept is what we call a *frame*. A frame is a rather complex, content-specific text structure. It has "slots" for the associated features of the generic concept. Each slot has a purpose or question associated with it. Table 4 presents examples of some science frames identified by Lunzer, Davies, and Greene (1980). The table gives the generic name of the frame, the generic purpose of the frame, and the questions associated with the attributes or slots of the frame.

One would expect, then, that an author responding to a question such as "What is photosynthesis?" would use a Process frame. The text responding to this question would contain answers to the following questions: "What is the name of the process?" "Where is it located?" "How does the process work?" "What is the function of the process?" There may be no particular order in which the author should address these questions, but a complete answer to the question "What is photosynthesis?" should contain *at least* the answers to the question slots of the Process frame. Note that some of the question slots can be answered with a single word or phrase (give the name of the function), while other question slots require a full text unit as a response (explain how the process works). Thus, a frame is an amalgam of single-word or sentence-length responses and more extended, full-fledged text units.

The Textbook Hierarchy

A textbook is a hierarchical arrangement of text units and frames. The author begins with some very broad purposes or questions. The responses to these questions suggest other component questions. As each question gives rise to a new frame or text unit, the hierarchy expands.

Research Evidence

Structure is the text feature that has received the most attention in the research literature. From a fairly extensive body of research, we know that structure or organization influences the *amount* as well as the *kind* of knowledge acquired from reading. With respect to the *amount* of knowledge acquired, the conclusion is straightforward: Better organized text is better remembered. (See Goetz & Armbruster, 1980; Meyer, 1979; Pearson & Camparell, 1981; and Shimmerlik, 1978.) Furthermore, information provided to the reader about the organization or structure of the text can facilitate recall (Meyer, 1979). Such information can be provided in two ways. One way is through "signaling." Meyer (1979) has defined signaling

TABLE 4
A Listing of Several Frames and Their Corresponding Questions
from Secondary Science Textbooks (adapted from Lunzer, et al. 1980)

Frame	Purpose of Frame	Question Slots in the Frame
1. Parts	To describe and explain structure or parts, for example, plant roots, teeth, nervous system.	Give the name of the part. Describe its location. Describe the part. Explain the function of the part.
2. Mechanisms	To describe and explain mechanisms such as the aneroid barometer, and the bicycle pump.	Give the name of the mechanism. Explain how it works. Explain its function. Describe its location.
3. Processes	To explain transformations over a period of time, such as the formation of limestone.	Give the name of the process. Describe when it takes place and its duration. Describe its location. Explain the function of the process.
4. Scientific Theory	To describe and explain patterns of thinking about observed phenomena in the world and tests of those patterns such as the theory of evolution and of spontaneous generation.	Give the hypothesis/question/problem. Describe the theory. Explain tests of its validity. Describe the scientist(s) who work with it. Explain applications of it.

as information in text that emphasizes certain aspects of the semantic content or points out aspects of the discourse structure. Types of signaling include: (a) explicit statements of the structure or organization, (b) preview or introductory statements, including titles, (c) summary statements, (d) pointer words and phrases, such as "an important point is . . . ," and (e) textual cues such as underlining, italics, and bold face. Another means of providing information about structure is through repeated, consistent use of a particular structure. Presumably, in this way the reader learns the structure and comes to expect that ideas will be organized in that particular way.

Structure of text also affects the *kind* of knowledge acquired from reading by influencing the way information is stored. The better organized the text, the more highly integrated the memory representation is likely to be. Highly integrated memory representations enable learners to consider related facts simultaneously, a necessary condition for higher-order cognitive processes such as inferencing, summarizing, and decision-making (Frase, 1972; Walker & Meyer, 1980).

In sum, the better the structure of the text, the more likely the reader is to remember the information and to engage in the higher-level cognitive processes that are usually considered to be the important outcomes of a learning situation.

Guidelines Related to Structure

1. *The author's topic, purpose or question, and structure should be readily apparent to the reader from titles, headings, and/or topic sentences.* By simply skimming the text, the reader should be able to determine the author's specific topics, the purposes the author is addressing with respect to those topics and the structure of the ensuing text. The reader should *not* have to guess at the author's intention from a title, heading, and/or topic sentence.

Examples

Poor Indication of Purpose	Improved Indication of Purpose
a. "What are the Chances?" [Suggests a list of probabilities consequent to a set of conditions.]	"An Explanation of Probability" [Suggests the topic and an explanation structure.]
b. "How fast are impulses?" [Suggests a number.]	"How do impulses travel?" [Suggests a process or explanation structure.]
c. "Finland is East of Sweden" [Suggests a true/false verification.]	"Finland: Climate and Geography" [Suggests a frame or descriptive structure.]
d. "New Genetic Types and Agriculture" [The use of "and" in this heading leaves the relationship between genetic types and agriculture vague. The author's purpose could be to describe both new genetic types and agriculture; to compare and contrast new genetic types and agriculture; or to explain some uncertain relationship between new genetic types and agriculture.]	"The Effect of New Genetic Types on Agriculture" [Suggests an explanation structure with an emphasis on effects.]
(e) "Chicago's suburbs grew and grew." [The author's purpose could be to give examples of suburbs that grew; to explain the causes of the growth of suburbs; or to explain the effects of the growth of Chicago's suburbs.]	"Chicago's suburbs grew for many reasons." [Suggests an explanation structure with an emphasis on causes.]

2. The actual structure of the text should match the author's purpose as implied by titles, headings, and topic sentences.

The following example shows a *mismatch* between implied purpose (to explain) and text structure (a description).

How do nerves carry signals?

Each nerve in the body is really a bundle of very fine nerve fibers. Nerve fibers are too thin to be seen except with a microscope. Each nerve fiber is part of a nerve cell.

dendrite
branch of a nerve that carries impulses to the nerve cell body

The nerve cell has a very irregular shape. It has a number of small branches sticking out, almost like the branches on a tree. These are called *dendrites* (den'drit). The word *dendrite* comes from a Greek word for "tree."

axon
a long nerve fiber that carries impulses away from the nerve cell body

At one end of the cell is a particularly long branch. It is called an *axon*. This axon is a single nerve fiber, as shown in the drawing.

The message that travels along the nerve cell is a small electrical charge. It usually starts at the dendrites, goes through the cell body, and then moves out along the axon. This electrical charge is called the nerve impulse.

synapse
a small gap between nerve cells

Nerve cells are strung together in chains. The branches of the axon of one cell come close to the dendrites of another cell. The parts of the different cells don't quite touch. There is a small gap between them that is called a a synapse (si'naps). (1)

The following excerpt illustrates another mismatch between title and text structure. Instead of tracing and elaborating on the decision-making process, the author chose to do something else.

The Pilgrims Decide to go to America

Finally the Pilgrim leaders said, "Why don't we go to America? Part of America is claimed by England. There we shall be able to educate our children in English ways. And we shall be able to worship in our own way."

The Pilgrims began to make plans. How could they get to America? They were hardworking and thrifty people, but they were not rich. They could not afford to buy supplies and hire a ship and crew. (2)

The next two examples illustrate a close correspondence between titles and text structure.

What did the People do to Solve the Arguments Among the States?

In 1787, 55 representatives from 12 states met in Philadelphia. This famous meeting is called the Constitutional Convention. The representatives met to discuss rules by which the states could work together as a strong, united nation . . . The representatives went to work. They soon decided to throw out the rules made by the Continental Congress and to make up a new set of rules for the new nation . . . We call this set of rules the Constitution of the United States.   (3)

Vision Explained

Light rays coming from an object pass through the cornea, enter the pupil, and reach the lens. The lens bends the light rays, which then form an image on the retina. This image is formed in the same way that a camera lens forms an image on film. The image on the retina produces impulses that reach the brain by way of the optic nerve. When the impulse arrives at the special area of the cerebrum that controls vision, we become aware that we see something.   (4)

3. *Text frames used repeatedly throughout the textbook should have a consistent structure.* The reader can learn to form expectations about content and structure if frames are used consistently. An example of such a text is one that organizes information about Latin American countries in the following parallel fashion: location, history, climate and landforms, natural resources, economy, people. An example of a consistent use of a frame in a biology textbook would be one that presented information on all systems of the human body (respiratory, circulatory, etc.) in the form: general functions of the system; component parts of the system along with the process that occurs in or as a result of each part; and comparisons/contrasts of the comparable system in other organisms.

COHERENCE

Definition

Coherence means "a sticking together." With reference to text, coherence refers to how smoothly the ideas are woven together. In a coherent discourse, the relationships among ideas must be clear enough so that there is a logical connection or "flow of meaning" from one idea to the next. Compared to an incoherent discourse, a coherent discourse makes it easier for the reader to perceive the message as an integrated unit.

Coherence operates at both global and local levels; that is, at the level of the whole text as well as at the level of individual sentences. At the global level, a text is coherent to the extent that it facilitates the integration of high-level ideas across the entire discourse. Features that might contribute to global coherence include titles and visual displays or diagrams.

At the local level, features related to coherence help the reader integrate the information within and between sentences. One important local feature is connectives or phrases that function conjunctively. These include linguistic connectives that make explicit the temporal, causal, spatial, or conditional relationships between propositions (Halliday & Hasan, 1976).

Research Evidence

With respect to *global coherence,* the research indicates that titles can have an important effect on comprehension (Anderson, Spiro, & Anderson, 1978; Bransford & Johnson, 1972; Dansereau, Brooks, Spurlin, & Holley, 1979; Schallert, 1976). In addition, visual displays, diagrams, and charts can facilitate comprehension, presumably because of their ability to portray the "big picture" at a single glance; i.e., lend coherence to the content (Gropper, 1970; Holliday, 1975; Holliday, 1976; Holliday, Brunner, & Donais, 1977; Holliday & Harvey, 1976).

Research relating to *local coherence* has demonstrated that an *explicit* use of connectives (rather than a statement that requires the reader to infer the connective) facilitates learning (Katz & Brent, 1968; Marshall & Glock, 1978–79; Pearson, 1974–75). Other research related to local coherence has indicated that repeated references and concepts that help to carry meaning across sentence boundaries can decrease reading time and increase recall of text as an integrated unit. (See Goetz & Armbruster, 1980, for a review of this literature.)

In sum, features of text contributing to both global and local coherence appear to help readers comprehend and recall the text as a structured, integrated unit.

Guidelines Related to Coherence

1. *Relationships among ideas should be explicitly stated.* As discussed in Anderson, Armbruster, and Kantor (1980), the use of short, simple sentences can often obscure the meaning of relationships. Readers are then forced to infer those relationships from their own knowledge. If the reader has the relevant background knowledge, comprehension is possible, but it requires more effort than it would if the relationships were explicitly stated. If the reader does *not* have the appropriate background knowledge, the intended meaning will be lost.

Examples

The following paragraph is an example of a text in which many of the connectives indicating relationships are missing and left to be inferred.

> In the evening, the light fades. Photosynthesis slows down. The amount of carbon dioxide in the air space builds up again. This buildup of carbon dioxide makes the guard cells relax. The openings are closed.   (5)

The paragraph below represents an attempt to improve the coherence of the text by making the relationships more explicit.

> What happens to these processes in the evening? The fading light of evening causes photosynthesis to slow down. Respiration, however, does not depend on light and thus continues to produce carbon dioxide. The carbon dioxide in the air spaces builds up again, which makes the guard cells relax. The relaxing of the guard cells closes the leaf openings. Consequently, the leaf openings close in the evening as photosynthesis slows down.

Here is another set of examples, with the second rewritten to improve coherence.

> Many of the farmers who moved in from New England were independent farmers. Land cost about a dollar an acre. Most men could afford to set up their own farms. Livestock farming was quite common on the frontier. Hogs could be fed in the forests. The cost of raising hogs was low.   (6)

> Most of the farmers who moved in from New England were independent farmers. Being an independent farmer means that the farmer can afford to own his own farm. Around 1815, most men could afford to own their own farms because land was cheap—it cost only about a dollar an acre. Many of these independent farms were livestock farms. For example, many frontier farmers raised hogs. Hog farming was common because hogs were inexpensive to keep. The cost of raising hogs was low because the farmer did not have to buy special feed for the hogs. The hogs did not need special feed because they could eat plants that grew in the surrounding forests.

2. *References should be clear.* The comprehension of certain words and phrases in text requires that the reader have knowledge of other ideas to which the words and phrases refer. Helping the reader keep these references straight is a prime responsibility of the author. Several types of words and phrases that require explicit referents are discussed.

Obscure *pronoun references* are common in textbooks. The following excerpt illustrates a confusing use of the pronoun *they*. The authors of this paper are still not certain whether *they* refers to "the people from the North" or "the Bronze Age people!"

The people from the North learned from the Bronze Age people. They were skilled workers and traders. They made fine tools and jewelry from metals. They traded their beautiful cloth and pottery to peoples around the Mediterranean. They kept records of their trade on clay tablets.   (7)

Quantifiers (for example, *some, many, few*) pose other potential reference problems. First, authors may omit the noun or noun phrase being quantified so that the reader has to infer it. Second, the intended quantity may be unclear, so that the reader does not have a good idea about the size of the object being referenced.

Problems with pronoun references and quantifiers are illustrated in the following excerpt. We suspect that readers may become confused when encountering four quantifiers and the pronoun *they* repeated seven times in this short passage.

Why Women Should Not Vote

"A woman's place is in the home!" many men said. Politics would have a bad effect on women's characters, they said. Women would soon be neglecting their homes.

Many said also that women's voting would cause arguments in the family. Arguments would weaken the family. Some believed that women were inferior to men by nature. They said that men were physically stronger and more intelligent than women. They said that women were too emotional. They were too excitable to vote wisely.

Many people attacked the women who were working for suffrage. They said that they were unattractive. They said that they were unhappily married and only wanted attention.   (8)

A *definite noun phrase* (e.g., "He saw *the accident*") without a clear referent is also a potential reference problem. The proper use of the definite noun phrase is predicated on the assumption that both the author and reader know the specific instance referred to. Thus, the sentence "He saw the accident" is unclear without prior mention of a specific accident.

A *verb phrase* may be the setting of another reference problem. For example, consider the following sentences. "When an Indian shot an arrow, he hardly ever missed. If he did, he might have to go to bed without his supper." It is not too difficult for an adult reader to infer that "If he did" means "If an Indian missed his target." But a young reader might not understand which preceding verb phrase is referred to by the *did*.

Other potential reference problems include the following:

a. the use of *also, too*, etc., when the preceding cases are uncertain.
b. the use of *but, however*, etc., when it is not clear what is being contrasted or qualified.

3. *In temporal sequences/processes and in explanations, the order of events should proceed in one direction only.* The sequencing of events should be unidirectional. The direction should generally proceed from earliest to latest in text for younger children. Young readers can become confused if the order of events in the text does not match the order of actual occurrence. For older readers, the direction may not be so critical. However, for most purposes, it would seem that the text should remain consistent and not skip around in time. Text that changes the time frame may send the reader on a wild goose chase; the reader may be unwilling to put forth the effort to figure out the chronological or logical order behind the rhetorical order.

The following is an example of a text that changes time frame. The sentences have been numbered so that the commentary is easier to follow.

> [1]Adult female alligators make large cone-shaped nests from mud and compost. [2]The female lays from 15 to 100 eggs with leathery shells in the nest and then covers it. [3]The heat from both the sun and the decaying compost keeps the eggs warm. [4]The eggs hatch in about nine weeks. [5]Unlike other reptiles that hatch from eggs, baby alligators make sounds while they are still in the shell. [6]The mother then bites off the nest so the baby alligators can get out. [7]When first hatched, baby alligators are about 15 to 25 cm long.   (9)

Note the many shifts in the temporal sequence. The first four sentences are fine; they present the order of events from earliest to latest. The fifth sentence reverts back to when the baby alligators were still in the shell. The time frame for the sixth sentence is when the baby alligators are sufficiently mature to leave the nest. The final sentence returns to when the baby alligators were first hatched.

Incidentally, Sentences 5 and 6 are confusing for another reason. In Sentence 6, "getting out" probably refers to leaving the nest. However, since Sentence 5 left the baby alligators "still in the shell," the reader might assume that the mother alligator's biting off the nest enabled the baby alligators to "get out" of the *shell*.

> [1]Photosynthesis·in the leaves starts with the morning sunlight. [2]Carbon dioxide was made during respiration all night. [3]It was stored in the air spaces around the spongy cells. [4]This carbon dioxide is used as the leaf starts to make sugar. [5]When a certain amount has been used up, the guard cells respond. [6]They become stiff, swell out, and make openings in the leaf. [7]They stay open all day.
> [8]In the evening, the light fades. [9]Photosynthesis slows down. [10]But respiration goes on. [11]The amount of carbon dioxide in the air spaces builds up again. [12]This buildup of carbon dioxide makes the guard cells relax. [13]The openings are closed.   (10)

In this example, the author has tried to grapple with the problem of describing a repetitive cycle consisting of a night phase and a day phase. The author chose to begin with the morning (Sentence 1), return to the previous night (Sentences 2 and 3), continue with the morning (Sentences 4–7), and then go on to the following night (Sentences 8–13). It would have been more considerate to begin by describing all events pertinent to the night phase in the first paragraph, and then describe the events of the day phase in the second paragraph, ending with a comment that the cycle is repeated.

It is interesting to note that only the reader who is able to connect "making sugar" with photosynthesis will know that Sentence 4 returns to the morning. Otherwise, the time frame for Sentence 4, and consequently for Sentences 5–7, is ambiguous.

UNITY

Definition

Unity refers to the degree to which the text addresses a single purpose. The author of a unified text has not strayed from the purpose by including irrelevant and distracting information.

Research Evidence

A case for the importance of unity can be made more firmly on theoretical than empirical grounds. Central to the theoretical argument is the notion of a limited capacity, short-term memory that can hold only about five to nine items at once (Miller, 1956). As reading proceeds, new information must be integrated with the few propositions stored in short-term memory. The more disunified the text, the lower the probability of integration. Comprehension will probably slow down and possibly fail. Presumably, the difficulties are compounded for the poor and beginning readers. In sum, text that is not well unified can theoretically create comprehension problems, particularly for less skilled readers.

Guidelines Related to Unity

1. *Each idea in the text unit or frame should contribute directly to the fulfillment of the author's purpose.* An idea that is not clearly contributing to the purpose but still merits inclusion should be indicated by using phrases such as "Incidentally, . . ." "As an aside, . . ." or "In case you were wondering about . . ." If there is a large number of irrelevant ideas, they should be edited out or they should form the basis of another text unit.

The following excerpt illustrates a text that includes information not contributing directly to the author's purpose.

The Dutch Come to America

[1]Other Europeans came to America besides the Virginia colonists and the Pilgrims. [2]The French traded and settled along the St. Lawrence River in Canada. [3]Spain had colonies in the far south. [4]Other European countries were claiming land and sending settlers, too.

[5]Dutch merchants in the Netherlands started a company. [6]They wanted to make money, too. [7]The Dutch colony sent people to the New World. [8]The people built a fort on a large island in the Hudson River. [9]They called it Fort Manhattan (man HAT n).

[10]Many Indians lived near Fort Manhattan. [11]Indians were good hunters and trappers. [12]They knew how to find wild animals in the forests. [13]When an Indian shot an arrow, he hardly ever missed. [14]If he did, he might have to go to bed without his supper.

[15]The Indians caught animals for their beautiful, soft furs. [16]The Dutch wanted the furs to sell in Europe. [17]The Dutch traded many things with the Indians. [18]Fort Manhattan became the center of the Dutch fur trade.   (11)

Apparently the author's purpose is to trace the history of Dutch settlement in America, including the establishment of the Dutch fur trade. The information about the Indians in Sentences 10–15, particularly Sentences 12, 13, and 14, does not contribute to the fulfillment of this purpose. In place of Sentences 10–16, we believe it would have been more considerate to say something like "The Indians living near Fort Manhattan were expert at hunting and trapping fur-bearing animals. The Dutch settlers wanted to obtain the beautiful, soft furs in order to sell them to Europeans who were eager to buy them." Although these two sentences are longer than others in this excerpt, we feel they are less distracting of the information-providing purpose of the author than the seven sentences they replace.

Incidentally, this excerpt also illustrates very well two guidelines related to coherence: Relationships among ideas should be clearly stated, and clear referents should be provided. The author has failed to specify the relationship between Sentences 5 and 6 and between Sentences 16 and 17. With regard to the latter, the adult reader can infer that the Dutch were trading "things" for *furs,* but the young reader of the text may fail to make this important inference. The author has also failed to provide clear referents for the "too" in Sentence 6 and the "Dutch colony" in Sentence 7. (We could find no prior mention of a Dutch colony. We presume the author meant the Netherlands itself rather than a colony of the Netherlands.) Also, the object of "shot an arrow" and "missed" in Sentence 13 is missing. It *may* be easy to infer that the Indian was shooting at the wild animal he "knew how to find" in the preceding sentence, but it was inconsiderate not to have supplied the information.

2. *Entire text units that are only slightly related to the main flow of prose in the textbook should be somehow set aside, for example, in boxed-in areas or appendices.*
Examples of such text units are those that:

a. Teach skills that are necessary for understanding a later text unit (such as reading maps or finding directions using a compass).
b. Relate content area ideas to knowledge with which students are already familiar.
c. Lend some authenticity to certain ideas in the text (such as excerpts from letters, diaries, notebooks, etc.).
d. Describe the people and personalities involved in the content area.
e. Have high interest value because of their unusual and/or attractive features (for example, including a unit about the "Venus flytrap," a plant that feeds on animals, in a chapter about animals that feed on plants).

These adjunct text units can be a valuable resource to textbook authors, who can use the units in a variety of ways to improve the textbook quality without increasing the risk of making the basic prose more difficult to comprehend. Even when written clearly, the prose of many content area textbooks is brutally boring, and many students understandably shy away from reading them frequently or for long periods of time. The solution to the problem of how to make textbooks more enticing and fun to read lies not in the manipulation of the basic text units, but rather in the cleverness that authors/editors can use to discover and develop intrinsically motivating adjunct units.

In the following paragraph, the author's purpose (as inferred from the context) was to trace the development of events leading to the establishment of tobacco as an important cash crop in the colony of Virginia:

> The Indians grew tobacco which they smoked in pipes. Smoking was probably brought to England in the late 1500's. It quickly became popular. Historians are not sure who brought tobacco to England. Some think it was Sir Walter Raleigh. (He named Virginia in honor of Queen Elizabeth, "the Virgin Queen.")   (12)

The last three sentences do not clearly contribute to the author's purpose. The last sentence is particularly out of place. The use of parentheses helps somewhat to set the last sentence apart from the main message of the text. However, we would go a step further and recommend that the last three sentences be removed from the text or at least relegated to a box.

Incidentally, the sentence "Historians are not sure who brought tobacco to England" also violates the temporal order. The succession of events is: "Smoking was brought to England"; then, "Smoking became popular"; then *back to* "Smoking was brought to England" (in the form of the sentence "Historians are not sure who brought tobacco to England").

AUDIENCE APPROPRIATENESS

Definition

Audience appropriateness refers to the extent to which the text matches the reader's knowledge base—knowledge both of the content and of discourse features such as syntactic and rhetorical structures.

In order to convey an idea of how sensitivity to different audiences is reflected in text, we have included the following examples of two treatments of the same topic, appropriate for different audiences. The texts differ with respect to concepts, vocabulary, and syntactic structure.

This is the text intended for sixth graders:

A Look Inside a Leaf

Suppose you magnified a small square patch of a green leaf. The top surface of a leaf is made up of a thin layer of tough cells. These cells protect the softer cells inside the leaf. This is what your own skin cells do. The tough ones on top protect the cells deeper down inside you. Beneath the tough surface cells in the leaf is a layer of long cells. These long cells have a rich supply of chlorophyll. It is the substance that makes green plants green.

When you pick up a leaf and look at it, all parts of the leaf seem to be equally green. But suppose you looked at a thin slice under a microscope. You would see that most of the chlorophyll is sandwiched in the middle layers of the leaf.

Just below the layer of long cells is a loose layer of cells. These cells also have lots of chlorophyll. Notice the air spaces among these loosely-packed cells. They make this layer look like a sponge. So they are called spongy cells.

If you followed one of the air passageways, you would see that it leads to an opening in the lower layer of tough cells. These openings let gases from the air get inside the leaf. And they let gases made by the green cells flow out of the leaf.   (13)

This is a text intended for older readers:

Structure of the Leaf

A microscopic examination of a leaf cut crosswise reveals five major regions: upper epidermis, lower epidermis, veins, palisade region, and spongy region.

1. Upper epidermis. The upper epidermis of the leaf consists of a single layer of cells. These cells secrete a waxy protective coating.

2. Lower epidermis. Except for the many pairs of guard cells, the cells of the lower epidermis are much like those of the upper epidermis. A stomate, or pore, lies between each pair of guard cells. The guard cells regulate the size of the pore.

3. Veins. Veins are composed mainly of xylem and phloem tubes, which are connected to the xylem and phloem of the stem and root.

4. Palisade region. The palisade region, which lies just below the upper epidermis, consists of one or more layers of elongated, boxlike cells. Each cell contains numerous chloroplasts, the bodies that bear chlorophyll. Most of the food of a plant is made in the palisade region.

5. Spongy region. The spongy region lies between the palisade layer and the lower epidermis. The cells of the spongy region are somewhat rounded and loosely arranged. These cells also contain chloroplasts and carry on some food-making. Large air spaces are scattered among the cells. The air spaces led to the stomates.   (14)

Research Evidence

The research most directly related to audience appropriateness has been concerned with the effect of prior content knowledge on comprehension. It is quite clear from the literature that possession of relevant topic knowledge prior to reading strongly affects comprehension (e.g., Anderson, Reynolds, Schallert, & Goetz, 1977; Spilich, Vesonder, Chiesi, & Voss, 1979).

Another line of research related to the effect of prior knowledge on comprehension has focused on vocabulary, or word knowledge. In their review, Anderson and Freebody (1979) conclude from many studies that "word knowledge is strongly related to reading comprehension." A considerable body of research on readability also supports the preeminent role of word knowledge in reading comprehension (see Klare, 1974–75 for a review).

In sum, the degree of the match between the text and the reader's knowledge appears to have strong effects on the comprehensibility of the text.

Guidelines Related to Audience Appropriateness

1. *Taking into account the prior knowledge of the readers, enough relevant ideas should be included in the text to form a complete answer to the author's purpose or question.*

The following is an example of a text in which there is not enough information to enable a young reader to form a complete answer to the question implied by the title.

How Blood is Transported Through the Body

The numerous arteries that branch off the aorta carry blood to various organs and systems. Then veins return the blood to the heart. Among these pathways are those to the digestive organs, the limbs, the head, the kidneys, and the walls of the heart.   (15)

The next paragraph gives a fuller, more considerate explication of the process:

How Blood is Transported Through the Body

Blood is transported by the circulatory system, which is composed of a network of tubes (arteries, veins, and capillaries), a pump (the heart), and a fluid (blood) which moves. The heart pumps the blood by a series of contractions and expansions from its chambers into the arteries. Arteries take blood to all organs of the body (brain, muscles, kidney, etc.) except the lungs. Blood enters an organ from the artery through capillaries or tiny tubes. Blood also exits the organ through capillaries which are connected to veins. Veins then conduct the blood back to the heart.

Here is another example of what we consider to be an incomplete text from a chapter entitled "The Water Cycle" in a fourth-grade science textbook.

A Change of Phase

Solids, liquids, and gases are phases, or forms of matter. Matter sometimes changes from one phase to another. Some matter can again change to the phase in which it first was. When this happens, matter changes phases in a cycle.

(An investigation involving the observation of condensation follows.)

Water Comes Out of Air

Water changes phases in a cycle. In one part of the cycle, water comes out of air. It condenses, or changes from a gas to a liquid. Many things make water condense.

Look at each of these pictures. (The accompanying three pictures are of a glass of ice water, a girl with mouth partially open, and a storm.) Look for evidence that water has changed from a gas to a liquid.

Why do you think that the water condensed?

1. Why do windows in your home sometimes steam up?
2. What can make a city by the sea foggy?   (16)

Water Goes Into Air

In one part of the water cycle, water condenses. It comes out of air. In the other part of the cycle, water goes into the air. It evaporates, or changes from a liquid to a gas. Many things make water evaporate.

Look at each of these pictures. (The accompanying three pictures are of waves breaking on a beach, steam coming from a teakettle, and haze or fog along a road.) Look for evidence that water has changed from a liquid to a gas.
Why did the water evaporate?
1. What do you think makes it humid on hot days?
2. What happens when wet clothes dry?

From the title, it would seem that the author's purpose is to inform the reader about the "water cycle" frame. Component purposes are to explain the processes of condensation and evaporation. However, the text does not provide enough information to fulfill these purposes. In fact, the author does little more than restate his/her own questions, leaving it up to the fourth-grade readers to somehow inform themselves.

The following example from a social studies textbook also suffers from incompleteness.

It took the invaders a long time to develop civilizations. They were much farther away than Greece from the old civilizations of the Fertile Crescent.
Another reason was the land of Italy. A chain of mountains runs along the peninsula. On the eastern side, these mountains are rough and steep. There were no good harbors along the east coast. Few ships visited this coast. (17)

The first paragraph needs to be expanded so that the relationship between time to develop civilizations and distance from existing civilizations is clarified. The second paragraph needs to be expanded to explain how and why the particular landforms of Italy retarded its development. The connection between landforms and development of civilizations is probably not apparent to the young readers of this textbook.

2. *Technical terms or other difficult vocabulary words should be introduced only if the learning of their meaning is an intrinsic part of learning the content. When such vocabulary is required, clear definitions should be provided.*

In the following excerpt, the term "vocational" is introduced in the title, but never defined. Although some students might infer the meaning from the many examples provided in the text, there seems to be no justification for simply introducing and not defining the technical term "vocational."

What Vocational School Training is Available?

Chicago has other special schools, too. Here girls and boys learn to do many kinds of work. There are classes to learn about cars and airplanes. Other classes teach about building houses. Some teach furniture making or shoe repair. There are classes that teach how to make clothes and cook. Many boys and girls learn to work in offices. Some learn to work in beauty shops. Most of these students will have good jobs someday.   (18)

In the following example, the technical term "responds to stimuli" is not defined and is not likely to be understood by the very young reader.

What is a Cell Like?

A cell is made of living stuff. It can grow. It takes in food and changes the food into more living stuff. A cell combines food and oxygen to make energy for all the things it does. The living stuff in a cell responds to stimuli. It moves.   (19)

The next example illustrates a considerate use of a definition in text. Note how and where the concept of relief is defined.

A plateau is an area of horizontal rock layers that has high relief. Relief is simply the difference between the highest and lowest points of a region. There is no fixed amount of relief for a plateau. As a rule, however, a plateau's relief is 1000 meters or more. Its high points may be well over 1000 meters above sea level. Its low points are the bottoms of its canyons and steep river valleys.   (20)

3. *Analogies, metaphors, and other types of figurative language should be used only if their referents are well known by the reader.*

Only familiar concepts can serve as referents for figurative language when the purpose of using the figurative language is to teach students about an unfamiliar concept. Otherwise, the student is left with the difficult task of comparing one unknown, the referent, with yet another unknown, the concept to be learned.

The statement that "haciendas are very similar to plantations in the southern part of the United States before the Civil War" will have no meaning to readers unfamiliar with the characteristics of antebellum Southern plantations. A potential comprehension problem is circumvented if the author presents a full comparison/contrast of the features of haciendas *and* antebellum Southern plantations. However, if the author's intent was to describe haciendas, there is no need to introduce southern plantations at all.

An example of an analogy or model used appropriately is found in a sixth-grade science textbook. The text is attempting to teach the concepts of repulsion, attraction, and static electricity. The students have just completed an exercise in which they (a) rubbed one balloon all over with wool and held it up to a wall, and (b) rubbed two balloons all over with wool, dangled the balloons from strings, and brought the balloons close together.

Have you ever played with bar magnets? If you have, you know that the two like poles of magnets push each other away. This is called *repulsion*.

repulsion
the act of repelling or pushing away

When the two unlike poles of magnets are brought together, they move toward each other. This is called *attraction*.

attraction
the act of attracting or pulling toward

In a way, the balloons you used acted as if they were bar magnets. You saw attraction and repulsion. The first balloon clung to the wall, as if the balloon and the wall were unlike poles of two magnets. In the second case, the two balloons repelled each other. They acted as if they were the like poles of two magnets.

But we should not confuse balloons with magnets. Balloons are not magnetized when they are rubbed with wool cloth. But some force must be at work. Some force had to hold the balloon to the wall, and some force had to cause the two balloons to repel each other. The force at work was static electricity.   (21)

TEXTBOOK EVALUATION CHECKLIST

The checklist presented in this section is an extension of the preceding ideas. The checklist represents an attempt to formalize some of the techniques of analysis that we have been using. At this stage in its development, the checklist is *not* an objective method of evaluating text; at best it helps the evaluator systematize his/her subjective judgments about text quality. We hope that in some way the checklist sensitizes the evaluator to some text variables that may be important in revising and editing texts and in selecting one textbook over another.

The checklist has two major purposes: (a) to determine the purpose of a text and how well it is fulfilled, and (b) to determine how considerate the passage is.

The parts are arranged in a hierarchy to maximize the efficiency of the evaluation. Progress through the checklist depends on the successful completion of a previous part. Thus, if a text sample fails the test of the first part of the evaluation, the analysis is terminated. In other words, if the text sample does not address relevant questions and contain adequate answers, there is no point in doing a more detailed analysis of the considerateness of the prose.

STEPS TO EVALUATE THE CONSIDERATENESS OF A TEXTBOOK

Step 1: Select three passages from the textbook that you intend to evaluate. Do NOT read the passages carefully during this selection process. Each passage that you select should:

a. have a title or heading,
b. be two or more paragraphs long,
c. have about 150 to 400 words,
d. cover content material that is important for students to learn,
e. cover content material you are familiar with,
f. not make reference to charts, figures, maps, and tables.

Step 2: Formulate a question or questions based on information found in the heading or title *only,* that you think will be answered in the remainder of the passage. (That is why it was important not to have read the passages carefully already.) Write those questions on the response form (see p. 225).

a. Decide whether the passage is a text unit (in which case you should have one main question) or a text frame (in which case you will probably have several questions that are all related to the content area being described).
b. When the title or heading is very general (i.e., sport cars, green plants, wagon trains), first assume that the author is using a frame (see p. 195 in an earlier section for information about frames). Try to anticipate the slots in the frame that the author will address, and write a question responding to each slot.
c. If you are unable to determine which slots should appear in a frame, look elsewhere in the textbook and see what frame the author used for a similar concept. For example, if you are puzzled about wagon trains, see what the author does with steamboats or freight trains.
d. If you are unable to determine which slots may be in a frame, consider the possibility that the passage will contain one or a few text units. In that case, try to guess what they might be. For example, the title "Eiffel Tower" might not readily suggest a frame, but it is reasonable to suspect that these two text units will be covered in the passage: Why was it built? How was it built?

Step 3: Read the passage carefully and underline the parts of it that are necessary to answer the questions formulated in Step 2. Also, draw a light line through those ideas that do not contribute directly to an answer. If the passage does not provide enough information for an accurate, complete answer to the questions, does the passage answer other questions better? If so, record those questions that correspond to other text units or frames. Then, start Step 3 again.

Step 4: Decide whether or not this passage meets the two most important characteristics of informative text, i.e., the passage provided a complete, accurate answer(s) to an explicit question(s). If the answer is YES, then continue with the next step, if NO, start again on Step 1 with another passage.

Step 5: Determine how clearly the author develops the structure of each *paragraph*.

a. First, determine that predominant structure you think the author intended for the paragraph.
b. Then, locate that type of paragraph from the list below, and answer the questions under each paragraph type.
c. Your answer will be entered on a rating scale. The 5-point scale ranges from low to high. If you are working with other evaluators, you may want to set some standards for these scales. If you are working alone, set your own standard and be consistent as you go from passage to passage and from textbook to textbook.

Paragraph Types

1. A *descriptive* paragraph, or *frame* paragraph
    (a) How clearly presented are the primary, distinguishing features, traits, and/or characteristics?
    (b) How well does the author explain the relationship(s) among these features, traits, and characteristics?
2. A *temporal sequence* paragraph
    (a) How effective are the time markers for establishing the temporal order of the events?
3. An *explanatory* paragraph
    (a) How effective are the time markers for establishing the temporal and/or logical order of the events?
    (b) How clear does the author make the relationship between each pair of events? Are they temporal, causal, and/or enabling relationships?
4. A *compare/contrast* paragraph
    (a) How clear is the author about which two or more ideas are being compared?
    (b) How clearly stated are the characteristics, traits, and features shared by the two or more ideas being compared?
    (c) How clearly stated are the *unique* characteristics, traits, and features of the two or more ideas being contrasted?
5. A *definition/example* paragraph
    (a) To what extent does the definition give the most important and distinguishing characteristics, features, and traits?
    (b) To what extent are the examples illustrative of the idea being defined?
    (c) How relevant are the examples to the readers' world knowledge?

6. A *problem/solution* paragraph
  (a) How clearly presented and described are the ideas that constitute the "problem"?
  (b) How clearly presented and described are the ideas that constitute the "causes"?
  (c) How clearly presented and described are the ideas that constitute the "solution(s)"?
  (d) To what extent is evidence presented that indicates whether the solution was tried or not, and whether it solved the problem or not?

Step 6: Determine how coherent this passage is.

a. To what extent are the connectives made explicit? Investigate the gaps between the sentences, and if a connective is not used determine whether or not the use of one would help clarify the intended meaning.
b. How effectively does the author use connectives? Search through the passage and draw a box around the connectives (*and, but, also, thus, therefore, because,* etc.). How many connectives can you locate? Then search for the ideas that are being connected. Can you find them? Are the ideas being connected properly?
c. How clearly are the pronouns referenced? Search through the passage and locate all of the pronouns. Circle each one, and then search for its referent (the word(s) in the passage that the pronoun stands for). If there are two or more cases where there is some confusion about the referents, the rating ought to be low.
d. How clearly referenced are certain nouns, noun phrases, and other phrases that require referents? Search through the passage and locate all other words, besides pronouns, that require a referent in order to be understood. If there are two or more cases where there is some confusion about the referents, then the rating ought to be low.
e. In those cases where it applies, how consistent is the temporal ordering of events? Are the events that are temporally related arranged in either an ascending or a descending order?

Step 7: Determine to what extent the ideas in the passage contribute to a single text unit or frame. Count the total number of words in the passage, and divide that number into the number of words that fail to contribute to that single text unit or frame. This latter number can be obtained by counting the words that have a light line drawn through them (see Step 3).

If more than $\frac{1}{4}$ of the words fail to contribute to the text unit or frame, then unity suffers and the rating should be low.

Step 8: Determine how appropriate the text is to the audience.

    a. To what extent are the words in the passage likely to be understood by the readers? Locate the hard words, including technical terms, that you think readers probably will not know when they first read the passage. Place a check mark by them. Also, look for easy words that may be used in unusual ways. Then determine whether the use of each word is necessary to advance the purpose of the passage: If it is necessary, is it defined in a previous or nearby section of text? If more than two words are used unnecessarily or are not properly defined, the rating should be low.

    b. To what extent are the analogies, metaphors, and other figurative uses of language made clear by the author? Check to see if this figurative language references knowledge that the students are likely to know. Also check to see if the figurative language is signalled so that the students will realize that it is to be interpreted metaphorically rather than literally.

CONCLUSION

The focus of this chapter has been on what authors can do to facilitate learning from content area textbooks. We suggested that authors may be "considerate" to their readers and provide text that can be read and understood with a minimum of cognitive effort. On the other hand, authors may be "inconsiderate" by creating text that requires a conscientious, highly skilled effort if readers are to comprehend it.

We organized our discussion around four text characteristics: structure, coherence, unity, and audience appropriateness. We defined and illustrated these characteristics and cited research relevant to their effect on comprehension and learning. We also included a set of guidelines and a checklist that might be helpful to editors and authors of textbooks and to people who select and evaluate textbooks.

We believe that the guidelines we offered for evaluating and writing text units and frames will help ensure that text is well structured, has coherence and unity, and is appropriate for its audience. Textbooks based on these guidelines, we believe, will be easily read and understood by students. We think that learning will increase both quantitatively and qualitatively and that this learning will occur *without* the heavy use of studying strategies. We think that such a textbook may help the teacher work *with* the textbook rather than around it; the teacher can use class time supplementing the textbook rather than translating or interpreting it. Finally, we believe that when learning from textbooks becomes easier, students will develop a more positive and receptive attitude toward the discipline.

REFERENCES

Anderson, R. C. & Freebody, P. *Vocabulary knowledge and reading* (Reading Education Report No. 11). Urbana: University of Illinois, Center for the Study of Reading, August 1979. (ERIC Document Reproduction Service No. ED 177 470)

Anderson, R. C., Reynolds, R. E., Schallert, D. L., & Goetz, E. T. Frameworks for comprehending discourse. *American Educational Research Journal, 1977, 14,* 367–381.

Anderson, R. C., Spiro, R. J., & Anderson, M. C. Schemata as scaffolding for the representation of information in discourse. *American Educational Research Journal, 1978, 15,* 433–440.

Anderson, T. H., Armbruster, B. B., & Kantor, R. N. *How clearly written are children's textbooks? Or, of bladderworts and alfa* (Reading Education Report No. 16). Urbana: University of Illinois, Center for the Study of Reading, August 1980. (ERIC Document Reproduction Service No. ED 192 275)

Bransford, J. D., & Johnson, M. K. Contextual prerequisites for understanding: Some investigations of comprehension and recall. *Journal of Verbal Learning and Verbal Behavior, 1972, 11,* 717–726.

Dansereau, D. F., Brooks, L. W., Spurlin, J. E., & Holley, C. D. *Headings and outlines as processing aids for scientific text.* Manuscript submitted for publication, 1979.

Frase, L. T. Maintenance and control in the acquisiton of knowledge from written materials. In J. B. Carroll & R. O. Freedle (Eds.), *Language comprehension and the acquisition of knowledge.* Washington, D.C.: Winston, 1972.

Goetz, E., & Armbruster, B. Psychological correlates of text structure. In R. J. Spiro, B. C. Bruce, & W. F. Brewer (Eds.), *Theoretical issues in reading comprehension.* Hillsdale, N.J.: Lawrence Erlbaum Associates, 1980.

Grice, H. P. Logic and conversation. In P. Cole & J. L. Morgan (Eds.), *Syntax and semantics* (Vol. 3): *Speech acts.* New York: Academic Press, 1975.

Gropper, G. L. The design of stimulus materials in response-oriented programs. *AV Communications Review, 1970, 18,* 129–159.

Halliday, M. A. K., & Hasan, R. *Cohesion in English.* London: Longman, 1976.

Holliday, W. G. The effects of verbal and adjunct pictorial-verbal information in science instruction. *Journal of Research in Science Teaching, 1975, 12,* 77–83.

Holliday, W. G. Teaching verbal chains using flow diagrams and texts. *AV Communications Review, 1976, 24,* 63–78.

Holliday, W. G., Brunner, L. L., & Donais, E. L. Differential cognitive and affective responses to flow diagrams in science. *Journal of Research in Science Teaching, 1977, 14,* 129–138.

Holliday, W. G., & Harvey, D. A. Adjunct labeled drawings in teaching physics to junior high school students. *Journal of Research in Science Teaching, 1976, 13,* 37–43.

Katz, E. & Brent, S. Understanding connections. *Journal of Verbal Learning and Verbal Behavior, 1968, 7,* 501–509.

Klare, G. R. Assessing readability. *Reading Research Quarterly*, 1974–75, *10*, 62–102.

Lunzer, E., Davies, F., & Greene, T. *Reading for learning in science* (Schools Council Project Report). Nottingham, England: University of Nottingham, School of Education, 1980.

Marshall, N., & Glock, M. D. Comprehension of connected discourse: A study into the relationship between the structure of text and information recalled. *Reading Research Quarterly*, 1978–79, *16*, 10–56.

Meyer, B. J. F. *A selected review and discussion of basic research on prose comprehension* (Prose Learning Series: Research Report No. 4). Tempe: Arizona State University, Department of Educational Psychology, Spring 1979.

Miller, G. A. The magical number seven, plus or minus two: Some limits on our capacity for processing information. *Psychological Review*, 1956, *63*, 81–97.

Pearson, P. D. The effects of grammatical complexity on children's comprehension, recall, and conception of certain semantic relations. *Reading Research Quarterly*, 1974–75, *10*, 155–192.

Pearson, P. D., & Camparell, K. B. The comprehension of text structures. In J. Guthrie (Ed.), Comprehension and teaching: Research and reviews. Newark, Del.: International Reading Association, 1981.

Schallert, D. L. Improving memory for prose: The relationship between depth of processing and context. *Journal of Verbal Learning and Verbal Behavior*, 1976, *15*, 621–632.

Shimmerlik, S. M. Organization theory and memory for prose: A review of the literature. *Review of Educational Research*, 1978, *48*, 103–120.

Spilich, G. J., Vesonder, G. T., Chiesi, H. L., & Voss, J. F. Text processing of domain-related information for individuals with high and low domain knowledge. *Journal of Verbal Learning and Verbal Behavior*, 1979, *18*, 275–290.

Walker, C. H., & Meyer, B. J. F. Integrating information from text: An evaluation of current theories. *Review of Educational Research*, 1980, *50*, 421–437.

TEXT EXCERPT CITATIONS

1. Bendick, J., & Gallant, R. *Elementary Science 6*. Lexington, Mass.: Ginn, 1980, p. 216.

2. Gross, H. H., Follett, D. W., Gabler, R. E., William, L. B., & Ahlschwede, B. F. *Exploring our World: The Americas*. Chicago: Follett, 1977, p. 119.

3. Gross, H. H., Follett, D. W., Gabler, R. E., William, L. B., & Ahlschwede, B. F. *Follett Social Studies: Exploring Our World: The Americas*. Chicago: Follett, 1977, pp. 193–194.

4. Lesser, M. S. *Life Science*. New York: Amsco School Publications, Inc., 1967, p. 127.

5. Bendick, J., & Gallant, R. *Elementary Science 6*, Lexington, Mass: Ginn, 1980, p. 71.

6. Senesh, L. *The American Way of Life*. Chicago: Science Research Associates, 1973, p. 149.

7. Dawson, G. S. *Our World*. Lexington, Mass.: Ginn, 1979, p. 29.

8. Senesh, L. *The American Way of Life*. Chicago: Science Research Associates, 1973, p. 245.

9. Berger, C. F., Berkheimer, G. D., Lewis, L. E., Jr., & Neuberger, H. T. *Houghton Mifflin Science (6)*. Boston: Houghton Mifflin, 1979, p. 55.

10. Bendick, J., & Gallant, R. *Elementary Science 6*. Lexington, Mass.: Ginn, 1980, p. 71.

11. *The Making of Our America*. Boston: Allyn & Bacon, 1974, p. 80.

12. Senesh, L. *The American Way of Life*. Chicago: Science Research Associates, 1973, p. 41.

13. Bendick, J., & Gallant, R. *Elementary Science 6.* Lexington, Mass.: Ginn, 1980, p. 63.
14. Lesser, M., Constant, C., & Weisler, J. J. *Contemporary Science, Book 1.* New York: Amsco School Publications, 1977, pp. 224–225.
15. Lesser, M. S. *Life Science.* New York: Amsco School Publications, Inc., 1967, p. 104.
16. Berger, C. F., Berkheimer, G. D., Lewis, L. E., Jr., & Neuberger, H. T. *Houghton Mifflin Science (4).* Boston: Houghton Mifflin, 1979, pp. 184–187.
17. Dawson, G. S. *Our World.* Lexington, Mass.: Ginn, 1979, p. 51.
18. Stanek, M. *Chicago—The City and Its People.* Chicago: Benetic Press, 1981, p. 95.
19. Bendick, J. *Ginn Science Program: Introductory Level C.* Lexington, Mass.: Ginn, 1973, p. 155.
20. Namowitz, N., & Stone, D. B. *Earth Science.* New York: American Book Co., 1978, p. 216.
21. Bendick, J., & Gallant, R. *Elementary Science 6.* Lexington, Mass.: Ginn, 1980, p. 151.

TEXTBOOK EVALUATION RESPONSE FORM

Textbook Title_____

Publisher_____ Grade Level_____ Copyright Date_____

Step 1: Title or heading of passage_____

        Page number _____

Step 2: Is this passage a text unit ____, or a text frame ____?

        Questions related to the unit or frame:

        1.

        2.

        3.

        4.

Step 3: After reading the passage carefully, is it primarily a text unit ____, or a text frame ____?

        Questions related to the unit or frame:

        1.

        2.

        3.

        4.

Step 4: Does the passage have adequate answers to relevant questions?

        Yes   Maybe   No   (circle one)

        Comments:

        If YES or MAYBE, continue on to Step 5.

        If NO, return to Step 1 with another passage.

Step 5: Write the name of the structure used in each paragraph, and then rate that paragraph using the appropriate questions (pp. 426–428).

Paragraph Number	Paragraph Structure	Question Number	Rating Scale Low				High
1	_____	1	1	2	3	4	5
		2	1	2	3	4	5
		3	1	2	3	4	5
		4	1	2	3	4	5
2	_____	1	1	2	3	4	5
		2	1	2	3	4	5
		3	1	2	3	4	5
		4	1	2	3	4	5
3	_____	1	1	2	3	4	5
		2	1	2	3	4	5
		3	1	2	3	4	5
		4	1	2	3	4	5
4	_____	1	1	2	3	4	5
		2	1	2	3	4	5
		3	1	2	3	4	5
		4	1	2	3	4	5
5	_____	1	1	2	3	4	5
		2	1	2	3	4	5
		3	1	2	3	4	5
		4	1	2	3	4	5

			Low				High

Step 6: Determine how coherent the passage is.

a. To what extent are the connectives made explicit?   1 2 3 4 5

b. How effectively does the author use connectives? (How   NA 1 2 3 4 5
many were used? ___)

c. How clearly are the pronouns referenced?   NA 1 2 3 4 5

d. How clearly referenced are certain nouns, noun phrases,   NA 1 2 3 4 5
and other phrases that require referents?

e. In those cases where it applies, how consistent is the tem-   NA 1 2 3 4 5
poral ordering of events?

Step 7: Determine to what extent the passage addresses a single   1 2 3 4 5
purpose. The computed proportion is ___.___.

Step 8: Determine how appropriate the text is to the audience.

a. To what extent are the words in the passage likely to be   1 2 3 4 5
understood by the readers?

b. To what extent are the analogies, metaphors, and other   NA 1 2 3 4 5
figurative language made clear by the author?

Step 9: Refer back to Step 2 and decide how difficult it was to   1 2 3 4 5
formulate questions based on the title.

Step 10: Refer back to Steps 2 and 3 and determine how consist-   1 2 3 4 5
ent your decisions were on the two steps. If you had to
formulate an entirely new set of questions after reading
the passage carefully, rate this step low.

Subject Matter Texts–Reading to Learn: Response to a Paper by Thomas H. Anderson and Bonnie B. Armbruster

Harold L. Herber
Syracuse University

My response to Anderson and Armbruster's paper (hereinafter called "the paper") is based on several strong beliefs about the notion of reading to learn. These beliefs have been formulated during two decades of working with content area teachers, developing instructional programs, designing instructional materials, and conducting research. The use of subject matter texts has been central to this work. My beliefs are that:

1. Reading to learn *is* different from learning to read, both for the learner and for the teacher.
2. Students need to be taught how to read to learn; transfer of skills gained in learning to read is not automatic.
3. Subject matter teachers can provide simultaneous instruction in reading skills and in course content.
4. Subject matter texts are instructional tools; students should not be expected to read them independently.
5. Comprehension is affected but not assured by the organization and content of the text; thus, creating better texts will not automatically produce better readers.
6. Students who are properly placed in a curriculum will find their texts "too difficult" to use independently; if they do not, they already know the subject and are improperly placed.
7. The difficulty of a text should be in its content, not in its organization; and one need not sacrifice the former in order to improve the latter.

8. The content of a text determines the processes by which it is read; thus, texts should be organized for the best presentation of content rather than to facilitate the teaching of a "given" or "specific" set of comprehension or study skills.

In bringing these beliefs to the reading of this paper, I respond with mixed feelings. The recommendations for improving texts are good, but I believe they are made for the wrong reasons. What follows is a review of the important recommendations in the paper and an analysis of their implications.

SIGNIFICANT RECOMMENDATIONS

Organization of Text. The heart of the paper is the recommendation that subject matter texts be better organized. Importantly, the paper explains how this can be done and provides an example. This is a refreshing approach to the issue of text adequacy. Most discussions are only complaints and lack positive suggestions for change.

The discussion of structure, coherence, and unity was thorough and well supported by research from psychology and information processing. One can also find support from research in reading education.

The use of graphic organizers to aid students in perceiving the organization or structure of the concepts being studied facilitates recall of the concepts and the text material (Alvermann, 1980; Barron, 1969, 1979; Earle, 1970). The structured overview, a graphic representation of the concept under consideration, can facilitate students' understanding of the relationships among the ideas that fit together to form that concept (Barron, 1969; Earle, 1970; Herber, 1978; Thelen, 1970). The structured overview aids students' perception of how the ideas in the text are woven together.

Guiding students' reading of text also helps them form concepts out of the relationships among selected pieces of information (Berget, 1973; Maxon, 1979; Sanders, 1970; Shablak, 1972). Guides also can facilitate students' use of the organizational patterns that exist in those relationships as an aid to comprehension (Vacca, 1973; Walker, 1975). Guiding students' reading develops their understanding of the relationships between the content of the text and the related reading processes.

Audience appropriateness is defined in the paper as "the extent to which the text matches the reader's knowledge base." It is not clear whether this is presented as a problem for textbook writers or for teachers. I assume that it is the latter. The concepts being studied in the text should be new to the students if they are properly placed in the curriculum; therefore, there will not be a match between the content knowledge of students and the text. However, when teachers help students activate relevant prior knowledge, students are more receptive to the study of the text and more readily understand the concept being developed (Herber, 1970, 1978; Herber & Nelson, 1976; Nelson, 1980; Nelson & Herber, 1981).

Anatomy of a Textbook.   This section is an illustration of the influence of prior knowledge (or lack of it) on comprehension. I was unfamiliar with the terminology used in the paper to describe textbooks. I tried to equate these new terms with old descriptors of parts of textbooks (unit, chapter, section, subsection, etc.) but quickly learned that the terms were not synonymous.

Here is what I understand to be the recomendation for the composition of textbooks. Since each discipline studied in school has content-specific frames that represent the major concepts addressed by that curriculum, then texts written for each discipline should utilize those frames.

Text units are representations of the author's purpose, including both the questions being asked and their answers. Six text units are identified, each defined as a function: (a) to describe, (b) to sequence events, (c) to explain, (d) to define and exemplify, (e) to compare and contrast, and (f) to relate a problem and its solution. The type of purpose or question addressed by the author dictates the type of function or text unit employed. Each text unit in a frame represents a different category of information.

One can see a clear relationship among all of the functions in the proposed organization of textbooks, and their purposes are explicated in the paper. What is missing, however, is an explanation of their relationship to the traditional descriptors for textbooks. Such an explanation would not change the paper's purpose, but it might change its impact and a reader's understanding.

Conceptual Relationships.   The paper's implicit and explicit emphasis on building concepts is important. Students need help in building an understanding of how concepts are formed, how ideas connect. Too often instruction in a content area emphasizes delivery, collection, and repetition of information. Too often, therefore, students fail to perceive the overarching ideas, the significance of the information they have collected, or its usefulness.

Content area lessons that successfully combine the teaching of subject matter and related reading processes are designed around "organizing ideas" (what the paper calls general frames or content-specific frames). With organizing ideas as the central focus, lessons have structure, purpose, and relevance (Herber, 1978; Herber & Nelson, 1976; Nelson & Herber, 1981). If textbooks were written as recommended in this paper, they could greatly facilitate this kind of conceptually based teaching.

Facilitation of learning. The motivation for this paper seems to be the production of textbooks that will facilitate the learning of course content, a laudable goal because many subject matter texts appear not to have been similarly motivated. Too often they are recitations of information, chopped into chunks of varied length to fit writing assignments among authors, frequently flawed by significant omissions, and well laced with redundancies. This paper presents a scheme for changing textbooks that could influence students' learning in a positive way.

SIGNIFICANT IMPLICATIONS

One's own background strongly influences the inferences one draws while reading. I freely admit that my response reflects the biases expressed in the list of beliefs presented earlier. It is possible, therefore, that what I infer was not intended. However, the inferences I draw focus on the issues that are critical to what the paper calls "reading to learn," or what is more generally called "reading in content areas." It is because of the implications for instruction that one can draw from the paper that I earlier expressed my belief that the paper was correct in its message but for the wrong reason.

Relationship Between Skills and Text. Are reading and study skills derived from textbooks or are textbooks organized around reading and study skills? Asked a different way, the question is: Do the organization and content of a text dictate how it should be read (reading and study skills used by the reader to assure comprehension), or do reading and study skills (preconceived notions about how students should read texts) dictate the organization and content of a text? The paper seems to support the position that skills dictate text.

As you will recall, researchers' interest in revising content area texts sprang from their inability to find texts suitable for training children how to study. This conjures up the image of a set of skills in search of a compatible text. Indeed, the researchers set about constructing a model of text that would support their notion of what constitutes study skills. While this procedure is consistent with traditional practices in the design of reading materials for teaching reading skills, it is contrary to current, successful practice in teaching reading skills through content area texts (Herber & Nelson, 1980).

Traditionally, the organizing element for the construction of *reading materials* is a set of skills derived from a combination of theory, logic, common sense, practice, and some research. Materials are designed to embody the skills and are used for teaching the skills. The subject matter is not the principal concern; organization for purposes of skill development is. One can readily infer that the paper's recommendations are guided by this tradition.

In contrast, current successful practice in teaching students how to read content area texts is influenced by the idea that "content determines process." The organization and content of the text determines what skills readers must use in order to comprehend that text. Comprehension is a dynamic process of interaction between the reader and the text. Therefore, the process fits any text, organized in any fashion, presenting any kind of content. Texts need not be designed to fit a preconceived notion of what constitutes the process of comprehension. Rather, texts can be organized for the clearest possible presentation of the concepts to which the texts are devoted. When used by teachers for instructional purposes, such texts serve to teach both the content of the discipline and the related comprehension skills.

Certainly the paper's recommended criteria for development of texts are important for improving the organization of their content. Structure, coherence, and unity are important factors in the presentation of any body of knowledge, no matter what the medium. But such criteria only clarify the content of the text, they do not dictate it. It remains for the reader to apply the appropriate comprehension processes to acquire an understanding of that content. This thought leads to the second implication.

Independence vs. Instruction. Implicity and explicitly the paper takes the position that subject area texts should be designed for independent reading by students. Note what is stated in the last paragraph of the conclusion:

> We believe that the guidelines we offered for evaluating and writing text units and frames will help ensure that text is well structured, has coherence and unity, and is appropriate for its audience. Textbooks based on these guidelines, we believe, will be easily read and understood by students. We think that learning will increase both quantitatively and qualitatively and that this learning will occur *without* the heavy use of studying strategies. We think that such a textbook may help the teacher work *with* the textbook rather than around it; the teacher can use class time supplementing the textbook rather than translating or interpreting it. Finally, we believe that when learning from textbooks becomes easier, students will develop a more positive and receptive attitude toward the discipline (pp. 223–224).

While such a position may be consistent with the traditional views of the reader's responsibility for reading content area texts, it is not consistent with currently successful practice (Herber & Nelson, 1980).

Texts that present concepts that are new to readers are hard books to read. They can be designed to be read "productively" but not to be read "easily." The assumption by teachers that students do not need instruction in how to read their texts is a root cause of the failure or poor performance of many students in content areas.

The paper suggests that the alternative to "easily read" texts is that the teacher must spend time "translating and interpreting." The alternative is a bad one, not because translation and interpretation are needed but because of who is doing the translating and interpreting. *Showing students how* to translate and interpret the text is the teacher's job, no matter how well the text is structured. The issue is who is doing the translating and interpreting and for whom, not whether it is necessary (Herber, 1978). This thought leads to the final inference.

Transfer of Training. The assumption that students can read content area texts independently implies that they have been taught how to read this kind of material in other classes and through other materials. This, too, is a rather traditional view of reading instruction and reading programs. It leads to the "blaming syndrome" prevalent among subject matter teachers and the general public. The traditional belief is that "learning to read" automatically transfers to "reading to learn," even though there is ample evidence to contrary. One need not worry about transfer when reading instruction is provided in content areas, using regular subject matter texts within the regular curriculum to develop students' understanding of course content and related reading skills (Herber & Nelson, 1980).

Significant Omissions. Logically extending from these implications is an awareness of two significant omissions from the paper: reading guides, and directions to teachers.

No reference is made to the inclusion of reading guides in the proposed textbooks, even though there is a brief review of research related to adjunct aids. This omission suggests that the authors assumed that teachers do not have to show students *how* to read the proposed text because students already know how.

The second omission—more understandable—is any reference to helping teachers learn how to use texts instructionally. It is understandable because this paper is not about teacher education. However, it is regrettable because it supports the inference that subject matter teachers need not teach their students how to read the text.

Both omissions are significant. Redesigned texts must include aids to comprehension that will help students learn course content and related reading skills, by facilitating teachers' instruction of same. Teachers must learn how to use such texts instructionally, and this is as much the responsibility of publishing houses as of teacher education institutions. The literature is replete with examples of such material (Nelson, 1980) and such teacher education programs (Herber & Nelson, 1976; 1980).

CONCLUSION

The suggestions in this paper for reorganizing and redesigning texts are important and useful. However, the assumptions on which the suggestions are based seem to reflect outmoded traditions, and the implications are contrary to recent, productive shifts in reading programs and practices in content areas. Even so, this paper illustrates the fact that a closer working relationship among publishers, practitioners, and researchers could be mutually beneficial—and ultimately helpful to our students, the objects of concern of us all.

REFERENCES

Alvermann, D. *Effects of graphic organizers, textual organization, and reading comprehension level on recall of expository prose.* Unpublished doctoral dissertation, Syracuse University, 1980.

Barron, R. F. The use of vocabulary as an advance organizer. In H. L. Herber & P. L. Sanders (Eds.), *Research in reading in the content areas, first year report.* Syracuse, N.Y.: Syracuse University, 1969.

Barron, R. F. Research for the classroom teacher: Recent developments on the structured overview as an advance organizer. In H. L. Herber & J. D. Riley (Eds.), *Research in reading in the content areas, the fourth report.* Syracuse, N.Y.: Syracuse University, 1979.

Berget, E. A. Two methods of guiding the learning of a short story. In H. L. Herber & R. F. Barron (Eds.), *Research in reading in the content areas, second year report.* Syracuse, N.Y.: Syracuse University, 1973.

Earle, R. A. *The use of vocabulary as a structured overview in seventh grade mathematics classes.* Unpublished doctoral dissertation, Syracuse University, 1970.

Herber, H. L. *Teaching reading in content areas* (1st ed.) Englewood Cliffs, N.J.: Prentice-Hall, 1970.

Herber, H. L. *Teaching reading in content areas* (2nd ed.). Englewood Cliffs, N.J.: Prentice-Hall, 1978.

Herber, H. L., & Nelson, J. *Reading across the curriculum.* Homer, N.Y.: TRICA Consultants, 1976.

Herber, H. L. & Nelson, J. *A network of secondary school demonstration centers for teaching reading in content areas.* Basic Skills Improvement Program, Title II, Grant #G008001963, 1980.

Maxon, G. *The effects of guiding reading using questions and declarative statements separately and in a particular order*. Unpublished doctoral dissertation, Syracuse University, 1979.

Nelson, J. *Meeting challenges*. New York: American Book Company, 1980.

Nelson, J., & Herber, H. L. A positive approach to corrective reading in middle and secondary schools. In J. Flood (Ed.), *Understanding reading comprehension*. Newark, Del.: International Reading Association, in press.

Sanders, P. L. *An investigation of the effects of instruction on the interpretation of literature on the responses of adolescents to selected short stories*. Unpublished doctoral dissertation, Syracuse University, 1970.

Shablak, S. *The effects of different types of guide materials and manner of presentation on ninth graders' curiosity toward and response to selected short stories*. Unpublished doctoral dissertation, Syracuse University, 1972.

Thelen, J. N. *Use of advance organizers and guide materials in viewing science motion pictures in a ninth grade*. Unpublished doctoral dissertation, Syracuse University, 1970.

Vacca, R. T. *An investigation of a functional reading strategy in seventh grade social studies classes*. Unpublished doctoral dissertation, Syracuse University, 1973.

Walker, N. *An investigation into the effects of graphic organizers on the learning of social studies readings in the middle grades*. Unpublished doctoral dissertation, Syracuse University, 1975.

7 Cultural Variation and Textbook Publication vis á vis Jelly Beans and Designer Genes

Thomas P. Pietras, Director, *Language Arts Department*
Ann Arbor, (Michigan) Public Schools

The decade of the 80's seems preoccupied with talk of jelly beans and designer genes,[1] with the former symbolic of politics and the latter symbolic of science. What they both seem to have in common is that they focus on human nature and the age-old argument about nature and nurture, that is, to what degree are people born a "certain way" as compared to what degree environment forms them a certain way.

It is well documented by the years of the Great Society that those who believe in changing society place their money on environment. The War on Poverty was essentially an assault on environment, with a myriad of social and educational programs designed to help "disadvantaged" citizens gain competitively more viable access to the opportunities of our society.

It now seems that in the forthcoming years of the Fiscally Responsible Society, those who believe in biology have control, and there is now an assault on social and educational programs because they have been judged ineffective, even detrimental, for the well-being of our citizens. Simply stated, man has to seek and he shall find, sow and he shall reap. It is he, to the measure of his own ability and motivation, that will determine his fate.

The reason that our society has these periodic great shifts in national political sociology and psychology is the fact that nobody really knows how much we are a product of our genes and how much we are a product of our culture. It is most likely that we are a combination of both, and

---

[1] The credit for this phrase belongs to syndicated columnist Ellen Goodman.

truth lies somewhere in between these two shapers of human existence. The argument, however, is fascinating because it is one more of politics than science. For example, the bilingual cause in this country, although begun and argued for as an academically humane program, is now a political issue. In the *Nation's Business* (December, 1980), an article, "One Nation, One Language for All," reports that in response to the question "Is there too much emphasis on bilingualism?", the readers of the periodical say yes by a margin of 20 to 1. The readership includes some "heavy" individuals from business and industry, and the two representative statements which follow illustrate the viewpoints of many of the respondents.

Our society has enough divisive forces already; language differentiation should not be another.

> Don Lundgren,
> Director of Corporate Personnel Development
> at the Scott Paper Company,
> Philadelphia

We should encourage all Americans—children and adults—to learn English to the best of their abilities. My company wants employees with a good grasp of English. A common language is one of our country's greatest assets. Bilingualism that diminishes the drive for a common language is counterproductive.

> William L. Matthaei
> Executive Vice-President
> for Marketing at the Roman Meal Company,
> Tacoma, Washington

And the following statement, most likely written satirically, reminds us of the issue of dialect variation and learning to read, which received national media attention via the Ann Arbor Black English court case during the 1979–80 school year.

If I ever move above the Mason-Dixon line, maybe I should demand that my children be taught a class in "how to speak Southern" so they won't lose part of their cultural heritage.

> Robert D. Brueckner
> Manager of Information Systems
> for Dorsey Trailers, Inc.,
> Elba, Alabama

The insight we receive from these kinds of responses is that language variation, be it foreign or dialect, receives little tolerance and understanding by the general public. As a result, public opinion on this issue is making it politically expedient for the new Federal Administration to no longer actively support nor advocate bilingual programs; its course seems one of benign neglect. However, before one begins to acrimoniously attack the presumed benighted behavior of those who have chosen this new course, let us remember that many in government who vigorously support bilingualism do not ignore the voter support of those who would presumably realize benefits from it.

So why argue? Why not leave such debate to the politicians and their "groupies" and get on with some data-based scientific recommendations for the issues confronting education generally and the language arts specifically? Unfortunately, scientific objectivity can often be as trendy as Madison Avenue. It is not difficult for us to pick and choose from among scientific-research-based ideas to support our beliefs about a certain educational issue, because scientists themselves often advocate one or another position as it fits their personal sociopolitical values. This seems especially applicable in the social sciences and education. As a result, it is challenging for us to find viable cause-and-effect dicta that we can apply to some of our long-standing issues in education, e.g., teaching *all* children to read at a functionally literate level let alone at grade level.

However, the foregoing discussion does not mean that we cease our quest for improved curriculum and instruction as it pertains to teaching children to read and to apply this skill to other school subjects. There exists valuable research data upon which language arts teacher educators and textbook publishers can base their syllabi and textbooks, but they need to temper their sociopolitical polemics and use the information that is both practical and applicable from a realistic rather than a utopian perspective. (One good source for such information is the Center for the Study of Reading at the University of Illinois.)

In the last 20 years, the disciplines of linguistics, psychology, psycholinguistics, and sociolinguistics have provided significant and educationally applicable information about the nature of language, the process of human communication, the process of language acquisition, the nature of dialectal language variation, the sociological effects of language diversity on human interaction, and the educational effects of language diversity on achievement in school. Not much of this information has been incorporated in a systematic broad-based manner into our teacher education programs (under-graduate, graduate, or inservice), and even less has been incorporated into the content of our language arts curricula. For example, most teachers and textbooks still treat dialects, usage, and semantics as "when and if we have time" projects outside the realm of the regular program. If we are ever to have a knowledgeable and understanding society regarding language, its education must occur in the classroom and not in the courtroom or legislative chambers. New knowledge about language is as important as the new math and the new science. These disciplines constantly revise their textbooks and train their teachers regarding new uses and discoveries concerning their content.

Thus, the following illustrative guidelines focus on some of the important information about language that is currently well documented but not generally known or understood by students, teachers, and the general public. This information should be an integral part of the content of our language arts textbooks, kindergarten through graduate school.

1. All languages, if they are living languages, change with time.
2. Any human infant exposed to human language and not suffering from a physical, mental, or emotional handicap will learn that language.
3. The relationship between words in a language and their referents is arbitrary, and analogic change, borrowing, and metaphor influence this relationship.
4. Concepts that can be expressed in one dialect of a language can be expressed in another dialect of that language.
5. No dialect of a language is inherently more elegant, more logical, more correct, or more crucial than any other dialect of the language, but situation and purpose relative to a specific communication act may require a certain form of the language.
6. Everyone speaks some dialect of a language, but most modern languages have a single written standard.
7. The grammatical differences among the dialects of English are very small compared to what those dialects share.
8. The few grammatical differences among dialects are the result of historical, geographical, and social accident, not of any intrinsically superior logic, expressiveness, or intellectual worth.
9. The linguistically minor grammatical differences between certain dialects and standard English not so inexplicably carry great social weight.
10. If speakers of nonstandard dialects do not learn to write coherently or clearly, it may be a consequence not of a few distinctive dialect features, but of teachers' failure to take into account what is known about the influence of dialect within the learning (school) environment.

This kind of knowledge can benefit competent teachers in two major ways: (a) It provides useful information on which they may rely when making instructional decisions for students who may be language variant speakers. (b) It provides subject matter information about the nature and functions of language in its various facets of everyday human communication and interpersonal relations which they can teach their students.

Regarding point one, a teacher knowledgeable about black vernacular English would be able to recognize the difference between a dialect shift and a decoding error as a child might read the following sentence as:

d(is)   s
"This a story about two boy

        d
and how they like to walk on

    trial   s
a trail in the wood."

In this example, the pronunciation of *th* as *d,* the omission of the linking verb *is,* and the omission of the plural marker *s* are all features of black vernacular English. Research regarding the reading process shows that dialect speakers render standard English print into their dialect pattern; this is known as a dialect shift. Also as part of this example, *trial* is not a dialect rendering of *trail* but is a reading decoding error.

This relates to the teaching of reading as follows. Dialect shifts do not ordinarily affect meaning; i.e., the students comprehend what they read, and the teacher can easily check their comprehension by asking them questions. If students understand what they read, then they know how to read, and the teacher should not spend time during reading instruction on dialect shifts as if they were decoding errors. However, if a dialect shift does cause a loss of meaning as can happen if, for example, *walked* is rendered as *walk* in a particular sentence and the student does not grasp that the event is past time, then the teacher should provide appropriate instruction to clarify the meaning of the sentence as he or she would do for *trail* read as *trial* in our example. The crucial issue in this instructional situation is whether or not the students understand the meaning of what they read. The matter of teaching the syntax of standard English is an issue of language instruction and should occur during the time allotted for it in the curriculum rather than taking time away from reading instruction.

Another aspect of the influence of language on learning is the way students pronounce their words and the manner in which their teachers may respond attitudinally, i.e., positively or negatively. New England speech patterns *(pahk, cah, pahtee)* usually receive an accepting response, as they represent the cradle of democracy, the Founding Fathers, the culture and refinement of the East. The speech patterns of the South *(ast, git, et, fixin, hep)* often receive a reserved acceptance, especially as these may seem to represent the poor, the uneducated, the uncultured. Or the speech patterns of an ethnic group such as the Polish-American *(tick, tin, dat, dose)* receive a negative response because these may seem to represent the unassimilated laborer, the ethnocentric adherent of a foreign (unAmerican) culture and tradition. In this last category we may generally include the hyphenated Americans that descend from Eastern Europe, Asia, Latin America, and South America. Interestingly, those who descend from Western Europe find that their speech patterns are quite acceptable as, for example, advertisers use French accented, Swedish accented, and British English to sell products to the middle and upper classes. A well-known and influential advisor to Presidents never found a strong German accent a detriment to his career. No doubt this is a result of the dominance that Anglo-Saxon culture has in American society. It seems obvious that language variation being understood and accepted is more a matter of which racial, ethnic, or social class group is doing the speaking than it is of language variation per se.

The human tragedy of this uneven, misinformed, and illogical response to language variation is that simply by the sound of their speech, some people are judged positively and others are judged negatively. This can be extremely serious when it occurs in school, and indeed, research in teacher expectancy (the Pygmalion effect) demonstrates that teachers can unconsciously have low expectation for students' ability to learn based on students' use of language, and that those students who speak one of the variants that elicit generally negative responses in society are the ones who usually get the same sort of response in the school environment. Language-knowledgeable teachers, however, seem not to fall victim to this kind of benighted behavior.

Moreover, if teachers are knowledgeable about language, they can incorporate this information into the curriculum and should do so, because it is important for students to know and understand the nature and functions of language in the various facets of everyday communication. What students *need* to learn is that either of the following two extremes regarding language is unacceptable.

1. There is one, best correct form of the language, and any variation is error and always socially unacceptable.
2. Because all variant forms of language (dialects) are co-equal, there is no need to learn a standard form.

The responsible position is for teachers not only to instruct students about the nature of language as previously discussed, but also to help them learn to use the standard dialect expected of persons who would participate in the institutional life of our society, particularly as it applies to writing standard English. It would be very beneficial to students if teachers had textbooks that enabled them to teach this important information.

Thus, one of the major challenges for the decade of the 80's in language arts textbook production is to provide content that takes language variation into account in a manner that recognizes American society as one that ideally respects diversity but realistically expects unity. It is not inconsistent to respect language differences but also to expect a standard language.

As textbook publishers address this challenge in our competitive profit-motive society, they will weigh and balance various factors before placing their "bets" on specific programs that they hope will satisfy the various constituencies (academicians, teachers, students, parents, the moral majority, women's lib, . . .) that often determine the success or failure of textbooks insofar as they are accepted and purchased for use in our nation's classrooms. Theirs is not an enviable task. Perhaps the following excerpt from *Ecclesiastes* puts their predicament into a realistic perspective.

> I returned and saw under the sun, that the race is not to the swift, nor the battle to the strong, neither yet bread to the wise, nor yet riches to men of understanding, nor yet favor to men of skill; but time and chance happeneth to them all.

Let us hope that the *swift, strong, wise, understanding,* and *skillful* among the publishers will prevail over *time* and *chance*.

8 Role of the Reader's Schema in Comprehension, Learning, and Memory

Richard C. Anderson
Center for the Study of Reading
University of Illinois at Urbana-Champaign

The last several years have witnessed the articulation of a largely new theory of reading, a theory already accepted by the majority of scholars in the field. According to the theory, a reader's *schema*, or organized knowledge of the world, provides much of the basis for comprehending, learning, and remembering the ideas in stories and texts. In this chapter I attempt to explain schema theory, give illustrations of the supporting evidence, and suggest applications to classroom teaching and the design of instructional materials.

A SCHEMA-THEORETIC INTERPRETATION OF COMPREHENSION

In schema-theoretic terms, a reader comprehends a message when he is able to bring to mind a schema that gives a good account of the objects and events described in the message. Ordinarily, comprehension proceeds so smoothly that we are unaware of the process of "cutting and fitting" a schema in order to achieve a satisfactory account of a message. It is instructive, therefore, to try to understand material that gives us pause, so that we can reflect upon our own minds at work. Consider the following sentence, drawn from the work of Bransford and McCarrell (1974):

The notes were sour because the seam split.

Notice that all of the words are familiar and that the syntax is straightforward, yet the sentence does not "make sense" to most people. Now notice what happens when the additional clue, "bagpipe," is provided. At this point the sentence does make sense because one is able to interpret all the words in the sentence in terms of certain specific objects and events and their interrelations.

Let us examine another sentence:

The big number 37 smashed the ball over the fence.

This sentence is easy to interpret. *Big Number 37* is a baseball player. The sense of *smash the ball* is to propel it rapidly by hitting it strongly with a bat. The fence is at the boundry of a playing field. The ball was hit hard enough that it flew over the fence.

Suppose a person with absolutely no knowledge of baseball read the Big Number 37 sentence. Such a person could not easily construct an interpretation of the sentence, but with enough mental effort might be able to conceive of large numerals, perhaps made of metal, attached to the front of an apartment building. Further, the person might imagine that the numerals come loose and fall, striking a ball resting on top of, or lodged above, a fence, causing the ball to break. Most people regard this as an improbable interpretation, certainly one that never would have occurred to them, but they readily acknowledge that it is a "good" interpretation. What makes it good? The answer is that the interpretation is complete and consistent. It is complete in the sense that every element in the sentence is interpreted; there are no loose ends left unexplained. The interpretation is consistent in that no part of it does serious violence to knowledge about the physical and social world.

Both interpretations of the Big Number 37 sentence assume a real world. Criteria of consistency are relaxed in fictional worlds in which animals talk or men wearing capes leap tall buildings in a single bound. But there are conventions about what is possible in fictional worlds as well. The knowledgeable reader will be annoyed if these conventions are violated. The less knowledgeable reader simply will be confused.

It should not be imagined that there is some simple, literal level of comprehension of stories and texts that does not require coming up with a schema. This important point is illustrated in a classic study by Bransford and Johnson (1972) in which subjects read paragraphs, such as the following, written so that most people are unable to construct a schema that will account for the material:

If the balloons popped the sound wouldn't be able to carry since everything would be too far away from the correct floor. A closed window would also prevent the sound from carrying, since most buildings tend to be well insulated. Since the whole operation depends upon a steady flow of electricity, a break in the middle of the wire would also cause problems. Of course, the fellow could shout, but the human voice is not loud enough to carry that far. An additional problem is that a string could break on the instrument. Then there could be no accompaniment to the message. It is clear that the best situation would involve less distance. Then there would be fewer potential problems. With face to face contact, the least number of things could go wrong (p. 719).

Subjects rated this passage as very difficult to understand, and they were unable to remember much of it. In contrast, subjects shown the drawing on the left side of Figure 1, found the passage more comprehensible and were able to remember a great deal of it. Another group saw the drawing on the right in Figure 1. This group remembered no more than the group that did not receive a drawing. The experiment demonstrates that what is critical for comprehension is a schema accounting for the *relationships* among elements; it is not enough for the elements to be concrete and imageable.

Trick passages, such as the foregoing one about the communication problems of a modern day Romeo, are useful for illustrating what happens when a reader is completely unable to discover a schema that fits a passage and, therefore, finds the passage entirely incomprehensible. More typical is the situation in which a reader knows something about a topic, but falls far short of being an expert. Chiesi, Spilich, and Voss (1979) asked people high and low in knowledge of baseball to read and recall a report of a half-inning from a fictitious baseball game. Knowledge of baseball had both qualitative and quantitative effects on performance. High-knowledge subjects were more likely to recall and embellish upon aspects of strategic significance to the game. Low-knowledge subjects, in contrast, were more likely to include information incidental to the play of the game.

Schema theory highlights the fact that often more than one interpretation of a text is possible. The schema that is brought to bear on a text depends upon the reader's age, sex, race, religion, nationality, occupation—in short, it depends upon the reader's culture. This point was illustrated in an experiment completed by Anderson, Reynolds, Schallert, and Goetz (1977), who asked people to read the following passage:

Tony slowly got up from the mat, planning his escape. He hesitated a moment and thought. Things were not going well. What bothered him most was being held, especially since the charge against him had been weak. He considered his present situation. The lock that held him was strong but he thought he could break it. He knew, however, that his timing would have to

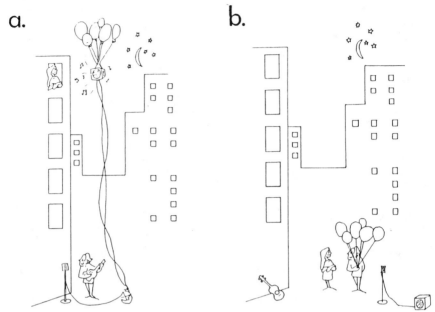

FIG. 1.   Illustrations from Bransford and Johnson (1972). Version "a" represents the appropriate context and version "b" represents the inappropriate context. See text for accompanying passage.

be perfect. Tony was aware that it was because of his early roughness that he had been penalized so severely—much too severely from his point of view. The situation was becoming frustrating; the pressure had been grinding on him for too long. He was being ridden unmercifully. Tony was getting angry now. He felt he was ready to make his move. He knew that his success or failure would depend on what he did in the next few seconds.

Most people think the foregoing passage is about a convict planning his escape from prison. A special group of people, however, see the passage an entirely different way; these are men who have been involved in the sport of wrestling. They think the passage is about a wrestler caught in the hold of an opponent. Notice how the interpretation of *lock* varies according to perspective. In the one case, it is a piece of hardware that holds a cell door shut; in the other it may be a sweaty arm around a neck. Males enrolled in a weight lifting class and females enrolled in a music education class read the foregoing passage and another passage that most people interpret as being about several people playing cards, but that can be interpreted as being about a rehearsal session of a woodwind ensemble. The results were as expected. Scores on a multiple choice test designed to reveal interpretations of the passages showing striking relationships to the subjects' background. Physical education students usually gave a wrestling interpretation to the prison/wrestling passage and a card-playing interpretation to the card/music passage, whereas the reverse was true of the music education students. Similarly, when subjects were asked to recall the passages, theme-revealing distortions appeared, even though the instructions emphasized reproducing the exact words of the original text. For example, a physical education student stated, "Tony was penalized early in the match for roughness or a dangerous hold," while a music education student wrote, "he was angry that he had been caught and arrested."

The thesis of this section is that comprehension is a matter of activating or constructing a schema that provides a coherent explanation of objects and events mentioned in a discourse. In sharp contrast is the conventional view that comprehension consists of aggregating the meaning of words to form the meanings of clauses, aggregating the meaning of clauses to form the meanings of sentences, aggregating the meanings of sentences to form the meanings of paragraphs, and so on. The illustrations in this section were intended to demonstrate the insufficiency of this conventional view. The meanings of the words cannot be "added up" to give the meaning of the whole. The click of comprehension occurs only when the reader evolves a schema that explains the whole message.

Schema-based Processes in Learning and Remembering

According to schema theory, reading involves more or less simultaneous analysis at many different levels. The levels include graphophonemic, morphemic, semantic, syntactic, pragmatic, and interpretive. Reading is conceived to be an interactive process. This means that analysis does not proceed in a stict order from the visual information in letters to the overall interpretation of a text. Instead, as a person reads, the interpretation of what a segment of a text might mean is theorized to depend both on analysis of the print and on hypotheses in the person's mind. Processes that flow from the print are called "bottom-up" or "data driven" whereas processes that flow in the other direction are called "top-down" or "hypothesis driven," following Bobrow and Norman (1975). In the passage about Tony, who is either a wrestler or a prisoner, processing the word *lock* has the potential to activate either a piece-of-hardware meaning or a wrestling-hold meaning. The hypothesis the reader has already formulated about the text tips the scales in the direction of one of the two meanings, usually without the reader's being aware that an alternative meaning is possible. Psychologists are at work developing detailed models of the mechanisms by which information from different levels of analysis is combined during reading (see Just & Carpenter, 1980; Rumelhart & McCelland, 1980).

The reader's schema affects both learning and remembering of the information and ideas in a text. Below, six functions of schemata that have been proposed (Anderson, 1978; Anderson & Pichert, 1978) are briefly explained.

A schema provides ideational scaffolding for assimilating text information. The idea is that a schema provides a niche, or slot, for certain text information. For instance, there is a slot for the main entree in a dining-at-a-fine-restaurant schema and a slot for the murder weapon in a who-done-it schema. Information that fits slots in the reader's schema is readily learned, perhaps with little mental effort.

A schema facilitates selective allocation of attention. A schema provides part of the basis for determining the important aspects of a text. It is hypothesized that skilled readers use importance as one basis for allocating cognitive resources—that is, for deciding where to pay close attention.

A schema enables inferential elaboration. No text is completely explicit. A reader's schema provides the basis for making inferences that go beyond the information literally stated in a text.

A schema allows orderly searches of memory. A schema can provide the reader with a guide to the types of information that need to be recalled. For instance, a person attempting to recall the food served at a fine meal can review the categories of food typically included in a fine meal: What was the appetizer? What was the soup? Was there a salad? And so on. In other words, by tracing through the schema used to structure the text, the reader is helped to gain access to the particular information learned when the text was read.

A schema facilitates editing and summarizing. Since a schema contains within itself criteria of importance, it enables the reader to produce summaries that include significant propositions and omit trivial ones.

A schema permits inferential reconstruction. When there are gaps in memory, a rememberer's schema, along with the specific text information that can be recalled, helps generate hypotheses about the missing information. For example, suppose a person cannot recall what beverage was served with a fine meal. If he can recall that the entree was fish, he will be able to infer that the beverage may have been white wine.

The foregoing are tentative hypotheses about the functions of a schema in text processing, conceived to provide the broadest possible interpretation of available data. Several of the hypotheses can be regarded as rivals—for instance, the ideational scaffolding hypothesis and the selective attention hypothesis—and it may be that not all of them will turn out to be viable. Researchers are now actively at work developing precise models of schema-based processes and subjecting these models to experimental test.

EVIDENCE FOR SCHEMA THEORY

There is now a really good case that schemata incorporating knowledge of the world play an important role in language comprehension. We are beginning to see research on differentiated functions. In a few years it should be possible to speak in more detail about the specific processing mechanisms in which schemata are involved.

Many of the claims of schema theory are nicely illustrated in a cross-cultural experiment, completed by Steffensen, Joag-Dev, and Anderson (1979), in which Indians (natives of India) and Americans read letters about an Indian and an American wedding. Of course, every adult member of a society has a well-developed marriage schema. There are substantial differences between Indian and American cultures in the nature of marriages. As a consequence, large differences in comprehension, learning, and memory for the letters were expected.

Table 1 summarizes analyses of the recall of the letters by Indian and American subjects. The first row in the table indicates the amount of time subjects spent reading the letters. As can be seen, subjects spent less time reading what for them was the native passage. This was as expected since a familiar schema should speed up and expedite a reader's processing.

The second row in Table 1 presents the number of idea units recalled. The gist measure includes not only propositions recalled verbatim but also acceptable paraphrases. The finding was precisely as expected. Americans recalled more of the American text, whereas Indians recalled more of the Indian passage. Within current formulations of schema theory, there are a couple of reasons for predicting that people would learn and remember more of a text about a marriage in their own culture: A culturally appropriate schema may provide the ideational scaffolding that makes it easy to learn information that fits into that schema, or, it may be that the information, once learned, is more accessible because the schema is a structure that makes it easy to search memory.

The row labeled *Elaborations* in Table 1 contains the frequency of culturally appropriate extensions of the text. The next row, labeled *Distortions,* contains the frequency of culturally inappropriate modifications of the text. Ever since Bartlett's day, elaborations and distortions have provided the intuitively most compelling evidence for the role of

TABLE 1
Mean Performance on Various Measures
(from Steffensen, Joag-Dev, & Anderson, 1979)

| Measure | Nationality | | | |
| | Americans | | Indians | |
	American Passage	Indian Passage	American Passage	Indian Passage
Time (seconds)	168	213	304	276
Gist Recall	52.4	37.9	27.3	37.6
Elaborations	5.7	.1	.2	5.4
Distortions	.1	7.6	5.5	.3
Other Overt Errors	7.5	5.2	8.0	5.9
Omissions	76.2	76.6	95.5	83.3

schemata. Many fascinating instances appeared in the protocols collected in the present study. A section of the American passage upon which interesting cultural differences surfaced read as follows:

> Did you know that Pam was going to wear her grandmother's wedding dress? That gave her something that was old, and borrowed, too. It was made of lace over satin, with very large puff sleeves and looked absolutely charming on her.

One Indian had this to say about the American bride's dress: "She was looking alright except the dress was too old and out of fashion." Wearing an heirloom wedding dress is a completely acceptable aspect of the pageantry of the American marriage ceremony. This Indian appears to have completely missed this and, has inferred that the dress was out of fashion, on the basis that Indians attach importance to displays of social status, manifested in such details as wearing an up-to-date, fashionable sari.

The gifts described in the Indian passage that were given to the groom's family by the bride's, the dowry, and the reference to the concern of the bride's family that a scooter might be requested were a source of confusion for our American subjects. First of all, the "agreement about the gifts to be given to the in-laws" was changed to "the exchange of gifts," a wording that suggests that gifts are flowing in two directions, not one. Another subject identified the gifts given to the in-laws as favors, which are often given in American weddings to the attendants by the bride and groom.

In another facet of the study, different groups of Indians and Americans read the letters and rated the significance of each of the propositions. It was expected that Americans would regard as important propositions conveying information about ritual and ceremony whereas Indians would see as important propositions dealing with financial and social status. Table 2 contains examples of text units that received contrasting ratings of importance from Indians and Americans. Schema theory predicts that text units that are important in the light of the schema are more likely to be learned and, once learned, are more likely to be remembered. This prediction was confirmed. Subjects did recall more text information rated as important by their cultural cohorts, whether recalling what for them was the native or the foreign text.

Of course, it is one thing to show, as Steffensen, Joag-dev, and Anderson did, that readers from distinctly different national cultures give different interpretations to culturally sensitive materials, and quite another to find the same phenomenon among readers from different but overlapping subcultures within the same country. A critical issue is whether cultural variation within the United States could be a factor in differential reading comprehension. Minority children could have a handicap if stories, texts, and test items presuppose a cultural perspective that the children do not share. An initial exploration of this issue has been completed by Reynolds, Taylor, Steffensen, Shirey, and Anderson (1982), who wrote a passage around an episode involving "sounding." Sounding is an activity predominantly found in the black community in which the participants try to outdo each other in an exchange of insults (Labov, 1972). In two group studies, and one in which subjects were individually interviewed, black teenagers tended to see the episode as involving friendly give-and-take, whereas white teenagers interpreted it as an ugly confrontation, sometimes one involving physical violence. For example, when attempting to recall the incident, a black male wrote, "That everybody tried to get on the person side that joke were the best." A white male wrote, "Soon there was a riot. All the kids were fighting." This research established that when written material has an identifiable cultural loading there is a pronounced effect on comprehension. It remains to be seen how much school reading material is culturally loaded.

In the foregoing research, schemata were manipulated by selecting subjects with different backgrounds. Another approach for getting people to bring different schemata to bear is by selecting different passages. Anderson, Spiro, and Anderson (1978) wrote two closely comparable passages, one about dining at a fancy restaurant, the other about a trip to a supermarket. The same eighteen items of food and beverage were mentioned in the two texts, in the same order, and attributed to the same characters. The first hypothesis was that subjects who received the restaurant passage would learn and recall more food and beverage information than subjects who received the supermarket passage. The reasoning was that a

TABLE 2

Examples of Idea Units of Contrasting Importance to Americans and Indians

American Passage		Indian Passage	
Idea Units More Important to Americans	*Idea Units More Important to Indians*	*Idea Units More Important to Americans*	*Idea Units More Important to Indians*
Then on Friday night they had the rehearsal at the church and the rehearsal dinner, which lasted until almost midnight.	She'll be lucky if she can even get her daughter married, the way things are going.	Prema's husband had to wear a dhoti for that ceremony and for the wedding the next day.	*Prema's in-laws seem to be nice enough people. They did not create any problem in the wedding, even though Prema's husband is their only son.*
All the attendants wore dresses that were specially designed to go with Pam's.	Her mother wore yellow, which looks great on her with her bleached hair, and George's mother wore pale green.	*There were only the usual essential rituals: the curtain removal, the parents giving the daughter away, walking seven step together, etc., and plenty of smoke from the sacred fire.*	*Since they did not ask for any dowry, Prema's parents were a little worried about their asking for a scooter before the wedding, but they didn't ask for one.*
Her mother wore yellow, which looks great on her with her bleached hair, and George's mother wore pale green.	Have you seen the diamond she has? It must have cost George a fortune because it's almost two carats.	There must have been about five hundred people at the wedding feast. Since only fifty people could be seated at one time, it went on for a long time.	*Prem's parents were very sad when she left.*

Note. Important idea units are in *italics*.

dining-at-a-fine-restaurant schema has a more constrained structure than a trip-to-a-supermarket schema. That is to say, fewer food and beverage items will fit the former schema; one could choose soda-pop and hot dogs at a supermarket, but these items would not be ordered at a fine restaurant. Moreover there are more cross-connections among items in a restaurant schema. For example, a steak will be accompanied by a baked potato, or maybe french fries. In two experiments, subjects who read the restaurant text recalled more food and beverage items than subjects who read the supermarket text.

The second prediction was that students who read the restaurant text would more often attribute the food and drink items to the correct characters. In a supermarket it does not matter, for instance, who throws the brussel sprouts into the shopping cart, but in a restaurant it does matter who orders which item. This prediction was confirmed in two experiments.

A third prediction was that order of recall of foods and beverages would correspond more closely to order of mention in the text for subjects who read the restaurant story. There is not, or need not be, a prescribed sequence for selecting items in a grocery store, but there is a characteristic order in which items are served in a restaurant. This hypothesis was supported in one experiment and the trend of the data favored it in a second.

Another technique for manipulating readers' schemata is by assigning them different perspectives. Pichert and Anderson (1977) asked people to pretend that they were either burglars or homebuyers before reading a story about what two boys did at one of the boys' homes while they were skipping school. The finding was that people learned more of the information important to their assigned perspective. For instance, burglars were more likely to learn that three 10-speed bikes were parked in the garage, whereas homebuyers were more likely to learn that the house had a leaky roof. Anderson and Pichert (1978; see also Anderson, Pichert, & Shirey, 1983) went on to show that the reader's perspective has independent effects on learning and recall. Subjects who switch perspectives and then recall the story for a second time recall additional, previously unrecalled, information important to their new perspective but unimportant to their original perspective. For example, a person who begins as a homebuyer may fail to remember that the story says the side door is kept unlocked, but may later remember this information when told to assume the role of a burglar. Subjects report that previously unrecalled information significant in the light of the new perspective "pops" into their heads.

Recent unpublished research in my laboratory, completed in collaboration with Ralph Reynolds and Paul Wilson, suggests selective allocation of attention to text elements that are important in the light of the reader's schema. We have employed two measures of attention. The first is the amount of time a subject spends reading schema-relevant sentences. The second is the response time to a probe presented during schema-relevant sentences. The probe is a tone sounded through earphones; the subject responds by pushing a button as fast as possible. The logic of the probe task is that if the mind is occupied with reading, there will be a slight delay in responding to the probe. Our results indicate that people assigned a burglar perspective, for instance, have slightly longer reading times and slightly longer probe times when reading burglar-relevant sentences. Comparable results have been obtained by other investigators (Cirilo & Foss, 1980; Haberlandt, Berian, & Sandson, 1980; Just & Carpenter, 1980).

IMPLICATIONS OF SCHEMA THEORY FOR DESIGN
OF MATERIALS AND CLASSROOM INSTRUCTION

First, I urge publishers to include teaching suggestions in manuals designed to help children activate relevant knowledge before reading. Children do not spontaneously integrate what they are reading with what they already know (cf. Paris & Lindauer, 1976). This means that special attention should be paid to preparation for reading. Questions should be asked that remind children of relevant experiences of their own and orient them toward the problems faced by story characters.

Second, the teachers' manuals accompanying basal programs and content area texts ought to include suggestions for building prerequisite knowledge when it cannot be safely presupposed. According to schema theory, this practice should promote comprehension. There is direct evidence to support knowledge-building activities. Hayes and Tierney (1980) asked American high school students to read and recall newspaper reports of cricket matches. Performance improved sharply when the students received instruction on the nature of the game of cricket before reading the newspaper reports.

Third, I call for publishers to feature lesson activities that will lead children to meaningfully integrate what they already know with what is presented on the printed page. From the perspective of schema theory, prediction techniques such as the Directed Reading-Thinking Activity (Stauffer, 1969) can be recommended. The DRTA would appear to cause readers to search their store of knowledge and integrate what they already know with what is stated. It must be acknowledged, however, that the empirical evidence for the efficacy of the DRTA is flimsy at present (Tierney & Cunningham, in press). Recently, Anderson, Mason, and Shirey (1983, Experiment 2) have illustrated that under optimum conditions strong benefits can be obtained using a prediction technique. A heterogeneous sample of third graders read sentences such as, "The stupid child ran into the street after the ball." Children in the prediction group read each sentence aloud and then indicated what might happen next. In the case of the sentence above, a frequent prediction was that the child might get hit by a car. A second group read the sentences aloud with an emphasis on accurate decoding. A third and a fourth group listened to the sentences and read them silently. The finding was that the prediction group recalled 72% of the sentences, whereas the average for the other three groups was 43%.

Fourth, I urge publishers to employ devices that will highlight the structure of text material. Schema theory inclines one to endorse the practice of providing advance organizers or structured overviews, along the lines proposed by Ausubel (1968) and Herber (1978). Ausubel, who can be regarded as one of the pioneer schema theorists, has stated that "the principal function of the organizer is to bridge the gap between what the learner already knows and what he needs to know before he can successfully learn the task at hand" (1968, p. 148). There have been dozens of empirical studies of advance organizers over the past 20 years. Thorough reviews of this bulky literature by Mayer (1979) and Luiten, Ames, and Ackerson (1980) point to the conclusion that organizers generally have a facilitative effect. Nevertheless, from within current formulations of schema theory, there is room for reservations about advance organizers. Notably, Ausubel's insistence (cf. 1968, pp. 148, 333) that organizers must be stated at a high level of generality, abstractness, and inclusiveness is puzzling. The problem is that general, abstract language often is difficult to understand. Children, in particular, are more easily reminded of what they know when concrete language is used. As Ausubel himself has acknowledged (e.g., 1968, p. 149), "To be useful . . . organizers themselves must obviously be learnable and must be stated in familiar terms."

A final implication of schema theory is that minority children may sometimes be counted as failing to comprehend school reading material because their schemata do not match those of the majority culture. Basal reading programs, content area texts, and standardized tests lean heavily on the conventional assumption that meaning is inherent in the words and structure of a text. When prior knowledge is required, it is assumed to be knowledge common to children from every subculture. When new ideas are introduced, these are assumed to be equally accessible to every child. Considering the strong effects that culture has on reading comprehension, the question that naturally arises is whether children from different subcultures can so confidently be assumed to bring a common schema to written material. To be sure, subcultures within this country do overlap.

But is it safe simply to *assume* that when reading the same story, children from every subculture will have the same experience with the setting, ascribe the same goals and motives to characters, imagine the same sequence of actions, predict the same emotional reactions, or expect the same outcomes? This is a question that the research community and the school publishing industry ought to address with renewed vigor.

REFERENCES

Anderson, R. C. Schema-directed processes in language comprehension. In A. Lesgold, J. Pellegrino, S. Fokkema, & R. Glaser (Eds.), *Cognitive psychology and instruction.* New York: Plenum, 1978.

Anderson, R. C., Mason, J. M., & Shirey, L. L. *The reading group. An experimental investigation of a labyrinth.* (Technical Report.) Urbana, U. of Illinois, Center for the Study of Reading, 1983, in press.

Anderson, R. C., & Pichert, J. W. Recall of previously unrecallable information following a shift in perspective. *Journal of Verbal Learning and Verbal Behavior,* 1978, *17,* 1–12.

Anderson, R. C., Pichert, J. W., & Shirey, L. L. Effects of the reader's schema at different points in time. *Journal of Educational Psychology,* 1983, in press.

Anderson, R. C., Reynolds, R. E., Schallert, D. L., & Goetz, E. T. Frameworks for comprehending discourse. American Educational Research Journal, 1977, 14, 367–382. *American Educational Research Journal,* 1977, *14,* 367–382.

Anderson, R. C., Spiro, R. J., & Anderson, M. C. Schemata as scaffolding for the representation of information in connected discourse. *American Educational Research Journal,* 1978, *15,* 433–440.

Ausubel, D. P. *Educational psychology: A cognitive view.* New York: Holt, Rinehart & Winston, 1968.

Bobrow, D. G., & Norman, D. A. Some principles of memory schemata. In D. G. Bobrow & A. Collins (Eds.), *Representation and understanding: Studies in cognitive science.* New York: Academic Press, 1975.

Bransford, J. C., & Johnson, M. K. Contextual prerequisites for understanding: Some investigations of comprehension and recall. *Journal of Verbal Learning and Verbal Behavior,* 1972, *11,* 717–726.

Bransford, J. D., & McCarrell, N. S. A sketch of a cognitive approach to comprehension. In W. B. Weimer & D. S. Palermo (Eds.), *Cognition and the symbolic processes.* Hillsdale, N.J.: Lawrence Erlbaum Associates, 1974.

Chiesi, H. L., Spilich, G. J., & Voss, J. F. Acquisition of domain-related information in relation to high- and low-domain knowledge. *Journal of Verbal Learning and Verbal Behavior,* 1979, *18,* 257–274.

Cirilo, R. K., & Foss, D. J. Text structure and reading time for sentences. *Journal of Verbal Learning and Verbal Behavior,* 1980, *19,* 96–109.

Haberlandt, K., Berian, C., & Sandson, J. The episode schema in story processing. *Journal of Verbal Learning and Verbal Behavior,* 1980, *19,* 635–650.

Hayes, D. A., & Tierney, R. J. *Increasing background knowledge through analogy: Its effects upon comprehension and learning* (Tech. Rep. No. 186). Urbana: University of Illinois, Center for the Study of Reading, October 1980. (ERIC Document Reproduction Service No. ED 195 953)

Herber, H. L. *Teaching reading in content areas* (2nd ed.). Englewood Cliffs, N.J.: Pren-tice-Hall, 1978.

Just, M. A., & Carpenter, P. A. A theory of reading: From eye fixations to comprehension. *Psychological Review*, 1980, *87*, 329–354.

Labov, W. *Language in the inner city: Studies in the Black English vernacular.* Washington, D. C.: Center for Applied Linguistics, 1972.

Luiten, J., Ames, W., & Ackerson, G. A meta-analysis of the effects of advance organizers on learning and retention. *American Educational Research Journal*, 1980, *17*, 211–218.

Mayer, R. E. Can advance organizers influence meaningful learning? *Review of Educational Research*, 1979, *49*, 371–383.

Paris, S. G., & Lindauer, B. K. The role of inference in children's comprehension and memory. *Cognitive Psychology*, 1976, *8*, 217–227.

Pichert, J. A., & Anderson, R. C. Taking different perspectives on a story. *Journal of Educational Psychology*, 1977, *69*, 309–315.

Reynolds, R. E., Taylor, M. A., Steffensen, M. S., Shirey, L. L., & Anderson, R. C. Cultural schemata and reading comprehension. *Reading Research Quarterly*, 1982, *17*, 353–366.

Rumelhart, D. E., & McCelland, J. L. *An interactive activation model of the effect of context in perception* (Part 2) (CHIP Technical Report). La Jolla: University of California, Center for Human Information Processing, 1980.

Stauffer, R. G. *Teaching reading as a thinking process.* New York: Harper & Row, 1969.

Steffensen, M. S., Joag-Dev, C., & Anderson, R. C. A cross-cultural perspective on reading comprehension. *Reading Research Quarterly*, 1979, *15*, 10–29.

Tierney, R. J., & Cunningham, J. W. Research on teaching reading comprehension. In P. D. Pearson, R. Barr, M. Kamil, & P. Mosenthal (Ed.), *Handbook of research in reading.* New York: Longman, in press.

Schema Activation and Schema Acquisition: Comments on Richard C. Anderson's Remarks

John D. Bransford
Vanderbilt University

Professor Anderson has done an excellent job of presenting the essentials of schema theory and of highlighting a number of its implications. My comments on his chapter are divided into two parts. First, I want to reemphasize some of Anderson's major arguments and elaborate on several of their implications. I then discuss some potential shortcomings of many versions of schema theory and suggest some modifications that seem relevant to the issue of understanding how people learn from texts.

Several of Anderson's points about schema theory can be reviewed by considering the processes involved in understanding, and later remembering, a simple statement such as the following: "Jane decided not to wear her matching silver necklace, earrings, and belt because she was going to the airport." In order to comprehend this statement, one must go beyond the information that was given and postulate a reason for the connection between airports and Jane's style of dress. People who are familiar with airports—who have a well-developed "airport schema"—might assume that Jane decided not to wear her silver jewelry because of the metal detectors in airports. In Anderson's terminology, their schemas provide a basis for interpreting and elaborating on the information that they heard.

Anderson also argued that schemas affect processes at the time of output as well as at input. For example, adults who attempt to recall the original "airport" statement three days later may rely on their knowledge of airports for a selective search of memory and then state that "Jane decided not to wear some metal jewelry because it could cause unnecessary delays at the airport." Note that this type of response reveals the comprehender's assumptions about important elements. It is the fact that

259

the jewelry was metal that was most important and not, for example, that it was expensive or pretty. Anderson also emphasized this function of schemas: They provide a basis for determining the important elements in a message or text.

Overall, Anderson discussed six functions of schemas. They provide a basis for (a) assimilating text information, (b) making inferential elaborations that fill in the gaps in messages, (c) allocating attention to important text elements, (d) searching memory in an orderly fashion, (e) formulating a summary of information, and (f) making inferences that can enable one to reconstruct an original message despite having forgotten some of the details. It may be possible to add to Professor Anderson's list of "schema functions," but the six functions he cited are sufficient to illustrate why the knowledge possessed by the learner has pervasive effects on performance. I might add that Dr. Anderson was not simply arguing that the activation of appropriate knowledge is a useful thing to do; he was asserting that it is a fundamental aspect of the act of comprehending and remembering. One clear implication of this position is that some children may appear to have poor comprehension and memory skills *not* because they have some inherent comprehension or memory "deficits," but because they lack, or fail to activate, the background knowledge that was presupposed by a message or a text.

It is instructive to note that there are many levels at which a child may lack the background knowledge necessary to understand a text. At one extreme, the child may have no information about a concept; he or she may know nothing about airports, for example. At another level, a child may know something about a concept (for example, airports) yet still fail to understand many statements that involve this concept. As an illustration, consider once again the simple statement about Jane's trip to the airport and her decision about her silver jewelry. A child may know that airports are "places where planes take off and land" yet have no knowledge that airports contain metal detectors. The child therefore knows something about airports, but his or her "airport schema" is still less articulated than that of most adults. The child's knowledge may be sufficient for understanding some types of statements about airports (e.g., John went to the airport because his aunt was coming to visit) yet insufficient for others (e.g., the earlier statement about Jane). The question of what it means for children to be "familiar" with the words used in a story is therefore more complicated than might be apparent at first glance.

Imagine another child who knows that airports are places where planes land and take off, and also knows that airports are often crowded and may be havens for thieves. This child may form the following interpretation of the statement about Jane and the airport: "Jane did not wear her expensive jewelry because she was afraid that someone might take it." This interpretation is quite different from one that focuses on the fact that airports have metal detectors. According to the "crowded airport" interpretation, the important elements are that the jewelry is valuable, visible, and easily accessible, rather than the fact that the jewelry is metal and hence may trigger a security alarm. Relatively subtle differences in people's schemas (in this case their "airport schemas") can therefore have important effects on the interpretations they make.

Consider some of the problems that can arise when two people form different interpretations of the same message. For example, imagine that a teacher forms a "metal detector" interpretation of the statement about Jane and that a child forms a "thief" interpretation. In a one-to-one conversation, these two individuals might well discover their differences in interpretation and agree that both are reasonable. However, extended one-to-one conversations are often impossible in an educational setting. Teachers are frequently forced to use assessment questions in order to evaluate students' comprehension. These questions may be supplied either by the author of a text or by the teacher. In either case, the phrasing of the question may reflect the question asker's initial interpretations of a message. For example, a question such as "Why didn't Jane wear something metal?" may stem from a "metal detector" interpretation, whereas the question, "Why didn't Jane wear her expensive jewelry?" tends to reflect a "thief" interpretation. My colleagues and I have found that even relatively subtle mismatches between a learner's initial interpretations and a teacher's or a tester's way of phrasing questions can cause considerable decrements in memory performance (Barclay, Bransford, Franks, McCarrell, & Nitsch, 1974). If my phrasing of a question is not congruent with a child's initial interpretation of an event, I may erroneously conclude that the child did not learn.

Mismatches between the phrasing of questions and a child's initial interpretations affect not only teachers' assessments of children's learning abilities; I am convinced that they also affect children's assumptions about their own abilities. Several years ago, Marcia Johnson and I conducted a study with college students that is relevant to this point (Bransford & Johnson, 1973). We created a passage about a man walking through the woods; nearly all our students interpreted the story as describing a hunter. They did not realize that the passage could also be interpreted from the perspective of an escaping convict. As Anderson noted, the perspective one takes on a story affects one's interpretation of the significance of information. For example, the story included information about it being muddy, hence the man's boots sunk in deeply. He then came to a little stream and walked in it for awhile. From the perspective of a hunter, this information suggests that the boots may have become caked with mud and that the man tried to clean them by walking in the stream.

From the perspective of an escaping convict, however, the same information suggests that the man was leaving footprints and must take precautions in order to avoid being tracked.

We asked one group of college students to read the story I have described but said nothing about the possibility of interpreting it as an escaping convict. They therefore assumed that it was about a hunter, and the story made sense from this point of view. After reading the story, we supplied students with questions and explained that these should help them retrieve the information they had studied. However, the questions were written from the perspective of the escaping convict interpretation. For example, one question was "What was the concern with the trail and what was done to eliminate it?" Not surprisingly, these questions did not help students remember relevant aspects of the story; instead they caused confusion. Many of the students thought about the questions for a considerable amount of time and eventually concluded that they had completely misinterpreted the story. Several apologized for having made such an error. In reality, however, they had not "misinterpreted" the story; their original interpretations had been perfectly reasonable. We eventually told the students this, of course, because it would have been unfair to let them think they had been in error. The point I want to stress, however, is that these mismatches between initial interpretations and the phrasing of questions can occur inadvertently in almost any situation. Furthermore, learners who do not realize why their performance suffered may mistakenly attribute their difficulties to their own inabilities to learn.

The preceding examples illustrate only a few of many important implications of schema theory, but I now want to consider some possible shortcomings of many versions of this theory. I refer to these as *possible* shortcomings because I am uncertain whether they are shortcomings of the actual theory or shortcomings that stem from my personal interpretation of schema theory (i.e., my "schema theory schema" may be only partially developed). At any rate, I believe that there are some issues concerning schema theory that need to be explored, especially when one begins to ask how teachers and authors might use this theory to help them avoid some of the text-student mismatches and question-student mismatches that have been discussed.

One possible approach to the problem of mismatches is to analyze carefully the materials presented to children and then to simplify them so that mismatches are much less likely to occur. There are some obvious merits to this approach, but it involves some potential problems as well. These problems revolve around the issue of what it means to "simplify" texts.

Several years ago, I participated in a conference where the topic of simplifying texts arose during one of the discussion periods. One of the participants at the conference expressed some concerns about the reading materials that his children had received in the elementary grades (see Kavanagh & Strange, 1978, p. 329–330). He felt that the content of the stories (e.g., about a milkman, mailman, etc.) was extremely dull. When he asked the teachers why the children received such uninteresting materials, he was told that the children were familiar with the "community helpers." The teachers had not read about schema theory, so they did not say, "These stories are written to be congruent with the children's preexisting schemas." Nevertheless, the teachers were emphasizing the importance of providing children with materials that were congruent with the knowledge they already possessed.

The conference participant went on to say that his children did not like to read stories about topics that were extremely familiar; they were much more interested in reading about novel situations. In addition, he asked how theories that emphasize the importance of assimilating information to pre-existing knowledge can account for the fact that it is possible to understand stories about novel situations. I think that this is a crucial question to ask schema theorists. It is especially crucial for those schema theorists who argue that comprehension involves the activation of a pre-existing schema that provides a coherent account of the givens in a message. Many schema theorists have very little to say about the processes by which novel events are comprehended and new schemas are acquired.

In his chapter, Professor Anderson mentioned two types of situations involving schemas. One involves the activation of pre-existing schemas. The second, which he noted was more interesting, involves the construction of new schemas. Since a major goal of education is to help students develop new skills and knowledge—to help them become able to understand things that they could not understand previously—the issue of schema construction or schema acquisition is extremely important. Nevertheless, nearly all the experiments used to support schema theory involve situations where students are prompted to activate pre-existing schemas. For example, students may be prompted to activate a "washing clothes" schema, "prisoner" schema, "fancy restaurant" schema, "homebuyer" schema, and so forth. We have seen that these schemas provide important support for both comprehension processes and memory processes. However, experiments involving these schemas "work" only because the students in the experiments have already acquired the necessary schemas. If a person knew nothing about washing clothes, for example, it would do no good to simply tell him or her that this is the topic of the washing-clothes passage. Similarly, imagine that a child is told that "Jane did not wear her silver jewelry because she was going somewhere" and is then given the cue "She is going to the airport." A child who knows only that airports are places where planes take off and land is still going to have difficulty understanding this statement. In situations such as this we confront the problem of helping the students develop new schemas or of helping them refine the structure of schemas that they have already acquired (e.g., Bransford & Nitsch, 1978; Bransford, Nitsch, & Franks, 1977; Brown, 1979).

Imagine that we want to help a child develop a more sophisticated "airport schema." We will assume that the child knows that airports are places where planes take off and land, yet is unaware that there are metal detectors in airports. A basic and time-honored procedure for helping the child acquire this new information is to tell him or her about it. One might therefore supply information such as "There are metal detectors in airports" either prior to the child's reading a text or in the text itself.

There are many reasons why a statement such as "There are metal detectors in airports" may be unhelpful to a child. An obvious reason is that a child may not be familiar with the concept of metal detectors. However, assume that our child is familiar with this general concept. He or she may still not benefit from the statement that "There are metal detectors in airports." The child needs to understand what the detectors are for and who uses them. Without this information, the child may assume that there are stores in airports that sell things, and hence conclude that most airports have "metal detector" stores. This is not the interpretation we want the child to make.

It seems clear that effective teachers or writers would do much more than simply state "There are metal detectors in airports." They would elaborate by helping the child realize that pilots guide planes to particular locations, that someone could try to force a pilot to fly to a different location, that this act may involve a gun or a knife, that these objects can be detected by metal detectors, that the detectors at the airport are designed to keep people from taking knives and guns aboard the plane and so forth. The amount of explanation needed will depend on the pre-existing knowledge base of the learner (e.g., a relatively knowledgeable child may need only be told that "There are metal detectors in airports in order to discourage hijacking"). The point I want to emphasize is that the goal of this instruction is to help the child develop a more sophisticated schema rather than simply to activate a schema that already exists. The teacher or author is attempting to help the child activate various pre-existing "packets" of knowledge that previously had been unrelated, and to help the child reassemble these "packets" of knowledge into an integrated schema. This schema should then provide support for comprehending and remembering subsequent events. For example, the child's interpretation of "the metal-detector repairman received a phone call and rushed to the airport" may now be more likely to involve the assumption that he was rushing to repair a machine rather than rushing to catch a plane or to meet someone arriving by plane.

At a general level, an emphasis on the importance of helping students activate sources of pre-existing knowledge that can be reassembled into new schemas is consistent with Ausubel's (1963; 1968) theory of meaningful learning. For example, he advocates the use of "advance organizers" in order to prepare students for texts. I think it's fair to say, however, that many aspects of this theory need greater articulation; in particular, the guidelines for writing advance organizers are relatively vague. One of the difficulties of constructing these guidelines is that advance organizers must differ depending on whether one is dealing with a problem of schema activation or schema construction. An advance organizer that is relatively general can be effective if learners have already acquired the schemas necessary for understanding a text; these general statements can prime concepts that learners might fail to activate spontaneously. When one is dealing with problems of schema construction or acquisition, however, advance organizers composed of general statements will not suffice.

Earlier, I emphasized some of the specific elaborations or explanations that may be required to help a child incorporate information about metal detectors into his or her airport schema. It seems valuable to explore this issue further by examining the processes involved in acquiring knowledge about a more complex domain. Imagine, therefore, that someone is familiar with the general terms "vein" and "artery," yet wants to learn more about them. (This is analogous to knowing something about airports, yet needing additional information.) Assume that the person reads a passage that states that arteries are thick, are elastic, and carry blood that is rich in oxygen from the heart; veins are thinner, are less elastic, and carry blood rich in carbon dioxide back to the heart. To the biological novice, even this relatively simple set of facts can seem arbitrary and confusing. Was it veins or arteries that are thin? Was the thin one or the thick one elastic? Which one carries carbon dioxide from the heart (or was it to the heart)?

Even the biological novice who is familiar with the terms "veins" and "arteries" may have difficulty learning the information in this passage. The problem the learner faces is that the facts and relationships appear arbitrary. It is possible to create an analogous situation by using concepts that are familiar to everyone. For example, imagine reading 10 statements such as those listed below and then answering questions about them from memory:

The tall man bought the crackers.
The bald man read the newspaper.
The funny man liked the ring.

The hungry man purchased the tie.
The short man used the broom.
The strong man skimmed the book.

College students do quite poorly when they are presented with these statements and are then asked memory questions such as "Which man bought the crackers?" (Stein & Bransford, 1979; Stein, Morris, & Bransford, 1978). The students rate each sentence as comprehensible, yet have difficulty remembering because the relationship between each type of man and the actions performed seem arbitrary. The biological novice is in a similar position because he or she sees no particular reason why an artery should be elastic or nonelastic, thick or thin. Note that to a child, a statement such as "Airports have metal detectors" can also seem arbitrary. The child may therefore have difficulty retaining the new information about airports; hence it will not be available for future use. This problem of retention becomes even more acute if we make the reasonable assumption that children are introduced to a number of new ideas during the course of a day. For example, they may receive new information about airports, fancy restaurants, dinosaurs, countries, and so forth. If these new facts seem arbitrary, it can be difficult to remember which things go with what.

In order to make the facts less arbitrary, we need to give a learner information that can clarify their significance or relevance (see Bransford, Stein, Shelton, & Owings, 1981). For example, what's the significance of the elasticity of arteries? How does this property relate to the functions that arteries perform? Note that our imaginary passage states that arteries carry blood from the heart—blood that is pumped in spurts. This provides one clue about the significance of elasticity—arteries may need to expand and contract to accommodate the pumping of blood. It can also be important to understand why veins do *not* need to be elastic. Since veins carry blood back to the heart, they may have less of a need to accommodate the large changes in pressure resulting from the heart pumping blood in spurts.

The process of clarifying the significance of facts about veins and arteries can be carried further. Since arteries carry blood *from* the heart, there is a problem of directionality. Why doesn't the blood flow back into the heart? This will not be perceived as a problem if one assumes that arterial blood always flows downhill, but let's assume that our passage mentions that there are arteries in the neck and shoulder regions. Arterial blood must therefore flow uphill as well. This information might provide an additional clue about the significance of elasticity. If arteries expand from a spurt of blood and then contract, this might help the blood move in a particular direction. Arteries might therefore perform a function similar to one-way valves.

My colleagues and I have argued that there are at least two important consequences of activities that enable a learner to understand the significance or relevance of new factual content (e.g., Bransford, Stein, Shelton, & Owings, 1981). First, people who understand the significance of facts develop knowledge structures that enable them to deal with novel situations. As an illustration, imagine that a biological novice reads a passage about veins and arteries and is then given the task of designing an artificial artery. Would it have to be elastic? A person who has merely memorized the fact that "arteries are elastic" would have little basis for answering the question. In contrast, the person who understands the significance or relevance of elasticity is in a much better position to approach the problem. For example, this person might realize the possibility of using a relatively nonelastic material that is sufficient to withstand the pressure requirements of spurting blood, plus realize the possibility of equipping the artificial artery with one-way valves that direct the flow of blood. This individual may not be able to specify all the details for creating the artificial artery, of course, but he or she at least has some appreciation of various possibilities and has an idea of the types of additional information that need to be discovered or acquired.

Activities that enable people to understand the significance of new factual content also facilitate memory. Facts that initially had seemed arbitrary and confusing become meaningful; the information is therefore much easier to retain. As an illustration, consider once again the earlier statements about the different types of men. I noted that college students have a difficult time remembering which man did what because the relationship between the type of man and the actions performed seem arbitrary. These same statements become easy to remember if students are supplied with information, or are helped to generate information, that renders these relationships less arbitrary (Stein & Bransford, 1979). For example:

> The tall man purchased the crackers that had been lying on the top shelf.
> The bald man read the newspaper in order to look for a hat sale.
> The funny man liked the ring that squirted water.
> The hungry man purchased the tie so that he could get into the fancy restaurant.
> The short man used the broom to operate the light switch.
> The strong man skimmed the book about weight lifting.

Elaborations such as these help people understand the significance or relevance of linking a particular type of man to a particular activity. They are therefore able to answer memory questions such as "Which man purchased the tie?", "Which man used the broom?", etc. In a similar manner, people who understand the significance of various properties of veins and arteries (e.g., the significance of the elasticity of arteries) are able to remember which properties go with what, and the child who understands the significance of having metal detectors in airports is better able to remember this fact.

It is important to note, however, that there are constraints on the type of additional information, or elaborations, that will enable students to understand the significance or relevance of new facts. As an example, consider the following list:

> The tall man purchased the crackers from the clerk in the store.
> The bald man read the newspaper while eating breakfast.
> The funny man liked the ring that he received as a present.
> The hungry man purchased the tie that was on sale.
> The short man used the broom to sweep the porch.
> The strong man skimmed the book before going to sleep.

These statements include elaborations that make sense semantically, but the elaborations do not help one understand why a particular type of man performed a particular activity. College students who receive a list of 10 sentences such as those above do *worse* than students who received the first list (the list *without* any additional elaboration; Stein & Bransford, 1979). My colleagues and I refer to elaborations such as those just noted as *imprecise* elaborations. In contrast, *precise* elaborations (such as those provided earlier) clarify the significance or relevance of facts (Stein & Bransford, 1979; Stein, Morris, & Bransford, 1978). Imprecise elaborations can make sense semantically; that is, they need not be nonsense. Nevertheless, they can actually produce poorer memory than a set of arbitrary statements that receive no elaborations at all. Note that there are many potential elaborations of facts about veins and arteries, airports, etc. that would also be imprecise. For example, the statement "Arteries are elastic so that they can stretch" does not help one understand why they need to be elastic, and the statement "There are metal detectors in airports that are used to check passengers" does not help one understand what is being checked or why.

An emphasis on the degree of precision necessary to help people understand the significance of facts is important for analyzing the issue of what it means to "simplify" texts. A text can be composed of relatively simple words and simple syntax yet still seem quite arbitrary. My colleagues and I asked metropolitan Nashville teachers to provide us with samples of some of the passages their elementary school students are asked to read, and found a large number that seem arbitrary. For example, one passage discussed the topic of "American Indian Houses." It consisted of statements such as "The Indians of the Northwest Coast lived in slant-roofed houses made of cedar plank . . . Some California Indian tribes lived in simple, earth-covered or brush shelters . . . The Plains Indians lived mainly in tepees," etc. The story provided no information about why certain Indians chose certain houses. For example, it said nothing about the relationship between the type of house and the climate of the geographical area, nor about the ease of finding raw materials to build houses depending on the geographical area. Furthermore, the story said nothing about how the style of house was related to the lifestyle of the Indians (e.g., tepees are relatively portable). If students either did not know, or failed to activate this extra information, the passage was essentially a list of seemingly arbitrary facts.

Other passages we examined discussed topics such as tools, animals, machines, and so forth. In each case, the passages contained a number of facts, yet frequently failed to provide the information necessary to understand the significance of the facts. For example, a passage describing two types of boomerangs—a returning versus a nonreturning boomerang—provided information about each boomerang's shape, weight, length, function, and so forth. However, it failed to systematically help the reader understand how the structure of each boomerang was related to its function (e.g., how the shape affected whether it returned to the thrower or not, how the weight was a factor in determining whether a boomerang could be used to hunt small versus large game, and so forth). The passages about animals also failed to help students focus on relationships between structure and function. For example, camels have a number of properties that help them adapt to certain aspects of desert life, including desert sandstorms. Facts such as "camels can close their nose passages" and "camels have thick hair around their ear openings" become more significant when one understands how they reduce problems caused by blowing sand. Students who are unable to make these connections on their own experience difficulty because the facts seem arbitrary. They also fail to develop a level of understanding that can provide support for learning subsequent materials. For example, a student who realizes how various properties of camels protect them during sandstorms is in a better position to understand a subsequent story about desert travelers who wear scarves over their faces even though it is hot.

It is important to note that passages such as the ones I have described do not necessarily seem arbitrary to someone who has already developed expertise in these areas. The expert not only already knows the facts but also understands their significance or relevance. Even new facts (e.g., camels can close their nose passages) can seem meaningful to the person whose pre-existing schemas provide a basis for understanding their significance (e.g., a person may already know that camels are adapted to survive in desert sandstorms). Adults who construct or evaluate passages for children are usually in a "schema activation" mode, but children who read these passages are usually confronted with the problem of constructing new schemas or of developing more detailed schemas. This is as it should be; the goal of the educator is to help children develop new skills and knowledge. However, we need to recognize that schema activation and schema construction represent two different problems. Our attempts to simplify texts can be self-defeating if we inadvertently omit the kinds of precise elaborations necessary for understanding the significance of the information. Indeed, we may sometimes need to introduce children to relatively sophisticated concepts that can provide a basis for more precise understanding. For example, the general concept of adaptation (of structure-function relationships) provides a powerful schema that supports the comprehension of new facts in a number of domains (e.g., structure-function relationships are important for understanding biological systems such as veins and arteries, tools such as different types of boomerangs, animals and environments such as camels and their desert habitats, and so forth). The careful introduction of core concepts such as this one may facilitate learning to a considerable degree.

SUMMARY AND CONCLUSIONS

I began by reemphasizing Professor Anderson's arguments about schema theory because they are extremely important. For example, Dr. Anderson's discussion of the six functions of schemas provided a powerful argument for the pervasive effects of students' pre-existing knowledge. I elaborated on two implications of his argument. One implication was that students may have developed partial schemas that are sufficient for understanding some types of statements but not for understanding others. We therefore need a more precise analysis of what it means for students to be "familiar" with the words in a text. The second implication was that pre-existing schemas affect the interpretation of teachers and authors as well as the interpretation of students, and that a person's interpretation can affect the way he or she phrases test questions. If there is a mismatch between the phrasing of a question and a student's interpretation of a passage, decrements in performance can occur.

Most of my comments were directed at differences between schema activation and schema construction. Professor Anderson noted that these represented two different (although related) problems. Most of the experiments he discussed dealt with schema activation because this represents the current state of the experimental literature. I emphasized schema construction because a major task for the educator is to help children develop new knowledge and skills.

The concept of precision provided the framework for my discussion of schema construction. To the novice, new facts can seem arbitrary unless they are precisely elaborated in a way that clarifies their significance or relevance. New facts that are not elaborated, or that are imprecisely elaborated, are difficult to remember and hence are not available for future use. In contrast, precisely elaborated facts can be integrated into new schemas that can provide support for the comprehension of subsequent texts. I also noted that texts can be composed of simple words and syntax yet can still seem arbitrary to the novice; the notion of what it means to "simplify" texts therefore warrants careful consideration. Indeed, we may need to introduce children to relatively sophisticated "core concepts" that can provide a basis for understanding the significance of a wide variety of new facts.

The final point I want to emphasize involves an issue that I have not mentioned but one that I feel is extremely important. I have noted that texts which are not precisely elaborated can seem arbitrary to the novice, but I don't believe that children's materials should always be elaborated explicitly. The reason is that children must learn to identify situations where they need more information in order to understand precisely, and they must learn to supply their own elaborations. More generally, I believe that they must learn about themselves as learners. This includes an understanding of how different texts and text structures influence their abilities to comprehend new information and to remember it at later points in time.

My colleagues and I have been working with fifth graders who are proficient at decoding but who differ in their abilities to learn from texts. In contrast to the successful learners in our samples, our less successful learners have very little insight into the factors that make things easy or difficult to comprehend and remember, and they rarely attempt to use information that is potentially available to understand the significance or relevance of new facts. Their ability to learn is therefore impaired. We have created sets of materials that enable these students to experience the effects of their own learning activities and that enable them to learn to modify their activities. We find that these exercises can improve their performance considerably. In order to do this, however, we purposely create materials that are arbitrary (we like to think of these as "advance disorganizers"), help the students evaluate these materials and experience their effects on memory, and then help them learn what to do to make the same materials significant or relevant. This seems necessary in order to help the students learn to learn on their own. The learning-to-learn issue is beyond the scope of Professor Anderson's paper and mine; Armbruster and Brown discuss this issue elsewhere in this volume. I simply wanted to mention the issue at this point in order to emphasize that the procedures necessary to make texts easy to learn are not necessarily identical to those necessary to help children learn to learn on their own.

ACKNOWLEDGMENTS

Preparation of this paper was supported, in part, by Grant NIE 6–79–0117. Many of the ideas discussed in this chapter were developed in conjunction with Jeffery Franks, Barry Stein, and Nancy Vye.

REFERENCES

Ausubel, D. *The psychology of meaningful verbal learning.* New York: Grune & Stratton, 1963.

Ausubel, D. *Educational psychology: A cognitive view.* New York: Holt, Rinehart, & Winston, 1968.

Barclay, J. R., Bransford, J. D., Franks, J. J., McCarrell, N. S., & Nitsch, K. Comprehension and semantic flexibility. *Journal of Verbal Learning and Verbal Behavior,* 1974, *13,* 471–481.

Bransford, J. D., & Johnson, M. K. Considerations of some problems of comprehension. In W. Chase (Ed.), *Visual information processing.* New York: Academic Press, 1973.

Bransford, J. D., & Nitsch, K. E. Coming to understand things we could not previously understand. In J. F. Kavanagh & W. Strange (Eds.), *Speech and language in the laboratory, school, and clinic.* Cambridge, Mass.: M.I.T. Press, 1978.

Bransford, J. D., Nitsch, K. E., & Franks, J. J. Schooling and the facilitation of knowing. In R. C. Anderson, R. J. Spiro, & W. E. Montague (Eds.), *Schooling and the acquisition of knowledge.* Hillsdale, N.J.: Lawrence Erlbaum Associates, 1977.

Bransford, J. D., Stein, B. S., Shelton, T. S., & Owings, R. A. Cognition and adaptation: The importance of learning to learn. In J. Harvey (Ed.), *Cognition, social behavior, and the environment.* Hillsdale, N.J.: Lawrence Erlbaum Associates, 1981.

Brown, A. L. Theories of memory and the problems of development: Activity, growth, and knowledge. In L. S. Cermak & F. I. M. Craik (Eds.), *Levels of processing and human memory.* Hillsdale, N.J. Lawrence Erlbaum Associates, 1979.

Kavanagh, J. F., & Strange, W. (Eds.), *Speech and language in the laboratory, school and clinic.* Cambridge, Mass.: M.I.T. Press, 1978.

Stein, B. S., & Bransford, J. D. Constraints on effective elaboration: Effects of precision and subject generation. *Journal of Verbal Learning and Verbal Behavior,* 1979, *18,* 769–777.

Stein, B. S., Morris, C. D., & Bransford, J. D. Constraints on effective elaboration. *Journal of Verbal Learning and Verbal Behavior,* 1978, *17,* 707–714.

9 Learning From Reading: The Role of Metacognition

Bonnie B. Armbruster
Ann L. Brown
Center for the Study of Reading
University of Illinois at Urbana-Champaign

Those of us who study reading in an attempt to help students learn to learn from text are humbled by the incredible complexity of the process of learning from written materials. Brown (e.g., Brown, 1982; Brown, Campione, & Day, 1981) has tried to capture this complexity in a tetrahedral model of learning. According to this model, four major variables enter into the learning situation. These are (a) the criterion task, or the endpoint for which the learners are preparing (completing a workbook exercise, taking a test, writing a report, solving a problem, performing an experiment), (b) the nature of the material to be learned (stories, informative text, directions, maps, tables), (c) the general characteristics of the learners (their prior experience, background knowledge, ability, interests, motivation), and (d) the activities engaged in by the learners (their strategies and tactics for making learning successful).

Efficient and effective learning depends on the orchestration of these variables. The orchestration is accomplished by a higher-order process, called *metacognition*. The purpose of this chapter is first to discuss the role of metacognition in learning from reading, and then to describe some promising results of attempts to teach students to employ metacognitive skills in learning from reading. Finally, we present suggestions for helping students learn to learn from reading.

METACOGNITION IN LEARNING FROM READING

In a recent review of the literature, Baker and Brown (in press) argue that it is necessary to distinguish between two closely related types of metacognition: (a) knowledge about cognition and (b) regulation of cogni-

273

tion. The first type of metacognition, knowledge about cognition, refers to knowledge readers have about their own constellation of component variables: their repertoire of abilities and activities and the compatibility between these and the demands of the text and the criterion task.

The second type of metacognition, regulation of cognition, consists of the self-regulatory mechanisms used by an active learner during reading. These mechanisms include planning one's next move, checking the outcomes of any strategies one might use, monitoring the effectiveness of any attempted action, and testing, revising, and evaluating one's strategies for learning.

Expert readers monitor their comprehension and retention; they evaluate their progress in light of the demands of the criterion task and text. The cognitive monitoring processes are not usually experienced consciously. That is, good readers proceed as if on automatic pilot until a comprehension problem is detected. Some triggering event (Brown, 1980; Collins, Brown, Morgan, & Brewer, 1977) alerts them to a comprehension failure. Then and only then does the understanding process slow down and become planful, demanding conscious effort. In less successful readers, on the other hand, the self-regulatory activities have not become automatic. These readers are much less aware of the need to be strategic, to plan ahead, and to monitor their own understanding. In other words, they have not yet learned how to learn from texts efficiently and effectively.

The importance of self-awareness and self-control during learning was recognized well before the current popularity of metacognitive theories; indeed, educational psychologists at the beginning of the century (e.g., Dewey, 1910; Huey, 1908/1968; Thorndike, 1917) were quite aware that reading involved the planning, checking, and evaluating activities now called metacognitive skills. For example, Dewey's system of inducing reflective thinking was essentially a call for metacognitive training. The aim was to induce active monitoring, critical evaluation, and deliberate "seeking after meaning and relationships." Similarly, Thorndike (1917) claimed that reading was reasoning and involved a great many activities now called metacognition.

> Understanding a paragraph is like solving a math problem. It consists of selecting the right elements of the situation and putting them together in the right relations, and also with the right amount of weight or influence or force for each. The mind is assailed as it were by every word in the paragraph. It must select, repress, soften, emphasize, correlate and organize, all under the influence of the right mental set or purpose or demand. (p. 329)

Although the term *metacognitive* may be new, the type of knowledge to which it refers has long been recognized.

Today we know that metacognitive skills develop gradually and emerge later than most other cognitive skills. For example, consider the metacognitive skill of selecting and studying the main idea of a text, a skill essential to efficient, effective learning from text. In a study by Brown & Smiley (1977), 8-, 10-, 12-, and 18-year-olds were asked to rate the ideas of complex folk stories according to their importance to the theme of the passage. The rating task entailed sorting each idea in the story into one of four groups ranging from least to most important. Only 18-year-olds could reliably distinguish four levels of importance or centrality to the theme. Twelve-year-olds assigned lowest scores to least important and highest scores to most important elements, but were not able to differentiate intermediate levels of importance. Ten-year-olds could only distinguish the highest level of importance from all other levels. Eight-year-olds could make no reliable distinctions between levels of importance.

After rating a story for the importance of its ideas, students were asked to read and recall another story. For students at all ages, the most important ideas were most often recalled, while the least important ideas were seldom recalled. Thus, even without conscious awareness of the relative importance of ideas, younger children still favored the important information in recall. Apparently, readers spontaneously abstract main ideas even when they do not deliberately attempt to do so.

These findings have important implications for learning from reading. In order to retain more than just a few main points, i.e., to achieve a more complete "fleshed-out" memory of the text, one must engage in active strategies to ensure increased attention to important material that will not be retained "automatically." This need for active intervention is particularly pressing if the contents of lengthy texts are to be retained over some period of time. This is the kind of demand that is typical of the school learning situation. If young children have difficulty distinguishing what is important, they will also have difficulty learning from reading. Quite simply, one cannot selectively attend to important information in the absence of a fine sensitivity to what *is* important.

In a follow-up study (Brown & Smiley, 1978), students were assigned texts to read and given extra time to study the texts. While children from seventh grade up improved their recall for important elements of text, children below seventh grade did not usually show such improvement, even when given extra time to study. An examination of the physical records provided by the students—underlining and notes—revealed that children who spontaneously underlined or took notes while studying tended to focus on important elements of the texts, while children who were *induced* to use one of these strategies took notes or underlined more randomly. Furthermore, the recall of spontaneous users of the strategies was much superior to that of induced users. Even fifth graders who spontaneously underlined showed an adult-like pattern and used extra study to differentially improve their recall of importance elements.

Brown and Smiley (1978) believe that older students and spontaneous strategy users are able to benefit from increased study time as a direct result of their insights into their own cognitive processes during reading and their ability to predict the important elements of the text. Younger students failed to distribute extra time intelligently. They did not concentrate on only the important elements of the text, since they could not predict what they were.

Another series of studies (Brown, Campione, & Day, 1981; Brown & Day, 1980; Day, 1980) were conducted to investigate the development of the ability to write summaries of texts. Summary writing requires the metacognitive skills of judging fine degrees of relative importance and of condensing ideas. Students from fifth, seventh, and eleventh grades, as well as college-age students, were asked to read and learn a story and then to summarize the story. Evaluation of their summaries showed clear developmental trends. Compared to the younger students, college students and eleventh graders showed a much greater propensity to plan ahead, to be sensitive to fine gradations of importance in text, to paraphrase words of the text, and to condense text by combining and rearranging ideas. Younger children tended to write summaries by deleting or retaining surface elements of the texts. Thus, just as with selecting and studying main ideas, the ability to produce an adequate summary of a lengthy text is a late-developing skill that continues to be refined throughout the school years.

We can conclude that when left to develop on their own, metacognitive skills such as selective attention to important information and summarizing may evolve only gradually and rather late. Fortunately, students can be systematically *taught* metacognitive skills that help them learn from text. The next section briefly describes some of the research that shows promising results for training in learning strategies that involve metacognition.

RESEARCH IN TRAINING METACOGNITIVE SKILLS:
SOME PROMISING RESULTS

We begin with a study on the training of summarization skills. In the series of studies on summarization mentioned previously, Brown and Day (1980) identified six basic rules that are essential to summarization: (a) Delete trivial material, (b) delete redundant material, (c) substitute a superordinate term for a list of items, (d) substitute a superordinate event for a list of actions, (e) select a topic sentence if the author has provided one, and (f) invent a topic sentence if the author has not provided one.

In a doctoral thesis, Day (1980) trained junior college students of varying abilities to summarize text in one of four conditions:

1. *Self-Management:* The students were given general encouragement to write a good summary, to capture the main ideas, to dispense with trivia and all unnecessary words—but they were not told rules for achieving this end. This type of instruction is quite typical of the routine classroom practice for "teaching" summarization (Bessey & Coffin, 1934).

2. *Rules.* The students were given explicit instructions in the use of the six rules for summarizing text listed above, and the rules were modeled for them. For example, students were given various colored pencils and shown how to delete redundant information in red, delete trivial information in blue, write in superordinates for any lists, underline topic sentences if provided, and write in a topic sentence if needed.

3. *Rules plus Self-Management.* The students in the third group were given both the general self-management instruction of Group 1 and the rules instruction of Group 2, but they were left to integrate the two sets of information for themselves.

4. *Rules plus Monitoring.* The students were given training in the rules and additional explicit training in the monitoring of these rules; that is, they were taught how to check that the rules had been used correctly and exhaustively. For example, the students were shown how to check that they had a topic sentence for each paragraph (either underlined or written in), to check, for example, that all redundancies were deleted, all trivia erased, and that any lists of items were replaced with superordinates.

The results of training were encouraging. All training had an effect in that students in all conditions exhibited a greater use of the rules. More advanced students needed less explicit instruction to show improvement. For students with more severe learning problems, the most effective condition was the most explicit training, i.e., training in rules and in self-monitoring in the use of the rules.

Other successful training studies have focused on teaching the skill of self-questioning during reading. In a study by André and Anderson (1978–79), high school students were assigned to one of three treatment groups: a group that was trained to generate questions about main points of the text, a group that was directed to ask main-idea questions but not trained how to do so, and a control group that simply read and reread the text. Findings included a significant main effect for treatment in favor of questioning-with-training. In addition, self-questioning was a particularly effective strategy for lower- and medium-verbal-ability students.

A study by Wong and Jones (1981) investigated the effect of training learning-disabled eighth and ninth graders and normally achieving sixth graders to generate questions while reading. Half of the students were trained in a five-step self-questioning procedure in which they learned to monitor their understanding of important information in text. Results of the study showed that for the learning-disabled students, training substantially increased awareness of important ideas, ability to formulate good questions about those ideas, and performance on comprehension tests over studied passages. However, training did not substantially increase the performance of the normally achieving sixth graders. A conjecture is that for this group, training may have interfered with their pre-existing successful studying strategies.

In a third study, Palincsar (1980) worked with four seventh-grade students who were decoding at grade level but whose comprehension was at second-grade level. During the study, each student experienced two interventions, corrective feedback and strategy training.

For the corrective feedback intervention, the students were asked to read a 400–word passage. They were then asked ten questions, five based on information that was implicitly stated (needed to be inferred) and five based on information explicitly stated. The investigator provided corrective feedback for incorrect responses by guiding the student to the paragraph or lines where the answer could be found. For those questions about implicit information, the investigator provided cues to help the student infer the answer.

The intervention of strategy training was influenced by Manzo's (1968) Request Procedure and a model-lead-test procedure (Carnine & Silbert, 1979). During strategy training, students read another 400–word passage. The passage was divided into five sections. First, the investigator modeled comprehension monitoring strategies by predicting the content of the entire passage from the title, summarizing the important content of the first section, and hypothesizing the content of the remainder of the passage. In addition, the investigator modeled how to generate questions about important information. Next, the students were encouraged to follow the procedures modeled by the investigator as they read the remainder of the passage. In a subsequent discussion, the student and investigator resolved any confusions the student had about the passage.

Students were tested on different passages after each instructional session in both conditions. Analysis of comprehension measures showed that corrective feedback improved comprehension ability and appeared to facilitate a readiness to use strategy training. Strategy training, however, had a greater and more enduring effect on reading comprehension performance than did corrective feedback. Thus, modeling in how to ask appropriate questions greatly increased the students' independent comprehension scores, to the delight of their teachers.

Research on summarization and self-questioning indicates that lower-achieving students can benefit from instruction in learning to learn from text that includes training in metacognitive skills. Furthermore, the most successful instruction for lower-achieving or less mature readers includes training in how to employ, monitor, check, and evaluate that strategy. In the next section, we present some guidelines for instruction in learning to learn from text that we hope will be useful to publishers in designing their instructional materials.

SUGGESTIONS FOR TEACHING STUDENTS HOW TO LEARN FROM READING

In our estimation, much current reading instruction is what Brown, Campione, and Day (1981) term "blind training." That is, students are not taught to be truly active, self-controlled participants in the learning process. They are induced to follow a rule or use a strategy without a concurrent understanding of the significance of that activity. Students are generally not fully informed about why, when, where, and how they should use the strategy.

The approach we advocate is *cognitive training with awareness*. The main aim of cognitive training with awareness is to make students cognizant of the complex interaction of variables that affect learning outcomes and of the need to adapt their reading/studying activities to the demands of the criterion task, the nature of the text, and their own characteristics. This self-awareness is prerequisite to self-regulation, the ability to monitor and check one's own activities while reading and studying.

Specifically, we recommend that training designed to help students learn to learn from reading include instruction in the four major variables of the tetrahedral model presented in the introduction to this chapter. Some suggestions for training in each of the four areas follow.

1. *Criterion Tasks.* Students should be instructed in the importance of knowledge of the criterion task. They should be taught the demands associated with various criterion tasks, how to determine the actual or probable task to follow a particular studying session, and how to match studying strategies and techniques to task demands.

2. *Texts.* Students should be taught about properties of text that affect learning. For example, one important property is structure or organization. A rather extensive body of research has established that students are better able to learn from text if they identify and use the inherent text structure (Goetz & Armbruster, 1980; Meyer, 1975, 1979; Shimmerlik, 1978; Walker & Meyer, 1980). Students should be taught the basic structures that underlie the texts they are expected to learn from in school. They should also be taught how to use devices such as headings, introductions and summaries, topic sentences, and key relationship symbols (i.e., *because, on the other hand, first . . . second, . . .*) to determine the structure of text. (See Anderson and Armbruster, this volume, for further discussion of these points.)

3. *Student Characteristics.* Students should be taught about the roles of background knowledge, ability, interests, and motivation in studying. They should be taught how to activate relevant prior knowledge, work with their strengths and weaknesses, and increase their motivation and concentration.

4. *Strategies and Techniques for Learning and Remembering.* Students should be taught some basic strategies, such as summarization and self-questioning, that can be applied in many learning situations. Students should be fully informed about the use of these strategies. That is, they should know *why, when, where,* and *how* to use strategies while reading and studying. With regard to the "how," students should be taught specific rules for applying the strategies as well as rules for monitoring and checking to ensure that the strategies are being used correctly and are resulting in the desired end-product.

We believe that if less successful students can be made aware of (a) the differing demands of a variety of tests to which their knowledge may be put, (b) simple rules of text construction, (c) the role of their own characteristics, and (d) basic strategies for reading and remembering, they cannot help but become more effective learners. A challenge for both researchers and publishers is to develop instruction that reflects these important factors.

REFERENCES

André, M. D. A., & Anderson, T. H. The development and evaluation of a self-questioning study technique. *Reading Research Quarterly,* 1978–79, *14,* 605–623.

Baker, L., & Brown, A. L. Metacognitive skills of reading. In D. Pearson (Ed.), *Handbook of reading research.* New York: Longman, in press.

Bessey, M. A., & Coffin, C. P. *Reading through precis.* New York: Appleton-Century, 1934.

Brown, A. L. Metacognitive development and reading. In R. J. Spiro, B. C. Bruce, & W. F. Brewer (Eds.), *Theoretical issues in reading comprehension.* Hillsdale, N.J.: Lawrence Erlbaum Associates, 1980.

Brown, A. L. Learning to learn how to read. To appear in J. Langer & T. Smith-Burke (Eds.), *Reader meets author/bridging the gap: A psycholinguistic and sociolinguistic perspective.* Newark, Del.: International Reading Association, 1982.

Brown, A. L., Campione, J. C., & Day, J. D. Learning to learn: On training students to learn from texts. *Educational Researcher,* 1981, *10*(2), 14–21.

Brown, A. L., & Day, J. D. *Strategies and knowledge for summarizing texts: The development of expertise.* Unpublished manuscript, University of Illinois, 1980.

Brown, A. L., & Smiley, S. S. Rating the importance of structural units of prose passages: A problem of metacognitive development. *Child Development,* 1977, *48,* 1–8.

Brown, A. L., & Smiley, S. S. The development of strategies for studying texts. *Child Development,* 1978, *49,* 1076–1088.

Carnine, D., & Silbert, J. *Direct instruction reading.* Columbus, Ohio: Merrill, 1979.

Collins, A., Brown, A. L., Morgan, J. L., & Brewer, W. F. *The analysis of reading tasks and texts* (Tech. Rep. No. 43). Urbana: University Illinois, Center for the Study of Reading, April 1977. (ERIC Document Reproduction Service No. ED 145 404)

Day, J. D. *Teaching summarization skills: A comparison of training methods.* Unpublished doctoral dissertation, University of Illinois, 1980.

Dewey, J. *How we think.* Boston: Heath, 1910.

Goetz, E. T., & Armbruster, B. B. Psychological correlates of text structure. In R. J. Spiro, B. C. Bruce, & W. F. Brewer (Eds.), *Theoretical issues in reading comprehension.* Hillsdale, N.J.: Lawrence Erlbaum Associates, 1980.

Huey, E. B. *The psychology and pedagogy of reading.* Cambridge, Mass.: M.I.T. Press, 1968. (Originally published, 1908.)

Manzo, A. V. *Improving reading comprehension through reciprocal questioning.* Unpublished doctoral dissertation, Syracuse University, 1968.

Meyer, B. J. F. *The organization of prose and its effects on memory.* Amsterdam: North-Holland, 1975.

Meyer, B. J. F. *A selected review and discussion of basic research on prose comprehension* (Prose Learning Series, Research Rep. No. 4). Tempe: Arizona State University, Department of Educational Psychology, 1979.

Palincsar, A. *Directed feedback and strategy training to improve the comprehension of poor readers.* Unpublished manuscript, University of Illinois, 1980.

Shimmerlik, S. M. Organization theory and memory for prose: A review of the literature. *Review of Educational Research,* 1978, *48,* 103–120.

Thorndike, E. L. Reading as reasoning: A study of mistakes in paragraph reading. *Journal of Educational Psychology,* 1917, *8,* 323–332.

Walker, C. H., & Meyer, B. J. F. Integrating information from text: An evaluation of current theories. *Review of Educational Research,* 1980, *50,* 421–437.

Wong, B. Y. L., & Jones, W. *Increasing metacomprehension in learning-disabled and normally-achieving students through self-questioning training.* Unpublished manuscript, Simon Fraser University, 1981.

10 Summary Discussion

Dorothy S. Strickland
Teachers College
Columbia University

What is reading comprehension? What factors influence its development? What is the role of the reader? The writer? The text? What does it mean to teach reading comprehension? These are some of the questions addressed in recent research at the Center for the Study of Reading. Moving away from the traditional view of reading comprehension as a set of separate and distinct skills toward a much broader concept focused on the processes involved, this research has added to our understanding of how learners construct meaning from print, and the implications for reading instruction.

In the field of education, where the gap between the emergence of new information and its application is often extremely wide, it is encouraging to see a significant attempt to share research information directly with those people who are most affected. The Tarrytown Conference for textbook publishers on "Learning to Read in American Schools" was successful in bringing researchers and a portion of their consumer public together. It will undoubtedly serve to lessen the inevitable knowledge gap between research and application. A summary of the proceedings follows.

The purposes and expectations of the conference were established through the welcoming remarks of William S. Hall, Center for the Study of Reading; Robert T. Rasmussen, Association of American Publishers; and Ralph Staiger, International Reading Association. The conference was designed to provide a forum for exchange between the Center and decision-makers in the publishing industry about recent advances in the study of reading comprehension and the challenges such advances hold for the development of reading programs.

An examination of dimensions that might affect comprehension in commercial reading materials was described by Isabel Beck. According to Beck and her associates, limitations related to vocabulary and prior knowledge have increased with the advent of more literary materials in readers for younger children. A wide range of problematic issues, ranging from direction-setting activities to after-reading questions, were explored and recommendations made. Publishers were warned that an attempt to be "all things to everybody" may be counterproductive. For example, while exposure to good art is important, an illustration will confuse the learner if if conflicts with the story. And, while the need for higher-level questions is important, such questions may cause confusion if they are unrelated to the text. Pearson's response to Beck's paper served to support the need for publishers to take a critical look at reading materials with this research in mind.

Bertram Bruce reported that the reader's limited experience with various story modes may affect comprehension. Authors and readers depend on a commonality of conceptual knowledge, social knowledge, and story knowledge in order to communicate. Problems can arise when there is a mismatch between the author's expectations of the reader and the reader's actual knowledge. Learners need to be exposed to a variety of story modes in their readers if they are to be expected to comprehend them effectively in trade books. There may even be a relationship between comprehension of certain types of story modes and cultural background.

The case was made, by Georgia Green, for unedited text beyond the middle of Grade 1. Her research revealed that children do respond to prose on the basis of linguistic and stylistic qualities. According to Green, children should be allowed to uncover vocabulary meaning naturally, while learning to read, just as they have for five years prior to entering school.

The inclusion of content that takes into account language variation, in a manner that recognizes and respects diversity, was presented by Thomas Pietras as a challenge to language arts textbook publishers. Teachers need assistance in instructing students about the nature of language and language variation so as to help them to use the standard dialect required to participate fully in American society. "It is not inconsistent," said Pietras, "to respect language differences but also to expect a standard language."

"Workbooks are widely used part of essentially every basal reading program." reports Jean Osborn. Stating that they could be improved, Osborn outlined a list of 20 recommendations for consideration by developers of workbooks. Her recommendations included these: (a) The need exists for paying closer attention to the relevance of workbook tasks to the instruction that is going on in the remainder of the unit or lesson, and to the reading level of the students using the materials. (b) The language used in workbook tasks should be consistent with that in the teachers' guides; for example, use of the terms *fiction* and *nonfiction* in the teachers' manual as opposed to *real* and *not real* in the workbook. (c) Workbook tasks should always opt for student response modes that are the closest possible to reading and writing.

Patricia Cunningham described a number of ways to make workbooks better through techniques that facilitate schema access and develop strategies for coping with a variety of text structures. Specific suggestions were given for the design of a series of workbook pages in which a decreasing amount of direction and guidance is given on each page designed to teach a specific strategy.

An explanation of schema theory and its implications for textbook writers and instruction was offered by Richard C. Anderson. Schemata, it was explained, are important both during and after reading for application and use of information. They provide the reader's basis for comprehending, learning, and remembering. John Bransford's discussion emphasized the need for instruction that fosters the acquisition of new schemata as well as the activation of those previously acquired. Examples were offered of situations in which children were thought to have comprehension problems when they actually lacked sufficient background for the task.

Publishers need to take a careful look at how they use, or misuse, readability formulas and at how they adapt text for the purpose of making it easier to read. The research of Alice Davison revealed serious problems in the use of readability formulas as predictors of difficulty and as guides to writing. Readability is relative rather than absolute. The use of readability formulas tends to take attention away from important features related to the content and structure of text. Davison suggested that subjective judgment is the best replacement available. This should be coupled with an informed view of psychology, linguistics, and information about how children learn.

Walter MacGinitie cautioned that by eliminating certain text characteristics we will, in the long run, insure that children will have trouble with them. The level of difficulty of a task largely depends on whether students have had previous experience with it. MacGinitie suggested that little guidance is given in manuals to help students use the language of the text in order to comprehend it. The fact that teachers tend to focus on content, rather than text construction, when a child does not comprehend was also pointed out.

The need for "considerate text" was discussed by Thomas H. Anderson and Bonnie B. Armbruster. They offered a variety of recommendations, with specific examples, for making textbooks more easily understood by students. A set of guidelines for use by authors was given.

A different perspective was taken by Harold Herber as he explained that comprehension is a dynamic process that should fit any text. Herber listed the characteristics of good texts: (a) Teaching and learning aids are built-in to facilitate comprehension. (b) Procedures are employed to promote response and interaction among students. (c) Any reorganization of the text by publishers does not dilute the content and is accompanied by help for teachers in reorganizing the text to facilitate comprehension.

Metacognition and the implications for helping children learn from reading were discussed by Armbruster and Ann L. Brown. Certain principles (drawn from the work of Brown) for helping children develop selective attention strategies were described. Students must be taught strategies for self regulation. Texts can be designed with built-in strategies (test, revise, evaluate) for students to monitor their reading.

Dolores Durkin's investigation of basal reader manuals revealed that manuals tend to give considerable help when it is least needed and virtually no help when help is needed most. Publishers were asked to review decisions about setting priorities and about the amount of practice given. Durkin challenged publishers to explain why so many procedures in manuals stop short of being instructive for comprehension.

Roger Farr pointed out that although researchers differ in their definition of comprehension, they generally agree that assignment giving, assessment, and practice are *not* the same as actual instruction. He claimed that we still know little about what teachers do to teach comprehension, and offered a set of questions for use by publishers in reviewing their basal reader manuals.

Although publishers had been cautioned early in the conference that they should not try to be all things to everybody, speakers on the publishers' panel indicated that this was precisely what they were being asked to do. Members of the publishers' panel described their frustration with the increasing demands of the textbook purchaser—demands that are frequently at odds with the research findings presented at this conference. They expressed hope, however, that the combined efforts of researchers and publishers might produce a more enlightened textbook consumer.

Rob Tierney's summary closed the conference on a note of optimism. While there is much to be learned, there is much that we already know and much that we can begin to do right now based on what we know. Our challenge is to help teachers to actually teach students rather than simply manage materials and to help students become more self-reliant and effective learners.

A Synthesis of Research on the Use of Instructional Text: Some Implications for the Educational Publishing Industry in Reading

Robert J. Tierney
Center for the Study of Reading
University of Illinois at Urbana-Champaign

This volume presents research findings and anecdotal evidence addressing an array of topics related to reading instruction and the use of texts in our schools. In general, these comments are critical of the present state of instruction, textbooks, and textbook use, and bear recommendations that at a glance may seem difficult to operationalize or, for various reasons, somewhat questionable. I plan to consider a few of the recurring themes and touch upon how these themes apply to basal and textbook development, as well as directions for future research. By drawing out several viable alternatives, I hope to counter any pessimism associated with the need for change as well as the task of implementing change. My comments relate to: (a) the quality of text material and criteria for text selection; (b) the shortcomings of the present comprehension curricula and skill objectives; and (c) the dearth of teaching procedures for the improvement of reading comprehension.

THE QUALITY OF TEXT MATERIAL AND CRITERIA FOR TEXT SELECTION

Several chapters highlight the shortcomings of text material used for instructional purposes, in particular basal readers, subject matter texts, and workbooks. For the most part, these criticisms touch upon one or more of three interrelated issues: the problem of "fit," the misuse of readability formulas, and the question of story quality. The issue of "fit" arises in response to the all-too-apparent mismatches that exist between (a) reader capabilities, (b) the information represented within basal readers, subject matter texts, and workbooks, and (c) the stipulated or inferred guidelines or suggestions for teaching. Examples of some of the more obvious mismatches are cited by Osborn in reference to workbooks, by Anderson and Armbruster in reference to subject matter text, and by Beck in reference to basal readers.

The second issue, the misuses of readability formulae, is discussed first by Davison, then Green, and then by MacGinitie. These writers point out how readability formulae may be misapplied, and the rather debilitating effects of such misapplications. They indicate that attempts to improve the readability of a selection by applying constraints derived from formulae based upon sentence length, syllable counts, and word frequency have been misdirecting changes in texts for some time and, unfortunately, have had an effect that is deleterious. Davison, Green, and MacGinitie present rather convincing evidence for avoiding the use of readability formulae and seeking the development of more linguistically based and contextually sensitive means for testing texts.

The third issue, story quality, is addressed by both Bruce and Beck. Within even the most up-to-date basal readers, particularly those designed for use in the lower grades, stories tend to be "stories" in a very restricted sense. The diverse roles of the narrator, described by Bruce, are virtually ignored. Furthermore, during reading instruction students are usually subjected to nonsystematic probes that fail to address what makes a story or why and how a story is likely to be read.

What are viewed as viable alternatives? Although several contributors suggest factors that might serve as guidelines for examining and improving text quality, no simple formula for doing so is provided. However, a very basic question has surfaced from the many suggestions made, a question that must precede and guide any text selection or revision task: Does the text (whether it be a basal reader, a subject matter text, or a workbook) work? That is, (a) are essential understandings adequately supported for those readers for whom the text is intended (those readers dealing with the text for those purposes for which a text is typically read)? (b) are relationships between ideas unambiguous and appropriately organized? and (c) is the text worth reading?

The algorithm one might use to equate text shortcomings with editing is not simple. Let me explain. For purposes of improving text quality, we need first to distinguish between what may be difficult, what may be deleterious, and what may be challenging. While publishers might examine the structural integrity of text for instances of unmarked topic shifts, for implicit relations, and for places where important information is rhetorically subordinated or where unimportant information is placed in superordinate positions, care must be taken in evaluating a text, the work of an author. For indeed, some unimportant information—for example, an interesting anecdote—may precede the main points and justifiably so. Similarly, implicit connectors may work as well as, if not better than, explicit ones, depending upon the topic and the purpose for which the text is intended. In addition, the use of adjuncts such as study guides and guiding questions might suffice for improving text, serving to challenge students, setting them up to read a text, or teaching them about certain aspects of text.

I would argue that any determination of text quality must be done in context, that is, in light of how a text is to be used, by whom, and for what purposes. We must consider: (a) how well the text fits with the intent of the instructional experience; (b) how well the text fits with the students for whom it is intended; and (c) how clearly the text is written, given the purposes for which it will be read. This suggests the need for some form of learner verification whereby materials are field tested in actual classrooms, in reading and in subject matter instructional settings. The guidelines provided by the various contributors to this book afford some direction for examining students' responses to text. However, lest the suggested criteria be applied rigidly, it should be reemphasized that the human element (the role of editors, teachers, teacher educators, and publishers) cannot be underestimated. For while readability formulae have been dismissed as viable tools for assessing and guiding text improvements, educated editorship must see to it that materials are properly piloted and, based upon such learner verification, must make decisions about which texts are appropriate, for what purposes, and in which settings.

SHORTCOMINGS OF COMPREHENSION
CURRICULUM AND SKILL OBJECTIVES

A second theme is reflected in the pervasive concern for reading comprehension instruction. If one examines the implications of research on comprehension and comprehension instruction against what exists, the present programs manifest a number of theoretical and practical shortcomings.

Both Anderson and Bransford point out that comprehension is an interactive process wherein the reader's background of experience, perspective, and active involvement have an overriding influence. They emphasize that a text is never fully explicit nor is reading comprehension merely the regurgitation of information presented on the page; rather, a reader's background knowledge has an immense influence on a reader's interpretation and, in fact, virtually determines the extent to which a reader can understand a text at all. Further, they emphasize that comprehension does not proceed piecemeal, rather the reader, driven by hypotheses, progressively refines a model or an interpretation that will account for the information represented by the text.

How do these notions of reading comprehension relate to present conceptualizations of comprehension in basal reading programs? Most reading programs appear to support a number of teaching practices that run counter to notions of reading comprehension emanating from this research. Consider, for example, how readers are typically set up to read a selection. While most programs encourage the use of activities (for example, vocabulary and purpose-setting activities) that may get the reader to activate appropriate schemata, the underlying assumption seems to be that all readers will bring the same background knowledge to the task, pursue the same purposes for reading, and have only word-level difficulties with accessing schemas during reading. Rarely are students encouraged to read text with their *own* reader-based hypothesis or perspective in mind. Before reading a basal selection, readers are typically set up to seek out right answers to predetermined questions that are more related to a teacher's objectives than to the reader's developing interpretation. During reading, readers are either given questions to keep them "on track" or word-level assistance if they appear to falter. After reading, a brief comprehension check is usually made to see that such answers have been acquired. Students are rarely encouraged to reevaluate hypotheses, explain their overall interpretation of the text, take alternative perspectives, reassess the author's point, determine the implications of newly acquired learnings from their reading, or to assess the efficiency with which they allocated their reading strategies to the task.

How might a more research-based model for comprehension be incorporated into the curriculum frameworks that presently exist? If a basal program must operate within the confines of a scope and sequence format, there are a number of objectives that could be included to ensure that at least some emphasis be placed upon skills that will count in the long run. Considering the importance of the readers' background of experience, they might include the following:

The reader is able to recognize and evaluate:

- the role of his or her background of experience in developing an understanding for a text;
- the purposes for reading prior to, during, and after reading;
- the nature of his or her interpretation, including the roles of perspective, background of experience, text-based and reader-based inferences;

- alternative perspectives and multiple interpretations;
- new learnings and their relevancy and application.

Considering the importance of strategies or behaviors that facilitate successful comprehension experiences, the following objectives ought also be included:

The reader is able to access selected behaviors that facilitate successful comprehension experiences:
- recall of related background experience;
- establish, verify, and refine predictions based upon prior experience and the text;
- self-generate questions prior to, during, and after reading;
- visualize events or descriptions prompted by reading;
- adopt alternative points of view including the ability to project oneself into a story as a character, observer, etc.;
- judge whether the text makes sense;
- adopt strategies for coping with misunderstandings or ambiguities;
- interrelate ideas by networking, outlining, and mapping;
- determine the nature of the reading task as well as the adequacy of the outcomes;
- and consider implications and applications of the ideas learned from the text.

Furthermore, in line with the need to extend the present skills listing to include text-based skills and the need to provide the students opportunities to recognize and evaluate text-based strategies as part of their repertoire of comprehension strategies, some of the following skills or strategies might be added. The reader is able to recognize and evaluate:

- the author's organization of ideas and their function in text;
- topical developments, focus, mood development, and shifts in mood;
- purposes for which texts are written and can be read;
- deficiencies within text (ambiguities and missing information, sudden shifts in topic and emphasis, faulty or inconsistent argument);
- the complexities of relationships (explicit and implicit) within a text.

Emphasis upon these text-based skills would serve two purposes: that of helping readers to develop a sense of authorship and readership (Bruce and Beck); and that of preparing readers to trouble-shoot text difficulties (Herber and Bransford).

Care must be taken, however, to avoid a piecemeal approach to reading comprehension or an approach which emphasizes outcomes rather than processes. If program developers wish to adopt an approach that coordinates the selective use of a variety of interrelated skills as well as process-oriented curriculum, the following criteria should be considered:

1. A comprehension program should be coordinated within and across lessons so that students may come to understand that what they did and learned in the previous lesson or lessons relates to what they are doing and learning now.
2. The teaching of reading comprehension should facilitate the development of a variety of skills and stress the relationships between skills. Reading experiences should highlight the fact that strategies are comprised of an array of skills, that strategies should be used selectively, and that it is the task of the reader to select the strategy that best fits the task at hand.
3. Teacher guidance associated with comprehension development should proceed as if the reader is refining a model for the text—adding details, noticing specifics, clarifying and structuring relationships, "filling out" scenarios—rather than building a model from "scratch" in a piecemeal fashion.

In essence, program developers should recognize the need for programs based upon what is known about comprehension. This goal, I suggest, requires activities that afford students opportunities to evaluate their own ideas, to recognize alternative perspectives, and to learn to recognize how their own background of experiences and purposes for reading influence what they understand. The burden of demonstrating whether a response is reasonable must shift away from the teacher to the student. Teachers must understand that answers will vary, and that the adequacy of a response must be assessed against the reasoning involved. Also important, it demands a reading comprehension curriculum that facilitates the acquisition of behaviors appropriate to learning from text. I believe that a major advance for reading programs would be a consideration of the process rather than simply the products of comprehension. How to convey this in the context of teachers' guides and students' books is a formidable task awaiting the creative enterprise of writers and editors.

DEARTH OF TEACHING PROCEDURES FOR THE IMPROVEMENT OF READING COMPREHENSION

From my perspective, by far the most disconcerting findings presented in this volume come from Durkin's examination of teaching practices in basal reading programs. Her findings detail how little actual reading comprehension instruction occurs in schools—comprehension instruction of any kind let alone the kind directed at helping students learn to learn from text.[1] We have suspected this for some time. Indeed, not so long ago, many assumed reading comprehension could not be taught. Fortunately, attitudes toward facilitating reading comprehension improvement have changed along with research findings that achieve successful outcomes as a result of instruction of one type or another. But, as one might expect, improvements in comprehension require careful instructional implementation, and it is for this reason that the findings reported in Durkin's study are distressing. The token comprehension instruction that seems to be characteristic of present practice will not suffice if we are to be earnest in our attempts to improve students' reading comprehension abilities.

What should developers of reading programs identify as instructional priorities? While Farr offers some suggestions, he does not offer many specific guidelines for deciding what to teach or how to teach. R. C. Anderson offers some suggestions for helping readers deal with text, but it is doubtful whether he intends his suggestions to extend to helping readers learn to learn from text. For such advice we need to examine the work of Brown, Bransford, and others recently summarized by Tierney and Cunningham (in press). The focus of their instructional suggestions has been upon the acquisition of self-monitoring strategies.[2] The significance of self-monitoring seems to lie at the very heart of learning to

---

[1] Practices for teaching reading comprehension can be represented by their instructional goals as intended either to increase learning from text or to increase a student's ability to learn from text. The former refers to the large array of instructional support techniques that are intended to improve students' ability to understand, recall, or integrate information from specific text passages. The latter relates to the notion of learning to learn or to those support techniques intended to improve general and specific reading comprehension abilities that will transfer to students' reading of passages they later encounter on their own. The concern with this group is with instruction aimed at improving students' self-control and self-awareness of their own learning processes.

[2] There are two dimensions to self-monitoring. One dimension relates to the student's development of an appreciation for the nature of his/her own understanding, the characteristics of the text, reader-text interactions, and factors that influence reading and the eventual acquisition of understandings. The second dimension relates to the student's self-management of any and all skills/strategies.

The development of these skills/strategies will vary according to the specific type of self-monitoring involved. For example, in order for students to develop an appreciation of perspective, they might be asked to read text from different viewpoints, *or* they might be asked to assess the accuracy of answers to questins. To develop self-management skills, readers might be given feedback or asked to respond to a checklist based upon the type of strategy/skill being emphasized. This would include the when, how, why, etc., of strategy usage. Within the context of skill features, workbooks, etc., these checklists can become a vital/integral feature of almost all instructional activities.

learn. It relates to the student's self-management of all skills and strategies; it takes students beyond teacher dependence to independence. As
Brown, Campione, and Day (1981) suggested:

> If learners can be made aware of (a) basic strategies for reading and remem-
> bering, (b) simple rules of text construction, (c) differing demands of a va-
> riety of tests to which their information may be put, and (d) the importance of
> activating any background knowledge which they may have, they cannot
> help but become more effective learners. Such self-awareness is a prerequi-
> site for self-regulation, the ability to orchestrate, monitor, and check one's
> own cognitive activities (p. 28).

Such an instructional emphasis requires an approach that extends far
beyond "mere mentioning" to careful guidance and facilitation. I would
argue that the crucial question for publishers intent on improving students' ability to comprehend what they read must be: "What can we do to
increase students' ability to comprehend or learn from new passages?"
Clearly, the concern must be with learning experiences that facilitate the
students' success as independent comprehenders. With this goal in mind,
Brown and her colleagues suggest the development of learning experiences where the utility of a skill or strategy is readily apparent. This
occurs when students recognize how a skill or strategy facilitates reading
and when and why it is appropriate. Brown et al. also suggest that it is
important for students to "try-out," appraise, and adapt their own skills,
behaviors, and strategies for learning from text. Effective learning, in
their view, does not occur when skills are mandated and drilled. Instead
the ability to use skills or strategies comes when skills and strategies are
used and monitored thoughtfully and somewhat idiosyncratically.

There seems to be general agreement that if our goal is to help students
become independent and self-initiating, then there is need for major
changes in instruction. Such changes do not necessarily entail the development of complex lessons and materials. On the other hand, as the
findings of Brown et al. suggest, they do entail using quality teaching time
to teach students strategies for dealing with text, even when the strategies
appear to be simple and straight forward.

A FINAL WORD

The research findings presented at the conference prompted a number of
rather diverse responses from those attending. The following remarks
capture the flavor of their responses. They are accompanied by my personal reaction to these concerns.

One response might best be characterized by the following statement: "You haven't told us anything we didn't already know, and your research findings regarding comprehension, text, and teaching are nothing more than common sense." I would argue that such a remark is misguided. The respondent underestimates the worth of empirically examining what appears to be common sense en route to identifying its subtleties. It is precisely that lack of respect for common sense that leads many not only to overlook the full ramifications of common sense, but to overlook what it is that makes such practices work in those instances when they are effective.

A second response might be described as a dismissal, that is, a dismissal of both research findings and their implications because of an apparent lack of "hard data." Certainly I would agree that many of the presenters offered hypotheses for which they had only hunches, sparse data, or anecdotal support. However, the major theses set forth at the conference, in particular, those which pertained to the misuse of readability formulae and the nature of comprehension, have a substantial data base. Furthermore, the majority of those ideas presented have a far more extensive and credible data base than much of what is presently being implemented in reading programs. While it may be wise to continue to insist upon "more" or "stronger" evidence, it would be foolish to underestimate what we do already know and possibly remain at a standstill as a result.

A third response is much less definitive than the previous two. While excited by many of the ideas presented at the conference, several respondents expressed concern for the nature of the political climate, questioning whether changes suggested by such ideas will, practically speaking, be "too different" for the market place. This is an issue to which the conference gave inadequate consideration. The history of change in American published reading programs needs to be addressed systematically as a research topic unto itself and evaluated against the research on change and dissemination being accumulated in the public and private sectors involved in education. In future conferences, such issues need to be considered more fully.

A fourth and rather frequent response to those ideas presented at the conference has to do with the "prescriptive" nature of the information presented. Many in attendance at the conference expected that a body of ideas would surface that could be considered for immediate adoption and implementation. Some participants would like to have been given model workbook pages, teacher's guide material, and readability guidelines that could be put to immediate use. The conference was not intended to be prescriptive in nature, nor could one expect the data presented at the conference to support such levels of generalizability. The purpose of this conference was not to prescribe, indoctrinate, or antagonize battles, but rather to create a forum for the flow of ideas. It was our hope that the dialogue this flow of ideas would sponsor would support (a) researchers' search for clarification, alternative perspectives, and issues in need of exploration, and (b) publishers' quest for improving the quality of their products en route to maximizing benefits for schooling.

In conclusion, the conference can and should be looked upon as an exciting moment in the history of American education. It has represented a unique gathering of those who influence and carry out research and those who influence and carry out practice. I believe the conference has set the stage for a long overdue working relationship between the two groups.

REFERENCES

Brown, A. L., Campione, J. C., & Day, J. D. Learning to learn: On training students to learn from texts. *Educational Researcher,* 1981, *10*(2), 14–21.

Tierney, R. J., & Cunningham, J. Research on teaching reading comprehension. In P. D. Pearson (Ed.), *Handbook on research on reading.* New York: Longman, in press.

Biographical Information about the Authors

RICHARD C. ANDERSON is a Professor of Educational Psychology and Psychology at the University of Illinois and a Director of the Center for the Study of Reading. He received his Ed.D. in Educational Psychology from Harvard University in 1960. He held various secondary school positions and taught at Rutgers University before coming to the University of Illinois. Professor Anderson's articles and books encompass a variety of research topics in instructional and cognitive psychology. His current interests include schema theory and discourse comprehension, and the role of context in word meaning. He edited (with Spiro and Montague) *Schooling and the Acquisition of Knowledge*. He is a member of the National Academy of Education and a Fellow of the American Psychological Association. He was a Fulbright Scholar in 1971–72.

THOMAS H. ANDERSON is an Associate Professor of Educational Psychology and a researcher at the Center for the Study of Reading and the Office of Guided Independent Study at the University of Illinois. He earned a Ed.D. in Education at the University of Illinois. He taught in secondary schools and was on the faculty at Arkansas Polytechnic University and Indiana State University. Professor Anderson has published articles on topics in computer-based instruction and studying strategies. His current research focuses on the interaction between young readers (ages 10–15) and the type of content area textbooks that are typically used in schools.

BONNIE ARMBRUSTER is a Visiting Assistant Professor at the Center for the Study of Reading. She earned her Ph.D. in Educational Psychology from the University of Illinois. Her major research interests relate to learning from informational text and issues concerning learning how to learn. She has written many articles dealing with text properties and instructional procedures.

ISABEL BECK is an Associate Professor of Education at the University of Pittsburgh and Co-Director of the Reading and Comprehension Unit at the Learning Research and Development Center (LRDC). Before coming to the University of Pittsburgh, she was a public school teacher. Her work at LRDC has involved the analysis of instructional practices associated with the teaching of decoding and comprehension and the design and development of reading and vocabulary programs. Presently Professor Beck is engaged in several studies about the development of instructional procedures that reflect current understanding of comprehension processes. Her publications include several chapters and articles about curriculum design and instructional strategies.

JOHN BRANSFORD is a Profesor of Psychology at Vanderbilt University. He received his Ph.D. in Cognitive Psychology from the University of Minnesota in 1970. Professor Bransford has published in a number of fields. His major interests include the role of prior knowledge, the acquisition of new knowledge, and the development of learning skills. He is the author of *Human Cognition: Learning and Understanding*.

ANN L. BROWN is a Professor in the Departments of Psychology and Educational Psychology at the University of Illinois. She also has an appointment at the Center for the Study of Reading. She received her Ph.D. from the University of London, Bedford College, and taught at the University of Sussex, England. Professor Brown has published in several areas of child development, but her main interests include memorial processes, metacognition, and strategies for understanding discourse. Her recent articles include "Metacognition and the reading process," and "Learning to learn how to read." She is co-editor of the *Advances in Developmental Psychology* series with Michael Lamb.

BERTRAM C. BRUCE is a Senior Scientist at Bolt, Beranek and Newman, Inc., in Cambridge, Massachusetts. He received his Ph.D. in Computer Science from the University of Texas (Austin). He taught in the Computer Science Department at Rutgers University and served as Senior Investigator for the NIH Research Resource on Computers in Biomedicine Project at Rutgers University. He is Principal Investigator for the BBN contract with the Center for the Study of Reading. His research interests include the study of text and discourse structure, the relation between oral and written language, and the role that plans and beliefs play in reading comprehension. He is co-editor with Spiro and Brewer of the newly published book, *Theoretical Issues in Reading Comprehension*.

PATRICIA M. CUNNINGHAM is an Assistant Professor of Education at Wake Forest University in Winston-Salem, North Carolina. She holds a Ph.D. degree from the University of Georgia. Professor Cunningham taught first and fourth grades and was a reading specialist, curriculum coordinator, and director of reading in the public schools of Florida, Indiana, and North Carolina. Her publications include research and applied articles, as well as two reading methods textbooks of which she is co-author. For the past two years, she has written the "Clip Sheet," a monthly materials review column in *The Reading Teacher*.

ALICE DAVISON is a Visiting Assistant Professor in the Department of Linguistics at the University of Illinois and also holds a position at the Center for the Study of Reading. She received her Ph.D. in Linguistics in 1973 from the University of Chicago, and taught at the State University of New York at Stony Brook. At the Center for the Study of Reading she has collaborated with other linguists in studies that examine the role of readability formulas in simplifying texts, and in experiments on how people process syntactic structures in relation to information available about their meaning. Professor Davison is interested in the study of sentence structures in relation to pragmatic, contextual information, as well as systematic patterns in language structure.

DOLORES DURKIN is a Professor in the Department of Elementary and Early Childhood Education and a member of the Center for the Study of Reading. She received her Ph.D. from the University of Illinois. She taught at the University of California (Berkeley) and Columbia University before returning to the University of Illinois. She taught in elementary schools in Chicago. She has written many articles and several books on reading, including *Teaching Them to Read, Phonics, Linguistics, and Reading,* and *Strategies for Identifying Words*. Her current work is on the evaluation of comprehension instruction in classrooms, the content of basal reading programs, and characteristics of minority children who are successful in school.

ROGER FARR is a Professor of Education and Director of the Henry Lester Smith Center for Research in Education at Indiana University. He received his Ph.D. from the State University of New York at Buffalo. He held various public school positions and taught at SUNY-Buffalo and Indiana University. Professor Farr has published on the teaching of reading as well as on the measurement and evaluation of reading and reading programs. He has written the book *Reading: What Can Be Measured?* and is the co-author of books and articles on national trends in reading achievement. He has also been involved in the development of classroom texts and reading materials. He is a past president of the International Reading Association and was co-editor of the *Reading Research Quarterly*.

GEORGIA M. GREEN is an Associate Professor in the Department of Linguistics and the Center for the Study of Reading at the University of Illinois. She received her Ph.D. in Linguistics from the University of Chicago in 1971. Her research interests relate to the study of English syntax, the relationships between syntax and discourse, and more recently, text properties. She is the author of the book *Semantics and Syntactic Regularity*.

HAROLD HERBER is a Professor of Education and Director of the Reading Language Arts Center at Syracuse University. He is also the Director of the Network of Secondary School Demonstration Centers for Teaching Reading in Content Areas. He received his Ed.D. at Boston University. Professor Herber has taught at the secondary school level and presently consults in several school districts. He has written a book *Teaching Reading in the Content Areas,* which is in its second edition, and has edited four monographs about research in content area reading. He is past director for the Commission on Reading of the National Council of Teachers of English and is a past member of the board of the International Reading Association.

JEAN OSBORN is a Senior Educational Specialist at the Center for the Study of Reading. She also works as a site consultant in several school districts implementing the Direct Instruction Follow Through Model, and has trained teachers in the United States, Canada, and England. She received an M.Ed. from the University of Illinois. Her research interests include language instruction, characteristics of successful schools, materials used to teach students to read, and time used in classrooms. She is co-author of several classroom programs in language and reading for elementary and high school students.

P. DAVID PEARSON is a Professor in the Department of Elementary and Early Childhood Education at the University of Illinois, where he also holds an appointment at the Center for the Study of Reading. He received his Ph.D. at the University of Minnesota. He taught elementary school in California and taught several years at the University of Minnesota, Minneapolis. He has published two books, *Teaching Reading Comprehension* and *Teaching Reading Vocabulary,* with Dale D. Johnson of the University of Wisconsin. With S. Jay Samuels of the University of Minnesota he edits the *Reading Research Quarterly*.

THOMAS P. PIETRAS is the Director of Language Arts, K-12, for Ann Arbor, Michigan, Public Schools. He received his Ph.D. in Education and English from Michigan State University. Dr. Pietras has had experience in the public school system at both the elementary and secondary levels. He has also taught at Purdue University and Texas A&M University. Dr. Pietras has written a number of articles dealing with teacher expectancy, sociolinguistics, and school policy.

DOROTHY S. STRICKLAND is a Professor of Education in the Department of Curriculum and Teaching at Teachers College, Columbia University. Her Ph.D. is from New York University. She has served on the faculties of Kean College of New Jersey and Jersey City State College. She has been a classroom teacher, reading consultant, and learning disability specialists. Her publications include articles and chapters on language arts and reading instruction. Dr. Strickland has held offices in the National Council of Teachers of English and the International Reading Association, of which she is a past president.

ROBERT J. TIERNEY is a Visiting Research Associate Professor at the Center for the Study of Reading. A teacher, consultant, and researcher in both the United States and Australia, he has taught at various grade levels (elementary through college) and has written articles dealing with educational theory, research, and practice. A recently published book is *Reading Strategies and Practices: A guide for Improving Instruction*. He is also co-author of a number of classroom reading programs.

Author Index

Subject Index